WOMEN, ISLAMISMS AND THE STATE

Also by Azza M. Karam

ISLAM IN EEN ONTZUILDE SAMENLEVING (*compiled by Ria Lavrijzen*)

Women, Islamisms and the State

Contemporary Feminisms in Egypt

Azza M. Karam

First published in Great Britain 1998 by
MACMILLAN PRESS LTD
Houndmills, Basingstoke, Hampshire RG21 6XS and London
Companies and representatives throughout the world

A catalogue record for this book is available from the British Library.

ISBN 0–333–68816–3 hardcover
ISBN 0–333–68817–1 paperback

First published in the United States of America 1998 by
ST. MARTIN'S PRESS, INC.,
Scholarly and Reference Division,
175 Fifth Avenue, New York, N.Y. 10010

ISBN 0–312–17501–9

Library of Congress Cataloging-in-Publication Data
Karam, Azza M.
Women, Islamisms, and state : contemporary feminisms in Egypt /
Azza M. Karam.
p. cm.
Includes bibliographical references and index.
ISBN 0–312–17501–9 (cloth)
1. Women—Egypt. 2. Women in politics—Egypt. 3. Feminism–
–Egypt. 4. Power (Social sciences) I. Title.
HQ1793.K37 1997
305.4'0962—DC21
97–7123
CIP

© Azza M. Karam 1998

This book is printed on paper suitable for recycling and made from fully managed and
sustained forest sources.

10 9 8 7 6 5 4 3 2 1
07 06 05 04 03 02 01 00 99 98

Printed and bound in Great Britain by
Creative Print and Design (Wales)
Ebbw Vale

I dedicate this book to
my mother and my father
in gratitude for their unparalleled love,
patience, support and wisdom

Contents

Contents
ix

Acknowledgements

I have many to thank and to whom I shall always, be deeply grateful, listing them all is impossible so the following are but a few.

Heartfelt thanks and an endless debt of gratitude and love are owed to my mother who inspired this research and whose wisdom and strength of character continue to enrich my life, as well as to my father who supported me unfailingly and is my guiding beacon in life.

The initial research for this book would not have been possible without the financial support and continued confidence in my abilities of Stichting De Zaayer; especially the wisdom, support, and faith in me that Mia Berden consistently maintained. Special thanks to the strong and humour-filled guidance of Joke Schrijvers, on the initial research for this book. I owe to my experiences of working with Dr Nawal Al-Sa'dawi, the concretization of the necessity and focus of this work.

Very special thanks to Jihan Abu-Zaid who personified everything a caring, careful friend and interviewee could ever be. To Jihan I owe the priceless debt of giving me faith in womanhood and Egyptianness and friendship all at the same time. Special thanks also to Amany Massoud and to Omayma Mostafa from Cairo University, Political Science Department, for being generous with their help and support.

To all those pioneering, hardworking women who made time in their impossibly full days to talk to me and bear my questions and my deliberations, I am forever indebted: Muna AbuSenna, Hala Mustapha, Laila al-Shall, Farida al-Naqqash, Asmahan Shukri, Awatef Wali, Amal Mahmud, Hoda Afifi, Farkhanda Hassan, Ayeda Saif al-Dawla, Iman Baybars, Amira Baheyy al-din (who also generously piled on me and trusted me with years of work not all of which was published – such dedication and good faith were heartwarming and will never be forgotten), Tahani al-Jibali, Atiyyat al-Abnoudi and Salwa Bakr (who gave me a unique woman-artist-intellectual's view on issues), Noha Radwan (the friend whose house was a sanctuary, and whose mind and spirit a close companion despite the distance), Ibtisam Kamel, Abeyya Badr, Heba Ra'uf, Safinaz Qazam and the Islamist women whose names I am bound not to reveal, but who will always be close to my heart as the ones who helped me learn and grow, because they enabled me to see difference and not to fear it. All these women mentioned here and countless others, taught me and continue to demonstrate by their existence and resilience so many of life's precious lessons: strength, perseverance and hard work. Through their lives and work, they taught me that nothing is impossible.

I owe a great deal to my friends from the Institute of Social Studies (ISS) who stood by me and encouraged me: Aurora Galindo, Judith Richter and Sabine Hausler. To my former MA supervisor and my mentor Jan Nederveen Pieterse, many thanks for the countless times I ran to him for advice. To Lisa Chason, my good friend who was always there in so many ways – professional editing not excluded! To Fatma Hassan who will always be my best friend and the source of so much strength and sustenance throughout this research and long, long before.

Thanks are owed to the central people who stood by me for endless technicalities: Jeff Glasgow and Rolf Pixley; as well as to my friends Caroliene Nevejan who was there from the big bang, and Halleh Ghorashi and Abdullah Mahmoud.

To all my cousins and family members who have inspired and paved the way for this research in ways probably unknown to them. Many thanks to my mother-in-law Melodie de Silva for her consistent prayers for me and to my father-in-law for his support and faith in me.

And last but by no means least, a very special debt of gratitude to my husband P.L. de Silva who was loving and patient throughout. To him the painstaking work on the Bibliography and the meticulous combing through of the rest of the text. Enormous thanks to my wonderful brother Mohammed, who was the best brother, research assistant and information analyst anyone could ever ask for. His sense of humour and his belief in me were the chirping birds, the gentle breezes and the gushing waterfalls throughout this journey – not to mention the comic relief!

A special thanks also for the patience and good humour of Anna-belle Buckley and Ruth Willats throughout the commissioning and editing of this book.

To all of those mentioned and to the many that quietly inspired, trusted and encouraged, my very warm thanks.

Glossary

Transliteration here has been a challenge but I have tried to be as consistent as possible, while attempting to allow for the colloquial as well as literary usages. I used the system adopted by the *International Journal of Middle East Studies* for the Arabic. Diacritics are omitted, but I use ' to represent the '*ayn*, as in *da'wa* and Al-Sha'rawi, and ' to represent the *hamza* as in *mar'a*. I drop the terminal *hamza* from words such as '*ulama*. The plural of words in languages that have 'broken' plurals is formed by adding an 's' to the singular, except in cases such as '*ulama*, in which the transliterated plural form has become standard. When persons or writers are known to have a preferred spelling of their name in a European language, I generally use this form.

All Arabic words in the text are itallicized.

Ahlam al-Siba:	Dreams of youth.
Al-Azhar:	Oldest mosque and religious university in Cairo in the Arab world.
Al-Da'wa:	*The Call*; Title of Islamist magazine edited by a member of the Muslim Brotherhood: 'Umar Al-Tilmisani.
Al-Farida Al-Gha'iba:	The Missing Commandment; title of a book by Islamist Abdel Salam Faraj.
Al-Mut'a:	A type of alimony for a divorced wife.
Al-Sha'b:	Newspaper of the Islamist-oriented Labour Party.
Al-Takfir wal Hijra:	Name of an Islamist group meaning excommunication and migration.
Al-Watan Al-Arabi:	Title of a magazine.
Al-Zawiya al-Hamra:	District in Cairo.
Asala:	Authenticity.
Bint Al-Ard:	Daughter of the Earth; name of a feminist non-governmental organization.
Dar Al-Harb:	House/abode of war.
Dar Al-Ifta':	Name of the institution where fatwas are issued; where the Grand Mufti works.
Dar Al-Islam:	House/Abode of Islam.

Dhimmi:	A free non-Muslim under Muslim rule.
Fatwa:	Religious opinion; *fatawi* (plural).
Fi Sabil Illah:	For the sake of God.
Fitna:	Seduction which leads to sedition.
Hadritik:	Polite and respectful way of saying 'you'.
Hamajiyya:	Lack of respect/barbarism/chaos.
Hijab:	A veil worn to cover hair, arms and legs and may be varied and colourful.
Hijra:	Migration.
'Idda:	A period of three months following a divorce wherein a wife is also entitled to alimony.
Ijtihad:	Independent reasoning.
Ishtibakat Hiwariyya:	Discursive clashes.
Islami:	Islamist; term used as a self-definition by some young Islamists.
'Isma:	Right to divorce.
Ittihad Ishtiraki:	Socialist Union; name of the ruling party during Nasser's time.
Jahili/Jahiliyya:	Term used to refer to pre-Islamic times; ignorant times; also used to refer to non-Islamic actions or eras.
Jama'at Islamiyya/al-Jama'at:	Name of an Islamist group, used interchangeably.
Jihad:	Struggle in the name of God; holy war; name of an Islamist group also used interchangeably with *al-Jihad*.
Jizya:	Tax payed by non-Muslims in early Islam.
Kafir:	Non-believer.
Khimar:	A stringent type of veil with a loose and long headscarf and long, long-sleeved and very loose dress/body garment usually of a drab and unitary colour.
Lajnat al-Tansiq al-Sha'biyya lil Tahdir li Mu'tamar Pekin:	National Popular Committee to Organize for the Beijing/Peking Conference.

Marakiz Al-Quwwa:	Power centres; used during Nasser's time to denote method of ruling.
Muhajjaba:	Woman wearing the *hijab*.
Munaqqaba:	Woman wearing the *niqab* (see below).
Murtadd:	An apostate or renegade from Islam.
Muslimun:	Muslims.
Muta'aslimun:	Term coined by Laila Al-Shall to refer to Islamists as those who 'put on' Islam.
Niqab:	Very severe form of veil, usually black in colour, entirely shrouds the head and body leaving only the eyes exposed.
Qadiyyat al-Mar'a:	The woman's issue.
Qanun al-'Ayb:	Law of Shame.
Qanun al-'Uqubat:	Criminal law.
Qawama:	Male control or leadership over women.
Ruz al-Yusuf:	Name of a longstanding leftist weekly magazine.
Shari'a:	Islamic laws.
Shudhudh:	Deviance, used when referring to homosexuals.
Sunna:	The Prophet Muhammad's actions.
Tajammu':	Leftist Progressive Unionist political party.
Takfir:	To denounce as *kafir* or non-believer.
Tarha:	Head scarf.
Tatabarraj:	Used by Islamist Sheikh Al-Ghazali to refer to a woman who does not veil.
Tatajammal:	Used to refer to a woman ornamenting herself.
Ulama:	Religious scholars.
Umma:	Islamic/Muslim nation.
Umm al-Dunya:	Name of the Nasserist Party's Women's Committee Newsletter, meaning Mother of the World.
'Urfi:	Used in reference to unofficial marriage.
'Uzla:	To distance, used by certain Islamist groups who preach withdrawal from society.

List Abbreviations

ADEW:	Association for the Development and Enhancement of Women
AHED:	Association for Health and Environmental Development
AUC:	American University in Cairo
AWSA:	Arab Women's Solidarity Association
CEDAW:	United Nations Convention for the Elimination of All Forms of Discrimination Against Women
FO:	Free Officers
FWWC:	United Nations Fourth World Women's Conference
ICPD:	International Conference on Population and Development
IMF:	International Monetary Fund
J:	*Jihad*
MB:	Muslim Brotherhood
NDP:	National Democratic Party (ruling party)
NGO:	Non-Governmental Organization
NMC:	New Marriage Contract
NPWC:	Nasserist Party Women's Committee
NUL:	New Unified Labour Law
NWRC:	New Woman Research Centre
PSL:	Personal Status Laws/Family Laws
PVO:	Private Voluntary Organization
PWU:	Progressive Women's Union (Tajammu' Party Women's Committee)
RCC:	Revolutionary Command Council
SAP:	Structural Adjustment Policies
WAF:	Women Against Fundamentalism (England)
WS:	Women's Secretariat at the National Democratic Party.

1 Background and Theoretical Considerations

INTRODUCTION

1985 witnessed a bizarre incident when women members and sympathizers of the Islamist current marched and demonstrated in Egypt against a Family Law, which had been introduced in 1979, and which ultimately gave women more rights than any other such law.[1] The protests and demonstrations, which were supported by conservative male Muslim clergy, eventually led to the Family Law being declared unconstitutional in 1985. The basis for this declaration lay in the fact that the way the law had been passed was in itself unconstitutional. Knowing and anticipating the likely opposition to it, President Sadat had passed the law by presidential decree rather than have it debated in Parliament as normal procedure dictated. After the intense opposition, during which it was pointed out that a presidential decree is valid only for when Emergency Laws were in force (which was not the case for the Family Law) the Supreme Constitutional Court declared it unconstitutional. As a result, Egyptian women were thrown back to seeking recourse to laws formulated in the 1920s.

Although the law was modified and reintroduced with government support, and eventually constituted as the New Family Code, the fact that it was so vehemently attacked by women who stood to benefit from it remains highly significant. Equally significant are the dynamics that were exposed during the debates for and against the 1985 Family Law. For, on the one hand, there was the rather ambiguous position of a state whose responsibility it was to have passed these laws and to see them implemented. And on the other, there was the convergence of Islamist and conservative Muslim thinkers to generate sufficient effective pressure on the state to withdraw from its previous commitment.

Why were women protesting? Why was the state forced to compromise with the Islamists, even if only in the short term? These are some of the questions that galvanized a great many activists within women's groups in Egypt to try to understand what was happening to Egyptian women after more than a century of feminism. The Family Law debates could be seen to have constituted a sort of

1

collective awakening for women's groups in Egypt, after many years of what seemed like quiet introspection and relative inactivity.

The debates highlighted certain 'realities' within Egyptian society and politics which had been evolving gradually over many years, effectively since the coming to power of President Sadat in 1971. The most dominant and significant of these is the extent to which 'Islam' had become the central feature of almost any discourse involving political, social, cultural and economic change. Indeed, the Islamization of discourse was the principal factor in the search for legitimacy and authenticity, which was and is plaguing the Egyptian polity.

In 1991, the Egyptian government, through its Ministry of Social Affairs (headed by Egypt's only woman minister at the time), banned the Arab Women's Solidarity Association (AWSA), a secular and openly feminist political organization.[2] The official reason given for the ban was its financial mismanagement. However, familiarity with the local political situation, as well as the Law of Associations under which AWSA was registered, indicated that by adopting openly political standpoints (such as actively organizing to mobilize opposition to the Gulf War), AWSA had gone against the letter of the law, as well as the spirit of 'the woman issue' (*qadiyyat al-mar'a*) according to government interpretation.

As if banning the AWSA was not harsh enough, the state then carried out another telling action: AWSA's assets were sequestered to a previously unheard of Non-Governmental Organization (NGO) titled 'Women in Islam'. Not only was this an obscure organization – and still is – but it had no political standpoint whatsoever. What did the government's action indicate? The attempt to answer this question is a large part of the motivation for and quest behind this book. Significant aspects of the AWSA incident are the following:

1. That the government, whilst allowing AWSA the status of an NGO after several years of failed attempts, denied the legitimacy of this association at the stroke of a pen, thus warning all other outspokenly *political feminist* organizations – not to mention other political organizations with openly anti-government positions.

2. That having banned AWSA, the government did not simply confiscate its considerable assets, but transferred them instead to an *Islamic* women's organization. 'Women in Islam' is a charity

concerned with helping less advantaged Muslim women, teaching them about the faith and doing this from within a relatively conservative framework.

In many respects, the Family Law debates as well as the AWSA incident reflected one of the sites where the interrelationships between the law, religion and feminism were continuously taking place. Since then, much has happened in the arena of women's issues in Egypt. Though the dynamics of the relationship between the three forces remain to the fore, the conditions of their power-plays are constantly changing.

Having become aware of the general ignorance about present-day Egyptian women activists (both in Egypt and abroad), I decided to become a part of the effort to highlight their contemporary struggles. What must be underlined here, however, is that this book does *not* deal with Islam *per se*, but rather with Islamism or political Islam. Although Islamism is understood by most of its adherents as a fundamentally religious movement, I regard it as a quintessentially *political* movement and ideology. Further, what interests me is the interrelatedness of Islamisms with the state and feminist responses in Egypt.

Questions surrounding modern-day women's activism in Egypt become especially interesting in the light of the current political situation. It is becoming increasingly difficult to ignore or marginalize the impact that Islamist groups and thought are having in today's Arab and Muslim societies as a whole. In fact, the apparent xenophobia within the Western world towards Islam and Islamism can be seen as a testimony to the perceived effect of political Islam on today's international polity. How are women faring in these increasingly politicized Islamist discourses? Events in Algeria, Iran and, to some extent, Tunisia and Turkey indicate that the relationships between the state, Islamists and women's organizations form important axes within the complex interplay of power and hegemony. Women's organizations (their effectiveness or lack thereof) feature as part of the power dynamics taking place, in so far as they are sites of shifting struggles.

In my analysis of power relations between feminists and Islamists and the state in Egypt, I rely on Foucault's analysis of power. In investigating this particular interplay of forces, I am repeatedly struck by the fact that there is a continuous response of one force to another, thereby prompting a reaction. In other words, power oscillates from one to the other in a series of reactions and counteractions. Islamists' power is a reaction to state power, as well as inherent to Islamist dynamics in itself. The same is true in reference to the relationship between Islamists and feminists, and between feminists and state. In fact, the power of Islamists, state laws and feminists lies in a complex interplay of resistances to each other. Foucault puts this succinctly when he says, 'when there is power there is resistance, and yet, or rather consequently, this resistance is never in a position of exteriority in relation to power' (Foucault 1978: 95).

Hence, I follow Foucault's suggestion of 'taking the forms of resistance against different forms of power as a starting point' to analyse relations of power (Foucault, in Dreyfus and Rabinow, 1982: 211). Herein lies the purpose of this book. Instead of viewing the power of the state, feminists or Islamists *per se* (i.e. as institutions, movements or groups), I propose to analyse the resistances resulting from the various antagonistic interactions. I shall look at the power relations involved by studying the relationships of resistance that take place between women activists and the state; women activists and Islamisms; and, to a lesser extent, Islamists and the state.

The book highlights the different forms of women's activism (resistances) in contemporary Egypt, by featuring some of these activists' perceptions vis-à-vis state laws and Islamist thought. The issues considered include women activists' perceptions of and debates on state laws which directly affect Egyptian women; an insight into the nature of the relationship between the Egyptian state and Islamists – highlighting the main Islamist ideologues and disciplinary techniques; and contemporary Islamists' conceptualizations of women's roles – contrasting the dominant male conceptualizations with those of some of the women activists.

FEMINISMS IN EGYPT

...But Why Feminism?

The women referred to in this book are all activists, in the sense that they are actively involved in articulating discourses on and of women, on a broad socio-political level. The principal aim of these discourses is to improve women's legal, social, political and economic *awareness* and *position*. I thus distinguish between women who carry out primarily charitable work (I do not deal with them in this research) and those who attempt to change women's lives by consciously participating in directly political activities (those I refer to as feminists).

Because the history and praxis of Egyptian feminisms has traditionally been grounded in and has emanated from charitable social work, such a distinction as the one I propose is admittedly both difficult and controversial. The difficulty arises in trying to clarify the fine line between social activism and political involvement, since sometimes both are intimately connected. The controversy arises in insisting on applying a term such as feminism(s), which is openly rejected as a self-definition by some women activists. Both difficulties are compounded by the fact that 'feminism as philosophy',[3] or as a theoretical tool of analysis, as opposed to activism *per se*, has yet to develop on the Egyptian – and indeed on the Arab – scene. The preoccupation, prevalent among women activists, of 'fighting for women's rights', or debating and resolving 'the woman question' (*qadiyyat al-mar'a*), effectively means that a feminist philosophy grounded in a literary discipline, and employed as a means by which textually and actively to critique and counter dominant practices, is absent. Prevalent are attempts at working at a variety of levels, on day-to-day issues of concern to women (e.g. literacy classes, legal awareness classes and income-generating projects).[4] Thus, conceptualizations of women's activism in Egypt must be seen as enmeshed in struggles for some form of 'women's rights'.

I understand and use feminism as *an individual or collective awareness that women have been and continue to be oppressed in diverse ways and for diverse reasons, and attempts towards liberation from this oppression involving a more equitable society with improved relations between women and men.*[5] The women I have chosen to refer to as 'feminists' are either affiliated to political parties or have stated political aims in their organizational and group agendas. By identifying and isolating certain forms of women's activism as 'feminisms', I am simultaneously highlighting differences, locating specificities, whilst placing them within a broader frame of reference. The latter facilitates recognition, and in so doing, permits comparison and inquiry. For ultimately, I do not unceremoniously label them all as feminists, but I take into account disparate nuances, as well as pronounced differences. Indeed, it is in these terms that I refer to the plurality and heterogeneity of feminisms, as opposed to one unified and universal philosophy.

The term 'feminism' is, to all intents and purposes, one that has originated in the West. Thus, in post-colonial Arab Muslim societies the term is tainted, impure and heavily impregnated with stereotypes. Some of these stereotypes are that feminism basically stands for enmity between men and women, as well as a call for immorality in the form of sexual promiscuity for women. Moreover, some former and present-day religious personalities (e.g. Muhammad Qutb (1991) and Muhammad Al-Sha'rawi (1992) among others) associate feminism with colonialist strategies to undermine the indigenous social and religious culture. In the opinion of such thinkers, colonizers used the 'woman question' as a tool with which to attack Islam and portray it as oppressive and backward. Hence, the association of 'feminism' with abuse of Islam. These stereotypes and associations have proved remarkably enduring. Not so much because of the limited grain of truth they encompass, but because such ideas appeal to pre-existing imagery and are effective tools in the attempt to discredit any means that legitimize and justify women's attempts to gain control over their own lives.

What seem today as taken-for-granted requests (e.g. women's right to education and to vote) were revolutionary when first introduced. Nevertheless, the quest for equal rights with men remains a thorny issue in most Arab countries. Hence the call, especially prominent during the lead-up to and holding of the UN's Fourth World Women's Conference (FWWC, Beijing 1995), of 'equity' instead of 'equality'. Though still ambiguous, the main difference between equity and equality seems to centre on affirming women's access to rights which do not necessarily equal those of men, as well as women's rights to differ from those of men without being subjected to any form of hierarchy. The supposedly alternative term equity was accepted and actually promoted by Muslim countries, and it was propagated and discussed during the FWWC by Islamists as well as their 'pro-family' religious colleagues.

Whatever the interplay of words and jargon, the fact that another term was needed to suit the enterprise of women's rights indicates that the terminology is more problematic than the efforts involved. In fact, whereas feminism is rejected as a term, some of its meanings and agendas are nevertheless adapted by the different actors within different historical and culturally specific contexts. If 'feminism' is rejected, this does not mean that a *feminist consciousness* and agenda are absent.

The term feminism is also questioned by many so-called Third World women. Feminist movements have been challenged on the grounds of cultural imperialism, of shortsightedness in defining the meaning of gender in terms of middle-class, white experiences, and in terms of internal racism, classism and homophobia (Mohanty 1991: 7). All these factors combined to make feminism a suspicious identity-definition as well as an analytical category. Clearly Western feminist discourse and political practice are neither singular nor homogeneous in their aims or analysis. But, as Mohanty argues, there are:

> various textual strategies used by particular writers that codify Others as non-Western and hence themselves as (implicitly) Western. [Certain] analytic principles ... serve to distort Western feminist practices, and limit the possibility of coalitions among (usually White) Western feminists and working class and feminists of color around the world. These limitations are evident in the construction of (implicitly consensual) priority of issues around which apparently all women are expected to organize.
>
> (ibid.: 52)

Mohanty elaborates her criticisms to identify Western feminist assertions on a 'monolithic notion of patriarchy or male dominance', which supposedly oppresses all Third World women in the same way. She proceeds to argue that

> It is in this process of homogenization and systematization of oppression of women in the third world that power is exercised in much of recent Western feminist discourse, and this power needs to be defined and named.
>
> (ibid.: 54)

Taking these criticisms a step further, one can argue that in so far as some Western feminism has essentialized, homogenized and universalized the means and outcomes of women's oppression, it has acted as a meta-discourse. As such, it has sought to legitimate itself by many means, both within academia and in the spheres of activism. An example is writing and analysing 'forms of oppression' on behalf of 'Other' women.[6]

Many women from developing countries have gone on to engage with feminism – even while sometimes rejecting the label. Amrita Basu notes that despite widespread resistance to feminism among women, it is

> equally striking how many women who believe that feminism is bourgeois or Western go on to identify indigenous alternatives to

Western-style feminism within their own cultural and political contexts.

(Basu 1995: 20)

Kumari Jayawardena, writing about feminist movements in Asia in the late nineteenth and early twentieth centuries, defines feminism as 'embracing movements for equality within the current system and significant struggles that have attempted to change the system' (Jaya- wardena 1986: 2). Jayawardena asserts that these feminist movements emerged in two formative contexts. One of these conditions was the formulation and consolidation of national identities during periods of anti-imperialist struggles. The other context was the re-creation of pre-capitalist religious and feudal structures in attempts to 'modernize' Third World societies.

In fact, as Mohanty points out, writings on feminism undertaken by women from the developing world have consistently focused on:

(1) the ideas of the simultaneity of oppression as fundamental to the experience of social and political marginality and the grounding of feminist politics in the histories of racism and imperialism; (2) the crucial role of a hegemonic state in circumscribing their/our daily lives and survival struggles; (3) the significance of memory and writing in the creation of oppositional agency; and (4) the differences, conflicts and contradictions internal to third world women's organizations and communities. In addition they have insisted on the complex interrelationships between feminist, antiracist and nationalist struggles.

(Mohanty 1991: 10)

This work falls in the cadre of Mohanty's second and fourth points and complements others, which endorse the importance of feminists of the Third World to rewrite history 'based on specific locations and histories of struggle of people of colour and postcolonial peoples, and on the day-to-day strategies of survival utilized by such peoples' (ibid.). Hence the advocation for feminisms devoid of hegemonic and universalizing characteristics, and open to differences of both interpretation and methodology.

I argue that there are diverse forms of feminism and multiple expressions for the activism advocated, which correspond to the types of oppression women perceive in different parts of the world. Particularly apt are postmodern conceptualizations of feminism, which advocate a theoretical outlook 'attuned to the *cultural speci-*

ficity of different societies and *periods* and to that of *different groups within societies* and *periods*' (Fraser and Nicholson 1990: 34, emphasis added). Other important features of such postmodern-feminist theorizing are its non-essentialism, non-universalism, pragmatism, and even its fallibility. But most importantly, in its denial of a single feminist epistemology, it creates space for contemporary feminist political practices, which would have been regarded previously as unorthodox. This understanding of feminisms has also been advocated to some extent by feminist anthropology. Nevertheless, it was due to the work of postmodernist feminist theoreticians that feminist critiques of Enlightenment discourses have been strengthened and refined. This has enabled diverse conceptualizations and articula-tions of feminisms (see Nicholson 1990 and 1991; Kristeva 1981 and 1982; Hekman 1992).

I have characterized three main 'types' of feminist thought and praxis operating in Egypt today. These are: *secular feminism, Muslim feminism* and *Islamist feminism*. Covering the broad political spectrum, this identification serves to highlight the multiplicity of voices through which Egyptian women activists speak and act. The distinctions, however, do not imply that these groups are clearly demarcated. On the contrary, I highlight their main characteristics while maintaining that often distinctions between the different feminists are in a state of flux, and are context- and issue-bound rather than clear-cut and immutable. Though on certain issues these feminists may converge and act together (e.g. appealing to the ruling National Democratic Party to lobby for the lifting of sanctions against Iraq) there are important differences among them. These differences include political convictions, social backgrounds, perceptions of the reasons behind women's oppression and the means advocated to counter this oppression. Nevertheless, I maintain the importance of seeing the commonalities of their struggles and goals despite their varied means.

Islamist Feminism

I use the term Islamist feminists because many of the Islamist women I interviewed are aware of a particular oppression of women, *and* they actively seek to rectify this oppression by recourse to Islamic principles. Nevertheless, most of the Islamist women interviewed will shy away from the term feminist, if not vehemently criticize it outright, as an irrelevant and inaccurate Western term. Though many still feel that feminism at best is ambiguous, and at worst is disrespectful to religion, what many women Islamists uphold is difficult to separate from what feminism, as defined here, connotes. I intentionally refer to these Islamist activists as feminists, not to homogenize them, but for the following reasons:

1. to distinguish them from their male and other women counterparts, who think differently, since not all Islamists are feminists by any means; and
2. to indicate later possible points of intersection with other women activists, an aspect I find crucial to the evolving power dynamics.

In the opinion of Islamist feminists, women are oppressed precisely because they try to be 'equal' to men and are therefore being placed in unnatural settings and unfair situations, which denigrate them and take away their integrity and dignity as women. For example, women are 'forced' to go out and compete in the labour market – a task which means that women may come into contact with men (as in public transport, for example) in a humiliating and inappropriate way.

It is the demands of a Western and culturally inauthentic ideology, made at the expense of Islamic teachings, which oppress women. As far as many of them are concerned, Western feminism, with its emphasis on the total equality of the sexes, results in women striving to be 'superhuman' and, in the process, losing much of their effort whilst taking on more burdens. For Islamist women, a just (Islamic) society is one that strives for a recognition and respect for compatibility between the sexes instead of competition.

Many of them, when directly questioned, are reluctant to distinguish between women's oppression and social oppression as a whole. They uphold that what is happening to women is part of a societal process wherein proper Islamic principles are absent, or at best are misused by a morally bankrupt and corrupt state regime. They see their mission as a 'structural *jihad*',[7] which is aimed at a 'change towards more Islamization', which in turn occurs through 'active participation in *all spheres* of life'.[8] This, then, is not merely a call for women to stay at home. Rather, it is a 'call to arms', which enhances and reconceptualizes women's role within the family (as mothers and wives), and gives women a sense of value, political purpose and confidence: they are not less than men, but equally important in different ways.

Islamist feminists are part of a political movement that is, on the whole, actively attempting to raise support for itself in its ultimate quest for the capture of state power and legislation. In their bid to combine the support of their organized and unorganized groupings, Islamists – particularly the moderates – cannot afford to lose the political, social and economic backing of these women, who actively participate in some of these Islamist movements. Simultaneously, Islamist women have successfully reversed traditional value judgements about women's space. Essentially, 'women's knowledge' of the home and child-rearing has been given a higher socio-political esteem than that of women working outside their home. Moreover, within the boundaries supposedly imposed by their understandings of Islam, women are still able to be active in the public arena.[9] In many respects, the Islamist movements resemble the nationalist movements of an earlier epoch, so far as their attempts to mobilize women for their cause are concerned. The end result of this is that, for the time being, attempts to curtail the public role of these women by the moderate male Islamists at least are not in evidence.

Muslim Feminism

Women activists whom I identify as Muslim feminists also use Islamic sources, like the Quran and the *Sunna* (the Prophet's actions and sayings), but their aim is to show that the discourse of equality between men and women *is* valid, within Islam. Muslim feminists also try to steer a middle course between interpretations of socio-political and cultural realities according to Islam and a human rights discourse.

Many of them will be proud to be identified as feminists, or at least have no problems with the term, in so far as it describes their main aims. As far as these women are concerned, a feminism that does not justify itself within Islam is bound to be rejected by the rest of society, and is therefore self-defeating. Moreover, Muslim feminists feel that to attempt to separate Islamic discourses from current discourses (whether they are accused of being 'Western' or not) can only lead to serious fragmentation within society, and is thus unrealistic. Such a separation, many argue, succeeds in preventing a process of mutual enlightenment between the two discourses, and in fact risks making the Islamic one more alienating and patriarchal, and the sole domain of the Islamists.[10]

Muslim feminists look upon the issue of the veil, for example, as one that should be based on a woman's choice and conviction. Islamist feminists, on the other hand, take the veil as an indisputable religious obligation, and, even more importantly, a symbol of the depth of religious conviction and solidarity with other Muslim – if not Islamist – women. For Islamist women, the veil is essential and without it, women have not made that necessary commitment to a particular ideal of authenticity of identity. In short, there are no unveiled Islamist women. More to the point, however, the veil is seen as a means by which to bridge the gap between the otherwise separate male and female domains. The veil becomes, therefore, not only a symbol of their identity, but a holy, sanctioned and acceptable means by which to broaden and further their political, social and cultural space.

Both Islamist and Muslim feminists argue for a form of *ijtihad*,[11] and many Islamist feminists agree with Muslim feminists, that women *are* indeed capable of taking on tasks involving the interpretation of Islamic jurisprudence and providing social and political leadership (previously thought to be the exclusive domain of men). In that sense, both these sets of feminists are arguing against existing patriarchal religious formations/hierarchies, and the implications of their interpretations on gender, and both use very similar 'tools' of analysis and argumentation. That is, both sets of feminists are extensively studying, analysing and referring to traditional Islamic texts, in order to validate and justify their arguments.

However, what distinguishes Muslim feminists from their Islamist counterparts is the former's willingness to contextualize religious (and particularly Quranic) injunctions, in order to allow for the possibilities of textual reinterpretation. This renders their socio-political positioning highly problematic: to refer to traditional authoritative religious texts is permissible and encouraged, but to attempt to reread the meanings is not. Reinterpretation involves challenging the traditional, hierarchical, institutional and predominantly male religious power structures, a task which women in general are not encouraged to do – *and especially not when these women have not gone through the traditional religious institutional training* (e.g. Al-Azhar). Given that many of the Muslim feminists are attempting to reconcile the discourses of Islam with human rights, they are further facing the same accusations of 'cultural inauthenticity' faced by other promoters of secular discourses. This can become a political handicap when faced with increasingly dominant Islamist and other discourses, which advocate the concept of *asala* (authenticity) 'at the expense of an appreciation of conjunctural and historical realities' (Al-Azmeh 1993: 72).

Muslim feminists are perceived by establishment Islam as a direct threat to almost all inherited religious values, and most of all, to its power-base. They thus lack popular political support from those who are influenced by Al-Azhar, as well as from Islamist ideologues who give themselves, as males in positions of authority, the rights denied Muslim feminists – i.e. to reinterpret religious texts. Moreover, as with the secular feminists, there is little support for these groups from the state. On the contrary, the state's often ambiguous role and its ill-defined position on women's issues,[12] only complicates matters for Muslim and secular women activists.

Secular Feminism   Human Rights discourse

Secular feminists firmly believe in grounding their discourse outside the realm of any religion, whether Muslim or Christian, and placing it, instead, within the international human rights discourse. They do not 'waste their time' attempting to harmonize religious discourses with the concept and declarations pertinent to human rights. To them, religion is respected as a private matter for each individual, but it is totally rejected as a basis from which to formulate any agenda on women's emancipation. By so doing, they avoid being caught up in interminable debates on the position and status of women within religion. Also avoided are potential accusations, levelled by religious conservatives, regarding their right to (re)interpret religious texts. None the less, a number of cultural and political criticisms are directed at them: they are clones of the West, implementers of imperialist agendas, and – the ultimate delegitimizer – non-believers.

Though they admit in theory to the need to maintain at least a dialogue with Islamist women, in practice secular feminists disagree totally with their points of view. Not surprisingly, secular feminists would *not* identify their Islamist counterparts as being even remotely feminist. In turn, as promoters of a secular discourse, they are not held in high esteem by the Islamists. Any strategic – let alone ideological – accommodation between them (e.g. to agree to disagree) is total anathema to all concerned. In short, they are political 'enemies'. Their relationship with Muslim feminists, however, is generally better. Though this tends to vary from moments of overlap and agreement (such as on the necessity to amend the Personal Status Laws) to moments of tension and dissent (e.g. on the relevance of an Islamic framework to such amendments).

OFFICIAL ISLAM AND ISLAMISM

An important distinction has to be made between official Islam and Islamism in Egypt. The former encompasses a wide variety of modes of operation and ideologies. Official Islam, otherwise referred to as 'Establishment Islam', is exemplified by the religious institution – Al-Azhar – and the *Dâr al-Ifta'*, the Office of the Grand Mufti. Al-Azhar is an Islamic institution which encompasses several functions: that of mosque, university, state legitimation, interpretive authority and centre of Islamic propagation all in one.

Traditionally, Al-Azhar has acted as the place of learning which produced the religious *ulama* who, in turn, went on to proselytize the faith in various ways. During the nationalist struggles of the early twentieth century, Al-Azhar had a relatively independent role from the state. Many Azharite *ulama* joined and actively participated in articulating nationalist aspirations at the time. After Nasser came to power, the independence of Al-Azhar was seriously curtailed as the staff – especially the head of the institution – effectively became government employees.

On several occasions, *fatwas* (religious opinions) were issued by the Sheikh of Al-Azhar in support of certain state policies, or actions, the most notable being Sadat's highly controversial peace initiative with Israel, his visit to Jerusalem and the modifications – reportedly made at the behest of his wife, Jihan Sadat – to the Family Laws that were passed by presidential decree.[13] As such, Al-Azhar came to be seen by many as the official mouthpiece of Islam, and the source of Islamic legitimacy to state power. This repetitive pro-government stance has undermined the legitimacy of Al-Azhar on several occasions – particularly in the eyes of Islamists.

The attitude of delegitimation accorded to Al-Azhar is prevalent among most Islamist ideologues and is exemplified by the opinions expressed by some leaders of different groups. For instance, Abdel Salam Faraj, an ideologue of the Jihad group, is quoted as having asked sarcastically in his book *Al-Farida al-Gha'iba* (the Missing Commandment), 'What did the ulama of Al-Azhar do when the troops of Napoleon were desecrating the Muslim soil of Egypt?'[14]

Mohammed Al-Ghazali, a leading member of the Muslim Brother-hood, remarked that there were two Islamic blocs in Egypt: the official one formed of Al-Azhar *ulama*, and one formed of 'Islamic groups/societies', and something along the lines of 'and never the twain shall meet'. Al-Ghazali added later that 'Al-Azhar society has gone to sleep and the Muslim society has followed them' (Al-Said 1977: 57).

Despite this perception, which has gained in strength over the years, Al-Azhar *ulama* are not totally disregarded by the rest of Egyptian public opinion. Statements by and opinions of the Sheikh of Al-Azhar, for example, still influence a great many people. During the ICPD,[15] for instance, it seemed as though everyone was waiting to hear the Sheikh's opinions on the various debates that had taken place there, ranging from the holding of such a conference in the first place to issues pertaining to reproductive rights and population policies. The role of this venerable institution in mainstream political discourse should not and is not being discounted here.

However, Al-Azhar's political profile has been surpassed by Islamist ideology, in so far as the former has been tainted by its connections with the state, and perceived as a dormant discourse. Islamisms, on the contrary, appear dynamic and aim for deep structural changes at all levels of society – they do not hesitate to challenge state power. Islamisms have politically and strategically outshone Al-Azhar by appearing to provide the long-lost political alternative to Egypt's woes. Moreover, with the passage of time and the improvement in the quantity and quality of social services offered to the poorer segments of Egyptian society by certain Islamist groups, Islamism has grown to prove itself a viable socio-political alternative.

Many of the boards of Egypt's traditional bastions of democracy – the professional syndicates[16] – are now presided over, not by Al-Azhar *ulama*, but by members of the Islamist Muslim Brotherhood. The Labour Party, just before the 1987 parliamentary elections, went into political partnership not with Al-Azhar *ulama*, but with the Muslim Brotherhood. Effective political opposition to the state is carried out not by Al-Azhar personnel, but by Islamists – both at the level of rhetoric, as well as of action. Quests for state power are not carried out by Al-Azhar male *ulama*, but by Islamist men and women. And finally, vocal demands for social change and alternative reinterpretations of Muslim women's roles, are voiced not by Al-Azhar *ulama*, but by women active within Islamist groups. Hence, in looking at the power dynamics between Islamists, women activists and the state, this book specifically concentrates on *political Islam*.

...But Why 'Islamism'?

The focus here is on the aspects of political Islam that claim to be 'moderate', and are also referred to as such by some researchers – notably Ibrahim (1980), Dessouki (1982), Binder (1988) and Kepel (1985) among others. I use the term Islamists because I feel it is necessary to refer to these groups in terms of the agendas that they themselves proclaim and in some cases implement. 'We can identify them and name them according to what it is they want', was the response of one Leftist Egyptian woman activist,[17] when questioned on her means of reference. Nikki Keddie, one of the first to use the term, asserted that Islamists form the essence of movements for political Islam, usually aiming at an Islamic state that would enforce at least some Islamic laws and customs, including those related to sex segregation, and some economic measures and Quranic punishments (Keddie, in Halliday and Allavi 1988: 15). Similarly, Habib Boulares uses the word 'in the precise sense of an action carried out by militant Muslims so that their concept of religion penetrates the *state* and *society*' (Boulares 1990: x, emphasis added).

Whether the strategy is the gradual Islamic re-education of the masses, until these masses themselves call for an Islamic government (as is the belief of the Muslim Brotherhood), or the forceful seizure of state power and replacement of the 'un-Islamic' leadership (as is the ideology of the Jihad, for example), the heterogeneous range of Islamist groups are united and agree on some form of *Islamization*[18] *of people and government*. The Islamist presence in Egypt, therefore, is a political phenomenon. Moreover, the term 'Islamist' is one which many Islamist activists themselves often identify with. As one young, middle-ranking activist of the Muslim Brotherhood said: 'It gives me a source of pride and satisfaction when I am referred to as an Islamist [*Islami* in Arabic]. All I seek is to see Islam implemented.'

The term more commonly applied by Western media and some researchers to political Islam is 'fundamentalism'. The latter term, however, is alien to the everyday realities of many of these male and female activists. As John Esposito lucidly elaborates:

> I regard 'fundamentalism' as too laden with Christian presuppositions and Western stereotypes, as well as implying a monolithic

threat that does not exist; more fitting general terms are 'Islamic revivalism' or 'Islamic activism', which are less value-laden and have roots within the Islamic tradition.

(Esposito 1992: 8)

The term 'fundamentalism', as Esposito pointed out was originally used to refer to a Christian Protestant sect. However, even with regard to Christianity, as Jan Nederveen Pieterse (1993) argues, the term 'fundamentalism' is a misnomer in most cases, and he makes a valid distinction between fundamentalism, pentecostalism and evangelicalism, as a means of bringing more clarity to his argument. Nederveen Pieterse also asserts that 'use of the term "fundamentalism" demonizes, homogenizes, polarizes, creates an enemy image ... makes phenomenon opaque, and blinds us with clairvoyance' (1993: 5–6). Demonization and enemy images particularly come to mind when senior politicians begin to reiterate the use of terms like 'Islamic fundamentalism' in the context of threats to the Western status quo – notably, Willy Claes, the former Secretary General of NATO, who is quoted as saying that 'Islamic fundamentalism is just as much a threat to the West as communism was'.[19] Not only is this homogenizing the differences between so-called 'Islamic fundamentalism', but it also aids the creation of enemy images of Islam as a whole. Samuel Huntington demonstrated this by stating in his influential article 'The Clash of Civilizations', that now that communism is beaten, the next great challenge to be confronted by Western civilization is Islam. This legacy of perceptions is adopted and its consequences enacted by US and European foreign policy decision-makers, as well as those researchers and consultants whose work is the stuff of cultural politics.

The term 'fundamentalism' serves to limit and homogenize different forms of Islamic thinking and practice. This is eloquently argued by Hippler, who points out quite rightly that in Western discourse, at least three diverse social and political phenomena are lumped under 'fundamentalism':

Firstly, the traditional Islamic clergy and their theology. These can be understood as conservative and therefore traditional. As a group they are hardly 'fundamentalist', even when, for political purposes, they sometimes use radical rhetoric ... Secondly the 'folk religion' of 'everyday faith', which per definition does not have much to do with official theology ... Thirdly the political religion of Islamists. They are principally in conflict with the traditional theologians and folk Islam. In this category are the real 'fundamentalists'.

(Hippler, in Hippler and Lueg 1995: 23)

Last but not least, I have found that the term fundamentalism, coined by non-Islamists to refer to a broad and diverse strata, is utterly rejected by its supposed adherents. Because of its negative connotations and the stereotypes it invokes, the term alienates both Islamist activists and their opponents, thus serving to create further obstacles to understanding the motivations and programmes of Islamist women and men, and the complexities, subtleties and nuances of their realities.

Having said that, however, it is important not to ignore the arguments *promoting* the validity and practicality of the term fundamentalism. Such arguments have been put forward by some women activists (e.g. from the Women Against Fundamentalism Group based in London), as well as from key compilers of a canon on the topic (i.e. Martin Marty and Scott Appleby, based at The University of Chicago).

In co-authored essays by Gita Sahgal and Nira Yuval-Davis (1994: 7–9), and Martin Marty and Scott Appleby (1991: vii-xiii) respectively, there is a general consensus that fundamentalism as a term used across religious convictions may homogenize phenomena. However, Sahgal and Yuval-Davis, in reply to Nederveen Pieterse's criticisms (noted above), insist that 'Fundamentalist movements rise in all major religions and are a reaction to the crisis in/of modernity' (1994: 8). Speaking from the standpoint of political activists and feminists, they maintain that there is

> Common ground in discourses within fundamentalist movements: the sense of danger from outside . . . the claim of purity and authenticity; the right to interpret the religious text and to insist that this is the only true version of it; the imposition of social control on members of the collectivity; and above all the use of state media and other resources to capture power and maintain control.

(ibid.)

Having specified the points of commonality, Sahgal and Yuval-Davis point out the differences inherent in the appearances and operations of fundamentalist groups. By arguing that concepts such as nationalism and socialism are equally liable to be used in a homogenizing and 'enemy-imaging' manner, Sahgal and Yuval-Davis further legitimize their use of the term.

Marty and Appleby, while arguing along the same lines, go further.
According to them,

> 'fundamentalism' is here to stay, since it serves to create a distinction over against [sic] cognate but not fully appropriate words such as 'traditionalism', 'conservatism', or 'orthodoxy' and 'orthopraxis'. If the term were to be rejected, the public would have to find some other word if it is to make sense of a set of global phenomena which urgently bid to be understood.
>
> (Marty and Appleby 1991: viii)

Other justifications for the term include the assertion that 'all words come from somewhere and will be more appropriate in some contexts rather than others' (ibid.); and, after years of research, 'no other term was found to be as intelligible or serviceable' (ibid.). Having clarified that each author in the canon on fundamentalism compiled by Marty and Appleby would voice her/his own reservations with the term, they say, 'It will be appropriate in virtually every case to picture individual quotation marks surrounding the term and then proceed with the inquiry and reading' (ibid.: ix). However, Marty and Appleby go on to present five characteristics of fundamentalism, which all centre on the word 'fight', a term that invariably evokes images of violence.

Starting with their generalization that fundamentalisms are *'fighting back'*,[20] the compilers of the canon then state that 'It is no insult to fundamentalists to see them as militant, whether in the use of words and ideas or ballots or, in extreme cases, bullets.' Moreover, they claim that *'Fundamentalists see themselves as militants'* (ibid.; emphasis added). Having spoken on behalf of almost all sorts of religious 'fundamentalists', Marty and Appleby then go on to say that fundamentalists also *'fight for'*. With some qualification, the authors however do concede that

> While some fundamentalists may be passive for a time, just wanting to be left alone, when the threat grows sufficiently intense they will fight for a changed civil polity.
>
> (ibid.)

One can only wonder whether Marty and Appleby have some definitive and general scale of measurement for this intensity. Fundamentalists, as Marty and Appleby state, *'fight with* a particularly chosen repository of resources which one might think of as weapons' (ibid.). What if one does not wish to use this not so subtle allusion? Knowing that fundamentalists' main characteristic revolves around fighting, one is not surprised to find the fourth point that fundamentalists *'fight against* others' (ibid.: x). In fact, they are supposedly 'the agents of assault on all that is held dear' (ibid.). Finally, fundamentalists, lest we should forget, also *'fight under* God'. In that category, Marty and Appleby hasten to remind us that 'particularly potent are those fundamentalists whose participants are convinced that they are called to carry out God's or Allah's purposes against challengers' (ibid.).

I am not averse to attempting to see the points of commonalities among different religious fundamentalisms, especially when, as in the Sahgal and Yuval-Davis case, there is a clear feminist project being undertaken. Women Against Fundamentalism (WAF), of whom Yuval-Davis is a member, openly states that they were set up in 1989

> [to] challenge the rise of fundamentalism in all religions. By fundamentalism we do not mean religious observance which we see as a matter of individual choice, but rather modern political movements which use religion as a basis for their attempt to consolidate power and extend social control, [to] resist the increasing control that fundamentalism imposes on all our lives... To struggle against religious dogma from whatever source which denies us our right to determine our own sexuality and justifies violence against women.[21]

As such, WAF, and similar organizations and groups, are implementing an activist agenda. Theirs is a quest, therefore, not unlike those of many women's groups in Egypt, which is to mobilize support 'on the ground' to push for certain issues. As an Egyptian secular woman activist was to tell me, 'When we are on the ground, we have to use universalistic principles to rally people. Slogans and general ideas are what the majority of people understand, and are prepared to gather around.'[22]

What is more problematic to accept, however, is the attempt to homogenize movements under an undefined agenda purporting to understand global phenomena, an agenda, moreover, that is coloured by antagonism to this generalized occurrence. It is canonizing all religious fundamentalist movements and ideas under a huge academic project, the premiss of which begins and revolves around the term 'fight'. Heavily loaded, the categoric terming already sets the stage, so to speak, for negative emotions and perceptions. The term 'fight' potentially evokes fear, anger and antagonism towards the projected perspectives on 'fundamentalism'.

Political Islam, or Islamism, is differentiated from 'Islamic fundamentalism' since it is my conviction that not all those who wish to live their lives by the book are actively participating in political movements aiming at State power. After interviewing more than 60 Islamist men and women in different parts of Egypt – members of groups ranging from the Muslim Brotherhood to Jihad – I cannot 'fit' these people into the overarching and antagonistic categories described by Marty and Appleby. Indeed there are some aspects which are similar, as is bound to be the case when such generalizations are made. Examples of such applicability are the 'selectivity' (ibid.: ix) employed by some groups in attempts to recapture their past; and the 'innovative power' (ibid.) employed by Islamists – though not to 'fight back' (ibid.), but logically and systematically to counter, in an often eloquent and articulate style, the arguments directed against them.

ISLAMISM AND POSTMODERNITY

Postmodernity is understood and applied here in two ways. First, as a political and academic shift away from universalizing Western meta-narratives (e.g. Marxism) which have been used to explain and legitimize social, political and economic trends and ideas. The above conceptualization is inspired by Jean-François Lyotard's analysis in *The Postmodern Condition* (1986). These large (his)stories of knowledge lost their significance as the sole legitimating frameworks for the events of the late twentieth century – particularly those related to colonialism and its modern forms. The truth purportedly given by universalizing meta-discourses is challenged by many scholars and activists on the basis of being (a) the only discourse of 'truth', and (b) denying legitimacy to many other less privileged voices, or multivocal, socially, institutionally and culturally specific 'truths' (Lyotard 1986; Foucault 1980). Instead, what is taking place is the rise of the smaller narratives – some of which are derivatives of larger meta-theories – which become the newer constructions of knowledge. An example of these smaller and diversified narratives more critical of the West is to be found in Islamisms. The latter being derivatives of meta-discourses of Islam.

Secondly, postmodernity is a form of 'deconnection' from hegemonic Western discourses, with their baggage of socio-political behaviour and analysis. Sayyid sees postmodernity as a 'decentring of the

West' (Sayyid, in Laclau 1994: 276). This is also the same sense in which Young (1990: 19–21) talks about poststructuralism, or an awareness of the specificity of European culture. In this respect, postmodernity would coincide with the project of the post-colonial, since both take up the deconstruction of the centralized, master narratives of the European culture. They break down the centre/margin binarism of imperial discourse.

Sayyid develops the concept of postmodernity in such a way as to make it applicable to Islamism, or the politics of the periphery. Basically, he argues that 'it is the change in the relationship between periphery and centre which is constitutive of post-modernity' (Sayyid, in Laclau 1994: 277). This change he terms 'decentring', following from his understanding that modernity itself is another means of privileging and prioritizing the West. Postmodernity then, is a shift from the centrality of the discourse of modernization/Westernization. Decentralization can also be looked at in terms of decolonization. The latter is by no means a homogeneous process, but is one of the 'main impetuses behind post-modernity and the revelation of the West's particularity behind its universalist façade' (ibid.: 278). Sayyid argues that the decentring of the West should be seen in Gramscian terms, wherein 'the hegemonic order that naturalized and sedemented a certain narrative structure has broken down, even though tremendously unequal power structures are still in place' (ibid.: 281). In other words, the West is being decentred, to the extent that its claim that there can be no other narrative of development, emancipation or progress other than its own, becomes irrelevant and inaccurate. In fact, seen in this light, 'Islamism does not become the "other" of postmodernity, but one of the possibilities of decentring of the West. Islamist movements are a *continuation and radicalization of the process of decolonization*' (ibid.; emphasis in the original).

Indeed, Islamist discourses can be seen as part-and-parcel of postmodernity, in so far as their proliferation and legitimation gain some legitimacy from the 'failure' of Westernization, and all its narrative baggage. It is the recognition of the non-universality of Western discourse, of the ability to think difference in a different way, that promotes the validity of Islamist discourse. No wonder, then, that in a country like Egypt, where nationalism, socialism and liberalism have been overstated and their usefulness questioned, that Islamism shines as a credible alternative. The Muslim Brotherhood's political slogan of 'Islam is the solution' serves only to represent this aspect of reality, and the recreation of knowledge.

THE EGYPTIAN STATE

For the purposes of this work, I adopt Gramsci's different uses for the word 'state': in a narrow legal-constitutional sense, as a balance between political and civil society, and as encompassing aspects of both. I see the Egyptian state as interventionist, where the lines dividing civil and political society can become blurred, particularly, as I argue throughout, when similar discourses of political power and legitimacy are being articulated and relied upon. Moreover, the state's use of particular laws (e.g. Law 32 of 1964, the Law of Associations) renders state control a defining aspect of the articulation of civil discourses.

The post-1952 interaction between the Egyptian state and the Isla-mists is a dynamic one which involves periods of covert encourage-ment on the one hand, and severe repression on the other. Chapters 3 and 4 will look at this Islamist–state interaction whilst analysing it from the Gramscian and Foucauldian standpoints wherein power and domination function in so far as those dominated consent to that domination. In other words, it is the consent of the state to allow the dominance of an Islamic discourse by participating and employing it, and the implied consent of some Islamists to work within state structures and institutions. The encouragement basically takes place at a time when Islamist activity can prove useful as a means to reach the ends of the state in terms of consolidating its ideological hege-mony. When these groups are seen to 'overstep the tolerance afforded' by the state, then a severe cycle of repression starts. Throughout this interaction, however, media reports and official literature give one the impression that a 'Muslim' state (which 'respects' Islam and is attempting to implement it in a modern way) is striving to fight off the evil monster of religious extremism. This impression implies a certain 'innocence' on the part of the state, whilst simultan-eously emphasizing the pressurizing potential of the Islamist move-ments.

As far as the relationship between women and the state is con-cerned, the view adopted here is that states incorporate facts of social power in societies in the form of law. In most state regimes, law is a particularly potent source and badge of legitimacy (MacKinnon 1989: 237). Hence, law is a site of power whilst being the arena through which power is exercised. Law is thus both a tool of oppression as well as of liberation, but in either case it is an instrument of political power. In both cases, the agency of women vis-à-vis the state (and vice versa) is critical (Schuler 1986: 4). In this regard, the secular feminist lawyer Mona Dhul-fiqar has said:

> We feel we can work with the government as partners, we have adequate laws and we are trying to use the laws as an instrument of progress... We have two fights in Egypt, a fight to change the [Family] law and a fight to implement the new law [but] when you get the approval of the government things happen more quickly.[23]

FURTHER THEORETICAL DELIBERATIONS

The struggles between all three intermingling forces studied in this arena are seen as projects involving power and hegemony. It is a struggle to *maintain* power (as in the case of the state), and a struggle to *gain* for themselves political power and hegemony (as in the case of the Islamists). As for the Egyptian feminists presented here, the issue is to *counter* the subordination of the discursive hegemony of both the state and certain Islamists, whilst seeking alternative discourses of empowerment. In the following section, I shall outline the main features of Gramscian (hegemony) and Foucauldian (power) ideas which I find enabling in conceptualizations of the complex interactions between feminists, Islamists and the state in Egypt.

Gramsci and Hegemony

Though not concerned directly with gender, Antonio Gramsci's work illuminates the power politics portrayed here. Gramsci's reflections on class relations and class struggle, written in the context of the growth of fascism and new forms of popular support for relations of inequality in the 1930s, give us an interesting insight into how power relations actually operate. For our purposes, his major innovation is the development of the idea of hegemony.

Gramsci uses the complex concept of hegemony as a description of the way relations of power work, both during ordinary times and during times of transition (see Gramsci 1971; Joll 1979; Sassoon 1980; Laclau and Mouffe 1985; Holub 1992; and Fontana 1993). Gramsci emphasizes the point that all power issues from a relationship, an interaction between two parties. Power is conceived as a dialectical interaction between unequal parties, one dominant and one subordinate, in which *both* parties have active roles to play. With the idea of hegemony, Gramsci explores the interplay of coercion and consent which forms the dynamic of relations of power. It is the relationship between unequals that is important for our analysis of the Egyptian situation. Neither Islamists, feminists nor the state actually share equal power relations. The state's hegemonic position is derived from, in Chomskian terms, its manufacture of consent. When analysing the relationship between Islamists and the state, both forces are effectively playing an active role. The state dominates (in the sense of force and coercion) this relationship. Islamists, through their successful social programmes and political alliances, are simultaneously hegemonizing political discourses of legitimacy, as well as attempting to Islamize state and society.

Gramsci argues that the hegemonic interaction, or power relationship, is most successful when force is not required and full consent of the subordinate party is achieved. Hegemony, therefore, describes the intellectual leadership of dominants, rather than the exercise of force, the framing of the ideas and visions of the subordinates which ensures the acceptance of inequalities. But the interesting point is that even this intellectual dominance does not entail a passive subordination within the power relationship; it requires an ongoing struggle which involves a process of negotiation, concession and underlying threat. Therefore, power in the Islamists' case is portrayed not as a possession of dominant groups, nor as the execution of force; it is, instead, the ongoing creation of a relationship which encourages the complicity and consent of the subordinate partner or partners. In these terms, the subordinates are often Egyptian feminists, who are continuously negotiating between and with Islamist thought and state laws.[24] This is not to argue that Egyptian feminists are constantly subjugated and victimized. On the contrary, their involvements in processes of negotiation entail dynamism and cycles when they exercise their own forms of power. Islamist feminists, for example, are not negotiating with and consenting to Islamist ideology in the same way that secular and Muslim feminists do. Gramsci's account, by focusing on the image of continuity in power relations and situations of inequality, forces us to reconsider the nature of power relations. The false image of stability conjured up by the apparent persistence of inequalities covers up a series of negotiations which are taking place. In these negotiations, subordinates, often including both Islamists and women, contest, negotiate and try to expand the boundaries of their experience, yet they also consent and accept their situation, often by believing themselves to be victimized and powerless. Power, in other words, involves a dynamic relationship in which women and Islamists, even as heterogeneous subordinate players, take an active role.

One of the drawbacks of Gramsci's theorizing is to visualize relationships of power and hegemony as essentially two-dimensional. The idea of one subordinate and one dominant actor may obscure the fact that, often, relationships of power are complicated and rendered less clear by the existence of more than two actors. When looking at a situation where Islamisms, state and feminists (not to mention countless others) are simultaneously involved in power relations, Gramsci's frameworks for conceptualizing power and hegemony are enriched and broadened by Foucault's articulations on power and related dynamics.

Foucault and Power

Foucault, like Gramsci, realized that subordinates as well as dominant individuals form the centre of intersecting forces of power, and that subordinate individuals are in many ways involved in the continual recreation of power. This suggests that there is a need to explore the complicated and contradictory ways through which subordinates pursue their ends in times of change. Of immediate relevance here is Michel Foucault's point:

> Power is not to be taken to be a phenomenon of one individual's consolidated and homogeneous domination over others, or that of one group or class over others. What, by contrast, should always be kept in mind is that power...must be analyzed as something that circulates...It is never localised here or there, never in anybody's hands, never appropriated as a commodity or a piece of wealth ...And not only do individuals circulate between its threads; they are always in the position of undergoing and exercising this power. They are not only its inert or consenting target; they are always also the elements of its articulation. In other words, individuals are the vehicles of power.
>
> (Foucault 1972: 98)

One of Foucault's drawbacks, however, was his overemphasis of the individual, which tends to underplay the often equally important role of collectivities. Foucault argues that power is productive and not primarily repressive; it is only so when it is frustrated: 'repressive power represents power in its most frustrated and extreme form. The need to resort to a show of force is more often evidence of a lack of power' (Sawicki 1991: 21). This corresponds to a certain extent with Gramsci's distinction between hegemony and domination. Domination, according to Gramsci, exists where force has to be used. These points are very relevant to the analysis of the relationship between Islamists and the state. State repression on all Islamists – whether moderates of the Muslim Brotherhood (e.g. the mass arrest of its members in the run-up to the November 1995 parliamentary elections) or extremists – illustrates these points clearly. For in its repression and recourse to force and violence, the Egyptian state is, in Foucauldian terms, manifesting a lack of power. In Gramscian terms, state discourse vis-à-vis Islamisms is dominant rather than hegemonic. In other words, state repression underlines the state's inability to obtain Islamists' consent to the status quo.

Further, Foucault focuses on how certain cultural and institutional practices have produced individuals. These are the practices of disciplinary power (which he associates with the rise of the human sciences in the nineteenth century). According to him, this disciplinary power is exercised on the body and soul of the individual. It increases the power, renders the individual stronger and more docile simultaneously (like basic military training). Examples of disciplinary power exercised by the state on women are evident in the laws. Such laws as exist today reproduce a masculinist discourse in which women are subordinate to men. Secular and Muslim feminists, whilst arguing against the injustices perceived in some laws, are actually arguing *within* the framework of the laws as they stand. Both groups of feminists, for example, do not dispute the legitimacy of the laws, but argue that they need to be amended, whereas Islamist feminists contend that these laws misrepresent the shari'a and are therefore more civil than Islamic, and hence should be scrapped altogether. Secular feminists, on the other hand, campaign for an exclusively civil law which is free of all religious references. In short, most of the feminists perceive state laws and disciplinary power as unfriendly to women, but their rationale and alternatives differ.

According to Foucault, power is circulated in modern society via the production of certain forms of knowledge (like the positivist human sciences) and also via disciplinary techniques which are used to control the individual. The latter include surveillance, examinations and discipline. Foucault isolates techniques of individualization such as the divisive practices found in medicine, psychiatry, criminology and their corresponding institutions – hospital, asylum and prison.

Disciplinary practices thus recreate the divisions within a society, which, because of the authoritative status (due to their link to culture, institutions, etc.), can be used as effective means of normalization and social control – e.g. sane/mad, legal/delinquent, healthy/ill. These practices may involve the literal dividing off of segments of the population through incarceration or institutionalization. Usually these divisions are experienced in the society at large in more subtle ways, such as in the practice of labelling one another or ourselves as different or abnormal.

In this regard, the Islamist policy of *takfir* is a disciplinary practice which aims at dividing people – i.e. literally, those who believe versus those who do not *(kafir)*; Muslims versus non-Muslims. Essentially, by labelling their enemies as *kafir* (non-believer), or *murtadd* (apostate), a disciplinary practice is created and practised, which is, in turn, a form and source of power. Effectively, this disciplinary technique creates divisions and affords a means of social control, which translates into empowering themselves (as Islamists) whilst marginalizing their opponents.

Power, Hegemony and Egyptian Feminisms

Foucault expands the domain of the political to include a heterogeneous ensemble of power relations operating at the micro-level of society. Jana Sawicki (1991) highlights the practical implication of Foucault's model by asserting that resistance must be carried out in local struggles against the many forms of power exercised at the everyday level of social relations. Egyptian feminisms represent these resistances. As several of them put it to me – and here I paraphrase – there is no one struggle against oppression, but there are many sites on an everyday basis. These struggles range from arguing against the division of labour with their partners and/or families in their homes, to refusal to (or insistence on, depending on the speaker) wear the veil, to organizing and petitioning publicly on certain issues.[25]

Foucault defines power as being dependent on resistance. He speaks of power in the following terms:

> I'm not positing a substance of power. I'm simply saying: as soon as there's a relation of power there's a possibility of resistance. We're

never trapped by power: it's always possible to modify its hold, in determined conditions and following a precise strategy.

(Foucault 1980b: 13)

Foucault rightfully claims that power exists everywhere. He describes the social field as a myriad of unstable and heterogeneous power relations. It is an open system which contains possibilities of domination as well as of resistance. He describes the social and historical field as a battlefield, a field of struggle. Power circulates in this field and is exercised on and by individuals over others as well as themselves.

In light of the above contentions, the resistance of Islamists to state domination is a form of power. But most significantly, *in their resistance to state laws and to certain elements of Islamist discourse, feminists are manifesting and proving their different forms of power.* This statement is both novel and crucial, because Egyptian feminists – whether they are secular, Muslim or Islamist – operate from the basis that they have yet to acquire power. The realization that by and in resistance there already is power has yet to be absorbed at the psycho-social and political level.

Foucault's analysis on the operations of power, such as his critical studies of the institutions of medicine, prisons and science, which have identified the body as a site of power through which docility and submission are accomplished, has been a useful way for feminist theory to understand the female body as a site of disciplinary power exerted by the male establishment of the medical fields and scientific fields (Holub 1992: 202). To ground this in Egyptian praxis, Islamists, both male and female, are also using the body as a site of power; whence their views on the necessity of veiling. Also with this dynamic in mind, looking at the triad of state, Islamism and feminists, an informative aspect comes to mind. Women who agree to wear the particularly severe form of veiling (the *niqab*)[26] and those Islamists (husbands or women) who coerce others into assenting, are, according to this interpretation, involved in the system of manufacturing consent to certain belief and value systems. However, it would be misleading to assume that 'everyone' is involved in the production of support for the status quo. For in this triad, all Islamists cannot be assumed to be supporting the status quo; rather, they are involved in attempting, via disciplinary means, to hegemonize in the power-game, and thus to engender their own alternative status quo.

Interestingly, Joan Cocks (1989), taking up from both Gramsci and Foucault, disagrees with radical feminism's dividing the world into black and white when it comes to power relations and access to power. She argues that radical feminism offers only a blunt and crude understanding of power, a representation of dominating power which is far from being emancipatory. This existence of power neglects the very real power relations among women whilst simultaneously oversimplifying the fact that individuals can occupy different positions along different axes of power simultaneously. It is for this reason that power can be dominating and oppositional at the same time. What is useful is Cocks' calling into question the often presumed innate virtue of women and their lack of will to (male?) power as implied by a good deal of radical feminism. This especially highlights the fact that feminist solidarity often crumbles unexpectedly when access to power in whatever constellation is dangled in front of some women's eyes. In fact, as Renate Holub points out, most of Foucault's work reminds us that we are all implicated in power, and that in many instances power can be gender-blind (Holub 1992: 202).

Gramsci's insistence on the ubiquitousness of power is of secondary importance when it comes to his analysis of the hierarchical structure of power relations. So that whilst power is omnipresent – as Foucault would have it – Gramsci would maintain that equally ubiquitous are unequal relations of power. As far as both Gramsci and Foucault are concerned, power and domination function in so far as those dominated consent to that domination. In other words, without consent there is no domination (ibid.: 199). This point was referred to above in the discussion of the interaction between Islamists and the state, but it is also relevant when analysing the relationship feminists have with both the state and Islamists. Its relevance lies in stressing the specific reality wherein women activists are not simply being subordinated and/or victimized, but play an active role in the negotiations of power that are constantly taking place.

STRUCTURE OF THE BOOK

The rationale behind this book, and the theoretical discussion of fieldwork and methodology takes place in Chapter 2. Also in Chapter 2, I situate myself as an author in this kaleidoscope whilst looking at the problematics of writing research. Since an overarching Islamization of political discourse is the *backdrop* to Egyptian feminisms, this is dealt with in Chapters 3 and 4, which look at interactions between the state and Islamists.

Chapters 5, 6 and 8 highlight Egyptian feminists in their diversities. Chapter 5 locates and describes different activism through identifying groups and individuals representative of the three feminisms. Chapter 6 presents the laws and congruent debates affecting women from the perspective of the women activists themselves.

In the next encounter between feminists and the backdrop, Chapters 7 and 8 analyse the respective affairs between gender and Islamisms. In these two chapters the opinions and rationales on various aspects of gender relations are elaborated and contrasted. In this instance only (Chapter 7), a concession has been made to include male voices. Even then, these voices are presented through selecting some of their writings (which is extensive) as opposed to what they could have said. In Chapter 8, Islamist feminist voices are presented by analysing their written material, as well as featuring their own words through personal and published interviews. Their ideas are introduced across three generations, and the continuities and changes in their ways of thinking highlighted. Chapter 9, in conclusion, summarizes the interplay of power between the forces, and suggests a politics of difference to face current and future power struggles.

2 Living Fieldwork, Writing Ethnography[1]

What does the ethnographer do? He [sic] writes.

(Geertz 1973)

In describing Melanesian marriage ceremonies, I must bear my Melanesian readers in mind. That in turn makes problematic the previously established distinction between writer and subject: *I must know on whose behalf and to what end I write.*

(Strathern 1987b; emphasis added)

In this chapter, I shall examine the process of conducting research and the underlying rationale for doing so in relation to this text. This is not and does not pretend to be 'classic ethnography' in the conventional sense of 'establishing relationships, and by learning to see, think and be *in another culture*' (Bell 1993: 1; emphasis added), partly because I was not in another culture as such, but actually studying in and about my own culture, and with those who form part of this subculture: i.e. a select group of Egyptian feminists. Nevertheless, much of this study involves characteristics of ethnographic writing. And it is for this reason that I have engaged in the task of examining 'living fieldwork' in the light of feminist ethnographic and anthropological writing. Furthermore, I find inspiration in the arguments put forward by certain feminist ethnographers (Strathern 1987; Visweswaran 1988; Mascia-Lees et al. 1989; Bell 1993; Schrijvers 1993; among others), who emphasize that the gendered self-awareness and situatedness of writers[2] structure processes of gathering as well as of writing/authoring.

In many ways, then, writing this research without writing myself in it is akin to attempting to paint a portrait without a brush. In the beginning, however, I resisted most emphatically the idea of situating myself. My reasons were motivated by the inherent possibility of falling into the pitfalls of 'navel-gazing', or into 'simple confessionals of field experience, or into atomistic nihilism' (Marcus and Fischer 1986: 68). My misgivings were compounded by Geertz's quote (above), especially by the '"he" writes' part. I was also alert to the romanticism that some anthropologists adopt when, in attempting to place themselves consciously within the text, they 'exoticise' their selves. As Mascia-Lees et al. put it, 'It is as if, finding the "exotic" closed off to him, the anthropologist constructs himself as the exotic' (1989: 26). Yet I realized that I did not see these women activists with whom I lived and worked as 'exotic', and in the same way I did not consider myself as remotely 'exotic'. Sandra Harding (1987) tells us that the feminist researcher is led to design projects that women want and need. Carrying out this study is something that many of these feminists themselves encouraged and continued to urge me to accomplish. The idea and project of this book is thus very much defined by the feminist struggles taking place in the Egypt of the 1990s.

It took me many years to come to terms with the fact that I could not attempt to 'evoke' these women in my text, without evoking myself in the discourse. For it is my experience in interacting with and writing about 'feminists, Islamists and the state' in Egypt, that such an evocation is a 'means of representing' these dynamics to the reader (Tyler 1986: 129–38). I start with situating myself – narrating the rationale behind this book – followed by a theoretical review of reflexivity, and the process of writing the text with its incumbent arguments of validity and the production of knowledge. This leads on to the final stage, which looks at details of the fieldwork carried out in Cairo.

THE AUTHOR AND HER RATIONALE

> I now recognize that while academic training does not offer us strategies for liberating 'our people', it empowers us to articulate and defend their interests, *if* we so choose.
>
> (Morsy, in Altorki and El-Solh 1988 73; emphasis in original)

As an Egyptian Muslim woman who identifies with at least these three aspects of my identity, debates and struggles concerning women's issues in Egypt and the ensuing repercussions (i.e. in terms of laws, attitudes and implications for status, religion and tradition) affect me directly. During the Family Law debates and later on when the AWSA was banned, I found myself questioning the effectiveness of the 'women's movement', which seemed as fragmented as it was barely audible in the fray. I was wondering who the inheritors of the 1880s feminists were, and why it was that when I needed a feminist from outside the family to discuss this with, I could see or hear of no one.

Many years later I was to become aware of the general buzz of feminist activism. The reason I had not heard of them was two-fold: I did not actively seek them and instead seemed to be expecting them to come to me; and, being brought up in a largely conservative religious milieu, the names of these 'modern day' feminists had not yet been written in 'decent' books or magazines, dealing with contemporary history and events, or alternatively, in religious books, and were thus unknown in the surroundings then familiar to me.

In Egypt, society leaves no other option but to situate oneself as a girl/woman firmly within the extended family for protection, identity, respect and empowerment. My family's catch phrase was increasingly 'all legitimate roads come from and go to Islam'. In this power-play, my quest as a woman for 'freedom' had to be grounded within certain norms and values – supposedly Islamic – which predetermined my subjectivity even before I had ventured to discover it myself. It was as if questions of my identity were determined for me by others, namely family and legislature, both of which functioned within a discourse that claimed moral, religious and patriarchal superiority, deriving legitimacy from a myriad of 'Islamic' interpretations of societal norms and values.

'Islamic' values and beliefs structure general behaviour, and the definition of possibilities and limitations of a woman's conduct in particular. None the less, these encoded 'Islamic' ideals were by no means universally agreed within the same family. There were always variations and nuances, and these were applied differently, with different results.

Let me give an illustration of what is meant here, by narrating the story of 'the three cousins'.

In the winter of 1987, I was in my final year as an undergraduate at the American University of Cairo (AUC). This university has a notorious reputation, despite its acclaimed academic standards, for being a Western secular establishment. AUCians are frequently criticized by many Egyptians as being too 'Western' and 'liberal' in their morals. At the same time, my veiled cousin Zaina, who comes from a country town in the Nile Delta, was completing her fourth year in medicine at the Islamic Al-Azhar University, also in Cairo. My other veiled cousin, Salma, was brought up in Cairo by a strong and determined divorced mother, and was completing her third year of commerce, at Cairo University. We are all three around the same age, give or take a year, and we have grown up in close emotional proximity to each other. Yet, 'Westernized' me, who had lived by that time in three European countries (always with my family), was not allowed to leave home except to go to university and back. Social visits beyond the family sphere were not encouraged. Zaina, however, though brought up in the country and moving to Cairo only for her university years, was given relatively more (controlled) freedom to socialize with her friends both in Cairo and in her home town, provided, that is, she had parental foreknowledge; early hours for doing so; and her companions were all females and known to the whole family – uncles and aunts included. As for Salma, she never even dared ask permission to socialize outside her home. Nevertheless, her female friends were allowed to come and visit her.

Effectively, my cousins and I ended up with different views vis-à-vis our respective situations. In my case, the sense of control over my movements and sense of personal space was frustrating. In Zaina and Salma's cases, they *felt* they had a choice. In fact, neither resented nor complained of any sense of limitation. The story continues.

In 1994, immediately after the International Conference on Population and Development (ICPD) in which the issue of female circumcision had been heatedly and publicly debated, I also spoke at length with my cousins. I asked Salma whether she would circumcize her daughter (she by then had one daughter and was pregnant again) and why. Her answer was simple: 'No, it is not necessary.' Zaina had completed her last year of medical college, was working as a trainee doctor in the town hospital and was about to be married. I asked her the same question. Her answer was, 'If they say and convince me that it is harmful, maybe I will not, but I have not heard that it is.' When asked to elaborate on the 'they', Zaina named religious scholars,[3] her immediate family and 'if there are any laws made by the government against it' – in that order.

The analogy with Islamisms and state authority is not difficult to distinguish from this statement. Nor is it difficult to see the order of legitimacy accorded them. Religious scholars and family are closely followed by state laws and constitute largely what Zaina considers most important before she changes her mind about an issue so close to her and part of her own experience. Also clear from her answers are precisely which aspect of 'state' power is given credibility. Our differing perceptions and those of our families – all of us believing ourselves to be 'good Muslims' – nevertheless translated into widely different power dynamics and reactions, not only within the family but without. Each one of us, despite our strong and deep bonds of friendship, has moved in totally different directions. Zaina at first chose to leave her job and not seek another one upon marriage. This despite the fact that her physician husband – who was also her choice *par excellence* – was extremely supportive of the idea of her working. Yet, she told me, 'I don't need to wear myself out'. A month later, however, Zaina was accomplice and witness to her sister-in-law, Nadia's attempt to assert her right to work. Though acquiescing that Nadia (the wife of her brother) should not work in order to be a better mother, Zaina herself promptly resumed her job at the hospital. She left the job only for maternity leave to deliver her baby daughter, fully intending to resume her job as soon as possible, and to continue with her Masters in Medicine. In this she is fully supported by the same mother who had her circumcized, who is also the mother-in-law adamantly opposed to her daughter-in-law Nadia's attempts to resume *her* job as a pharmacist.

Salma took it for granted that her prospective husband would be chosen first by her mother and maternal uncle, and only then would her approval be solicited. Despite these seeming limitations, she was able to state her preferences quite clearly. Salma rejected the principle that a fiancé would attempt to meet and see her without constant parental chaperoning – even if her brother were present. On the occasion of a surprise visit (and therefore unattended by her mother) by one over-eager fiancé, she did not hesitate to jump out of the window of her home in order to escape, and left him to socialize with her distraught brother. Luckily, they were living on the ground floor.

Despite bureaucratic difficulties, Salma insisted that she go on working until she gave birth, and only leave work with paid pregnancy leave, or with unpaid leave to accompany her husband on his work. Her advice to another young bride – a pharmacist and wife of a male cousin of ours[4] – was: 'Beware of God in all your actions with your husband and in your married life. As long as you do that, God will not let you down.' And here I am today, a woman activist in the field of women's rights, carrying out research, in an attempt to understand and analyse the dynamics that have shaped, and continue to influence, our lives.

In that respect, debates concerning religion, law, circumcision and women's rights in general are also a mirror of many other debates taking place within the social fabric of Egyptian society, in which the interrelationship of state, religion and feminism intermingles and takes shape. Since these debates took place, much has happened in the arena of women's issues in Egypt. Though the dynamics between these three complex and heterogeneous forces remain prominent, conditions and sites of their power-play are constantly changing and shifting. By viewing the scenario from the point of view of its most interesting contenders – feminists – I am attempting several things. First, to bring out the diversity of feminist voices, whose silence is to be seen as relative to the coverage that both state and (male) Islamists persistently receive in both scholarly and journalistic works, Secondly, I highlight the importance and diversity of women's activisms in an area often portrayed (by certain researchers, the global media and even many international activists) as mostly devoid of feminisms and populated by oppressed women. And thirdly – though by no means lastly – to understand the dynamics of power that motivate and shape the lives of many Egyptian women in contemporary Egypt. In many ways then, this study is an appraisal and in recognition of contemporary Egyptian women activists.

WRITING RESEARCH

The term 'ethnography' is not clearly defined in common usage and there is disagreement about what are considered examples of it. What is more, the meaning of the term overlaps with that of several others, such as 'qualitative method', 'interpretative research', 'case study', 'participant observation', 'life history method', etc.; and these terms are themselves not very precisely defined either. What this diversity and looseness of terminology reflects, in Hammersley's opinion, is

> some dissensus even on fundamental issues among advocates of these approaches. More than this, though, it results from a certain vagueness in thinking about methodological issues that arises from a widespread emphasis among ethnographers on the primacy of research practice over 'theory' about how to do it. Sometimes this amounts to an anti-methodological and anti-theoretical prejudice. Ethnographers tend to distrust general formulations, whether about human social life or about how to do research, in favour of a concern with particulars. But however much one distrusts philosophy, one cannot escape it.
>
> (Hammersley 1990: 1)

With this inescapability of dealing with philosophy in mind, I am fascinated by the distinction (and discrimination) between 'Self' and 'Other' (see Bell et al. 1993; Kandiyoti 1996) – particularly with regard to Western feminist ethnographical theorizing, which in some cases assumes certain aspects of what traditional male ethnography is accused of. More precisely, the work of white Western feminist ethnographers on 'Third World [sic] women' – where the distinction between 'Self' and 'Other' is clear-cut – is often regarded as evidently ethnographic. Meanwhile the ethnographic work of 'indigenous' feminists is scrutinized on more detailed grounds, in an attempt to question the validity of both the knowledge-gathering and writing processes. In other words, Western feminist anthropologists and ethnographers are credited with 'gendering the fields' and pioneering diversity in ethnographic methodology, as well as resisting traditional male, highly structured knowledge-gathering techniques. Yet in my experience, and that of other indigenous researchers in Western academia, Western feminist criteria for such anthropological/ethnographical work, when carried out by indigenous feminists in their own societies, become more rigid and frustratingly limiting (see Lorde 1984; Ong 1988; Chow 1991; Mohanty 1991). The expectations are that indigenous feminist ethnography/writing must be limited in scope (e.g. to life-stories only, or to in-depth daily descriptions of particular aspects of life) and must – as Hammersley points out – be wary of theoretical material. Put differently, it is as if the indigenous 'Other' is firmly and incessantly being 'Othered' and continuing to 'Other', whilst to the Western 'Self' is attributed the responsibility of widely researching and ultimately 'saving' this 'Other'. Rey Chow succinctly expresses a similar point:

> Vis-à-vis the non-Western woman, the white woman occupies the position, with the white man, as investigator with 'the freedom to speak'. This relation, rather than the one that says 'we are all women', is particularly evident in disciplines such as anthropology and ethnography. What has become untenable is the way Western feminism imposes its own interests and methodologies on those who do not inhabit the same sociohistorical spaces, thus reducing the latter to a state of reified silence and otherness.
>
> (Chow, in Mohanty et al. 1991: 93)

That the politics of social research and academia are an important ingredient of the *how* and *why* certain texts are written is not new. Steven Sangren has already shown that academic politics condition the production and reproduction of ethnographic texts. According to him,

> whatever 'authority' is created in a text has its most direct social effect not in the world of political and economic domination of the

Third World by colonial and neocolonial powers, but rather in the academic institutions in which such authors participate.

(Sangren 1988: 411)

Mascia-Lees et al. point out that patriarchal social orders prevail in the academy and influence the choice and method of writing. In fact, they argue that some postmodern writings are an attempt by some to 'score' higher than others who inhabit the halls of anthropology departments and thereby secure future jobs (Mascia-Lees, Sharpe and Cohen 1987). This criticism of male-dominated academia and its eschewed literary and intellectual output resonates with arguments made in both the United States and Britain for the femininization of the academy. Adrienne Rich's 'Towards A Woman-Centered University' (1980) attacks the ways in which education is used as a weapon of colonization, whilst arguing that the solution lies in feminist pedagogy. The latter could, Rich maintains, legitimate personal experience and begin to change the reproduction of knowledge in academic institutions, and the content and priorities of research.

Marcia Westkott (1983) takes this further by arguing for feminist research that is *for* women rather than *about* women, and hence calls for engaging in 'negations [of current social realities which marginalize women] that yield transcendence [of these realities and into newer presumably more egalitarian ones]'. Westkott argues that 'by engaging in 'negations that yield transcendence' our Women's Studies classes are educational strategies for change' (Westkott, in Humm 1992: 396). Westkott also argues that to achieve Rich's call for a 'woman-centered university', women have to be at the university and *in positions of power* within the university, in order to bring about change for other women. In short, a body of feminist pedagogy emerged and developed, which outlines the problems, strategies and encounters between feminists/women's studies and patriarchal structures, within academia and the educational field in general (see Luke and Gore 1992).

However these arguments serve to point out above all the problems faced by *Western* researchers in Western academia. What is yet to be sufficiently researched and which is of vital importance in this study and others like it, is the extent to which Western academia and including Western feminists within academia, influence research writings by native feminists on native feminisms. The paucity of written material on this subject, despite its importance and relevance to the whole process of the production of knowledge, rendered it necessary to begin investigations. I spoke to ten native researchers[5] in a preliminary attempt to compare experiences as native/indigenous[6] researchers in Western academia. What unfolds in these situations is a power dynamic, wherein the traditional 'Other' of Western academia namely feminists, are dealing with this relatively newer 'Other', native feminists, who study their own societies (in which they are simultaneously 'Self' and 'Other') from within the halls of Western academia. The complexities involved are compounded if native or indigenous feminists do not share or profess the same discipline as their Western academic seniors, but are involved in multidisciplinary research.

What I contend is that whilst the possibilities of learning from each other are vast, the 'Othering' processes undertaken by some Western academics in positions of power in Western academia can be potentially counterproductive. For essentially those researching are coming under direct authority from Western academics and the obvious power positions therein are, to say the least, imbalanced. Based on discussions with colleagues from different Western universities, certain common mechanisms whereby our work is devalued and silenced, and our academic identities Othered, were identified. The latter include various ways of delegitimating the native researcher's work by Western academics. In some instances this delegitimation takes place by outright denial of the 'objective' validity of the work carried out, or simply by neglecting to acknowledge or refer to the input, analysis and sometimes even the physical presence of the native researcher. In other instances the native researcher's work is simply appropriated (thus denying the originality of the ideas presented and ignoring the researcher's labour). Yet in other cases, the sources and methods used by the researcher are questioned, demeaned and thus invalidated. Misunderstandings and lack of awareness of the situation of the 'Other' may prompt denigration and delegitimation from a position of imposing power and ultimate right to approve written texts, which can lead to the 'reification of the silence' of the native researcher as 'Other'. This academically sanctioned power balance highlights serious problems of privilege/underprivilege, which still divide Western feminists from their Southern, non-Western and native counterparts.

Effectively, Western academia is another field where the Self/Other issue goes beyond Man/Woman and firmly enters multiple layered domains of Western academics/Indigenous ('non-Western') academics. The latter is a realm with its specific baggage of power relations, which in turn have direct epistemological implications for writing research. My research is intended not only for the readers – feminist and otherwise – back home and in the general Western audience. But in fact, what I must keep in mind is that this has to be read *and approved* by Western academicians before it is even accepted as research at all. These are very important considerations, which I cannot afford to ignore. The implications of this reality on my own academic and feminist convictions, as well as on the end-product of writing, are stimulating at best, frustrating at worst.

Keeping this imbalance of power in mind, similar (and more radical) criticisms of feminist pedagogy are registered by Black feminists in Western academia. Gloria Hull and Barbara Smith state that

> women's studies has become both more institutionalized and at the same time more precarious within traditional academic structures, the radical life-changing vision of what women's studies can accomplish has constantly been diminished in exchange for acceptance, respectability, and the career advancement of individuals.
>
> (Hull and Smith, in Humm 1992: 400)

Hull and Smith state clearly that 'we cannot change our lives simply by teaching solely about "exceptions" to the ravages of white-male oppression' (ibid.). In other words, white feminist pedagogy may fall into the same pit as its initial oppressor, and actually end up oppressing 'the Other' – using the same techniques. Bell Hooks talks of a similar dilemma when insisting that it is not simply the creation of an alternative or new discipline within academia that will lead to emancipation or freedom from oppressive structures of creating knowledge. In fact, Hooks argues that

> as individual critical thinkers, those of us whose work is marginalized, as well as those whose work successfully walks that elusive tightrope with one foot on the radical edge and one foot firmly rooted on acceptable academic ground, must be ever vigilant, guarding against the social technology of control that is ever ready to co-opt any transformative vision and practice.
>
> (1990: 132)

Some Western feminist researchers who have themselves carried out ethnographic fieldwork among the 'Other', *and are sensitive to the power dynamics involved*, may be capable of enriching and stimulating the native researcher's text. This is reflected during the fieldwork and post-fieldwork processes, when a less involved insight and yet related expertise are instrumental in sorting out the complex web of information gathered.

There is much to be said about the power relations between native feminists and Western feminists in Western academia, and consequent implications on the production of knowledge process (see Hooks 1990: 127–33; and Karam 1997). In the following pages, however, I focus on further intricacies of writing oneself into the research.

Writings in anthropology have long been haunted by the authorial presence in the text. In other words, there is a revolving question within each text as to where and how to situate the author, and to what extent the presence of the author affects the information being presented. This question has been posed, not from within the framework of narratology, or 'how best to get an honest story told', but rather, as an epistemological issue. As such, the emphasis, or the line of questioning, for a long time revolved around how to present 'objective' facts without letting subjective views colour them (Geertz 1988: 9).

Objectivity in my opinion may be a more relevant discussion in the realm of the physical sciences. Even then, as the discursive practices of the science remain attached to the theorist it may be coloured by her/ his hypothesizing, and the manner in which s/he conducts and presents the findings. In fact, this whole discursive practice may well be labelled after the founder/explorer/scientist her/himself (Foucault, in Rabinow 1984: 113–17). I thus tend to opt for an analysis that advocates less the 'expressive value' of discourses, but rather evaluates discourses according to how it is that they came to be formed (ibid.). In this regard, my analysis of the different feminist discourses is one which looks at both what these activists have to say and the differing circumstances that surround them. To illustrate this, the research is structured in such a way as to give voice to a number of feminists representing a diversity of political opinions, whilst also highlighting the dynamics that surround this discourse in the form of feminists– state–Islamist power struggles and interactions. I find the description that 'the task of the ethnographer is not to determine "the truth" but to reveal multiple truths apparent in others' lives' to be particularly apt here (Emerson, Fretz and Shaw 1995: 3).

Following Foucault's suggestion would point to discussions that are less focused on their claim to a delusion called 'objectivity' and more centred on the historical development of discourse. In other words, by studying how a particular discourse comes into being, one is able to learn about the dynamics that structured, influenced and/or created this discourse. Similarly, the previous section, in which a history of who I am, and how and why I came to write this particular research, is aimed at clarifying this writing process. It is not inconceivable that a researcher's background, motivation and means of carrying out the research can reveal a great deal about the manner and content of the written work. 'So long as the self is rigorously split off and secreted in diaries, then self-analysis in anthropological practice is perceived as loss of professional armour' (Okely, in Okely and Callaway 1992: 7). In the end, I refer to an old adage told me by my grandmother, which paraphrased and translated says: 'What a person says about others, sometimes reveals more about himself [sic]'.

Indeed my grandmother's saying points out the dilemma faced when trying to relate an experience. One is reminded of a saying of Galileo, though with slightly different implications: 'Find me a place to stand and I will move the earth.' For what ethnographers try to do is not to change images so much as to attempt to portray a particular 'reality' as experienced by them and as they think it is experienced by others. In that sense, most 'realities', or 'truths' for that matter, are extremely subjective, since each will see and translate events, information and knowledge, based ultimately on personalized experiences and comprehension. This is in turn and to a certain extent a factor of the manner in which the researcher/writer presents her/his material. There is, therefore, a definite challenge of being alternately insider/outsider, in both processes of participant observation, as well as writing. This constantly moving pendulum has certain implications on the process of ethnographic writing. Okely correctly contends that 'in an academic context, the personal is theoretical' (Okely, in Okely and Callaway 1992: 9).

Clifford has recognized four processes at work in ethnography, or as he refers to them, 'modes of authority' – experiential, interpretive, dialogical and polyphonic (Clifford 1988: 21–54). The experiential model can be said to have been represented by Malinowski (1961 and 1967), who created the image of the fieldworker as a kind of scientist, who collects data and presents his findings in the form of an experimental report. The interpretive model, exemplified by Geertz (1973), tended to privilege the 'native', as opposed to 'scientific' knowledge. The more recent dialogical models are represented by Rabinow (1977) and Rosaldo (1984). The latter model, closely tied to the polyphonic one, emphasizes self-reflexivity and the rhetorics of the self, and subjects itself to literary criticism (see Battaglia 1995).

Indeed, it is *reflexivity* that is here regarded as a pertinent aspect in the writing of this text.

To date, discussions concerning reflexivity have tended to come from anthropologists who are *not* indigenous to the field they are studying (Tedlock 1983; Hastrup 1990; Callaway 1992; Hervik 1994). The non-indigenous status may account for the fact that reflexivity has often been argued in terms of 'cross-cultural encounters' (Hervik 1994: 93).

None the less, I maintain that as a 'continuous mode of self-analysis and political awareness' (Callaway 1992: 33), reflexivity is an important aspect of any ethnographic fieldwork and research. Important, because the information presented is then questioned by its writer, so that the awareness acts as a form of self-censorship, literary criticism and examiner of information. In fact, individual reflexivity on the part of the anthropologist is accompanied by the social reflexivity of those we are mediating for and trying to understand. In other words, our presence on the field itself leads to a certain kind of reflexivity on the part of those we are with and interviewing. Hence, reflexivity is also inherent in the experiential space of those with whom one is interacting, who are themselves changing positions and reflecting all the time.

An example of this can be seen among the many Islamists and feminists I came in contact with. Self-reflexivity plays a role in the questions I chose to ask, those I questioned, and the manner in which I asked them. Though I had a prepared a tentative list of questions, I invariably ended up with a great deal of different questions that emerged as a result of the open-ended discussions I had with most of the women I interviewed. In many cases, my original questions were reformulated and replaced in the heat of the debates and discussions that took place. Indeed almost none of the encounters were purely question-and-answer sessions, but more like a tug-of-war of thoughts and ideas. Both I and the people I talked to were continuously thinking about what we were saying. I remember a particular interview with an Islamist feminist, in which the question I posed – entirely a result of our discussion – almost silenced her since she was too busy thinking of the answer. The silence grew long and uncomfortable and I moved on to something else. Not only was this an indication of both of us acting reflexively, but I also had in mind that she was after all from my mother's generation, and I did not feel it appropriate to embarrass her by my question. In other words, the responses I received were not automatic. On the contrary they were a result of a series of reflexive processes on the part of myself and those

I spoke to. As Rabinow lucidly puts it: 'The data we collect is doubly mediated, first by our own presence and then by the second order self-reflection we demand from our informants' (Rabinow 1977: 119). It is not only the verbal interaction within the fieldwork process, however, that is mediated by reflexivity. The writing process itself is similarly mediated, this time by the author and her/his perception of the *possible* readership. I have reflected, questioned, criticized and consciously decided on what to write and how to write it, all the while keeping in mind my likely readership. This 'imagined community' of readers that I have formulated in my mind, consists not only of academic supervisors, but also of those I am now engaged in writing about. It is the latter who, in my mind, I have set up to act as forms of censors on what I write. The image of my cousins, for example, was constantly in my mind, as I wrote about them here; their words and their expressions were a constant companion to the words and sentences I considered. My mental dialogue with them was continuous.

Self-reflexivity, therefore, must also take account of the writer's own projections of the reflexivity of others. In other words, one is dealing with multiple forms of reflexivities – both real and imagined. One implication of this is my choice to write of women activists as 'feminists'. Not only is this a conscious decision on my part, but part of the process of writing them in this text as *feminists* has had implications for the way in which I justify the use of the term and the words I chose to describe them. Anticipating some of the responses of these women to what I am writing is part of the process of reflexivity that takes place.[7]

Another aspect of reflexivity is the awareness (or lack of it) of both author and those in the field of the changing nature of the relationships. So that in effect the data we collect are mediated by unequal power relations, and by both the aim and subject that are being asked from our informants and the manner in which they are asked. Hence, reflexivity can be interpreted as the world between ourselves and the others (Tedlock 1983: 323; cf. de Silva 1995a), as well as between ourselves and ourselves. When interviewing Islamist men, there was a definite power dynamic taking place, which was constantly shifting. On the one hand, I had requested and sought after 'him' (I am generalizing here to describe what I found was a similar situation often replicated while dealing with the men). However, it must also be pointed out that the dynamics are affected by a great many other factors – such as the ranking or hierarchy within the organization and the closeness to the mediator. Considering that I was able to talk to mainly middle echelon activists, the Islamist men interviewed were favouring me by their presence. But, on the other hand, I was the one posing the questions and the unspoken knowledge lay between us that, whatever was said, I would be doing the writing (this was reflected in the sentence that invariably came after each interview: 'We hope you report our words correctly when you are writing them'). To what extent all those who were interviewed realized this particular implication and twist to the power scenario is extremely difficult to determine.

Such awareness of shifting balances of power and the inherent reflexivities also occurred in my interactions in the field with feminists. In some instances, meeting the older feminists incurred a certain awe and respect on my part. This meant in practice that I had to take special care not only in my choice of questions, but also the manner in which I appeared to them and how the questions were levelled. I recall a meeting with an elderly activist member of a political party, for example. After the initial moments, I realized that she was voicing rehearsed answers in a bored manner – regardless of what my questions were. Moreover, I was also aware that some form of self-censorship, a result of having studied and heard about her a great deal, was playing a formative part in the extent to which I was interrupting (or not) and repeating (or not) the questions.

As Callaway argues, reflexivity is not imposed from outside, but is a result of shared social experience. Accordingly, it is not dictated by outside ideas, but is rather a consequence of one's subjective engagement in the practices, discourses and institutions which lend importance to the events taking place (Callaway, in Okely and Callaway 1992: 37). I refer here also to what Okely describes as 'embodied knowledge', which comes with actively participating with others during fieldwork and creates both shared and inner experiences. Not just a privilege of a practitioner, embodied knowledge is an outcome of working with those one is observing (Okely, in Okely and Callaway 1992: 16–24). It is by being a working practitioner that certain forms of knowledge are gained and shared. These experiences can often be contradictory and in turn reflect on the process of being, during fieldwork, as well as writing. For instance, on one occasion I was gently admonished by an Islamist for not being veiled despite my being a Muslim woman. Henceforth I noticed I took special care to appear *muhtashima* (modestly dressed), meaning that I tried to wear skirts which came to below the knees more often and to make sure that if I wore trousers, they would be loose and I would cover my hips and thighs with a long shirt. Also, I rarely let my hair down and the most skimpy of outfits became a short-sleeved T-shirt. On the other hand on one occasion when I had my hair in a wide hair-band and tied in a bun, I was asked – with noticeable alarm – by a secular feminist, whether I had become veiled. It was not so much a question as a horrified speculation.

One's subjective experiences become significant as an indigenous fieldworker, faced with the problematic of detachment and distance. Cassell notes that indigenous fieldworkers may be confronted with an inability to remain emotionally detached when researching in their own communities (Cassell 1977). This is a somewhat eschewed reading of the position of an indigenous fieldworker. For the implicit and not so subtle assumption is that an outsider can maintain this 'distance' more easily. However, it is not the insider/outsider dynamic *per se* that is shaped by and shapes issues of distance, but matters of the topic under research, the kinds of ties established within the society, the means of collecting and disseminating information about those studied as well as about oneself, to name but a few (see de Silva 1995b).

Furthermore, 'distance' itself is difficult to specify. One can be an 'outsider' to a certain group of people, but an 'insider' to their discussions or topic or activism, so that the positions of Insider/Outsider and Self/Other are continuously changing. For on the one hand, I am the woman activist working with women activists and identifying with them as with myself. Yet on the other hand, I am the researcher/ 'Other'. In some interviews with those closest to me ideologically – Muslim feminists – I am as if in a dialogue with myself, whereas in that same dialogue I am the one theorizing the Other (Muslim feminism) and thus being 'the Other' (the researcher and analyst from academia). Effectively, therefore, with every shift in these positions there is also a corresponding shift in the narratives used to communicate these positions and the manner of articulating them on and off the field.

Thus, distance may be emotional, physical, cognitive and personal, and it may range from moments of complete identification to total hostility. In my interactions with feminists, for example, I alternated between moments of identifying totally with them, which occurred mostly with both Muslim and secular feminists (not with Islamist feminists). I also experienced the other extreme of feeling almost alienated in certain discussions, for example, during certain board meetings of secular feminists, as well as discussions between

Islamist feminists. My feelings of identification/alienation stemmed primarily from the subjects being discussed and in some cases from the manner in which certain issues would be dealt with. In one board meeting of a secular feminist group, of which I am a member, the names of other people and groups came up whom I knew, and a certain antagonism was expressed towards these people. At that time I felt alienated and rather uncomfortable. Yet during the same meeting with the same group, when it came to discussing action on an issue we all felt strongly about, I found myself tied to the cause and committed to cooperate with other members in taking action. Self-reflexivity is part and parcel of being able to recognize this distance, understand its implications and relate it within the text, as an author.

In this research, the issue of distance structured a great deal of the evoking and writing of this text. My involvements both personally and emotionally in the different debates going on was and is inevitable, considering that what is being discussed, debated, set up or brought down is affecting me as an Egyptian Muslim woman – and one married to a foreigner at that.[8]

Nevertheless the opportunity to leave Cairo and return to Amsterdam after 3–4-month sojourns, afforded me what I consider a trump card. By being able to manoeuvre physically both inside and outside, I was also able to shift my positions as insider/practitioner and outsider. The physical distancing was to prove one of the most effective ways in which to overcome a disadvantage of emotional involvements, since by leaving the scene itself, I was in fact enabled to reflect on the processes taking place. In other words, the distance enabled me to take a look at my field notes, which effectively are the first written indication of individual self-reflexivity. This in turn was 'the first step on the road towards anthropological discursive reflexivity' (Hervik 1994: 92). On the other hand, it was and is precisely these emotional, personal, physical and cognitive involvements which spurred me on during moments of depression. The linkages, involvements and the sense of dedication I saw and felt during the fieldwork were also strongly imprinted in my mind.

In that respect self-reflexivity becomes important in understanding the dynamics of relating not only to oneself during the research process, but also to relating to those in the field, and then to the writing of the ethnographic text. Reflexivity forces us to think through the consequences of relating to others – whether they are relations of reciprocity, inequality or even potential exploitation. After all in many cases, when so many women were generously giving me of their time, their resources, their writings and their hospitality, I was not always repaying them in any sense. In fact in many cases, I had to fight very hard not to feel that I was exploiting their time and energy. When it comes to writing I am in a way forced to choose what will be represented in this text and what will remain as information for future writing projects. As Okely lucidly puts it, 'there are choices to be made in the field, within relationships and in the final text' (Okely, in Okely and Callaway 1992: 24).

Being a member of some of the groups I study and being a Muslim feminist among feminists, I am a practitioner in the scene studied. In this respect, Hammersley points out that practitioners have a number of 'advantages': knowing their own intentions; long-term experience of the studied scene; previously established relationships with contact people in the field; and the consequent ability to test theory to practice (Hammersley 1992: 144).

While concurring with these points, I nevertheless largely agree with what Hammersley lists as the countervailing disadvantages. The certainty one has about one's own knowledge need not be infallible. Also long-term experience is usually derived from a particular role or roles, and one should not assume any omniscience as to all that is taking place. Moreover as far as relationships available to a practitioner are concerned, they do not necessarily occlude constraints or exclusion from other aspects of information. And finally, 'What is required to test theoretical ideas may well conflict with what is needed for good practice' (ibid.: 145). With respect to the latter, an aspect of my fieldwork experience is revealing. My theoretical perception that women activists were altering their discourse because of Islamist influences could not very well be articulated so bluntly in my questions. For were I to ask them directly if this were the case, the immediate answer, in most instances dictated by pride and propriety, would be outright denial. Instead, I let them talk about Islamism in particular and air their grievances/support of it and through that analyse the extent to which their discourses were accommodating/rejecting it. In other words, I could not ask the question directly, but instead I was sometimes performing somersaults with words, in order for them to reveal their opinions and thereby confirm or refute my ideas.

Hammersley's critique of a practitioner's capacity to test hypotheses is not in itself sufficient to undermine that advantage. However, one tends to recognize that any position has both advantages and disadvantages, which reflect on the material and data collected. As Hammersley himself states:

In general, I think that the chances of the findings being valid can
be enhanced by a judicious combination of involvement and
estrangement. However, no position, not even a marginal one,
guarantees valid knowledge; *and no position prevents it either.*
(ibid.; emphasis added)

Hammersley's points are illustrated and critiqued through my fieldwork experience. Two specific facets of my multiple identities, that of
researcher and activist, accorded me enormous advantage. To all
those approached and interviewed I was primarily 'the researcher'.
Yet being a member of a group, I was also privy to certain details of
interactions that would not be easily accessible to researchers only. To
put it quite simply, some women felt more comfortable sharing their
grievances about each other in front of me, since I was seen by them
as being 'one of us'. Others, knowing or suspecting my affiliations, felt
the need to educate and enlighten me as to the multiplicity of viewpoints and present 'their version'. In fact, I realized I was lucky to
have the two most appropriate aspects required in this field. I feel
fortunate to admit that I made good friends during this researcher/
activist interaction, which might otherwise have been difficult if I were
only a researcher or an activist.

On the other hand, there were certain drawbacks: being a friend of
someone from group 'A' with which group 'B' had a longstanding
argument could be problematic. This entailed a certain reserve, which
was occasionally overcome by stating that I was there primarily as a
researcher seeking information for my research and not as a representative of another group. This was actually quite a productive tack,
though I did question the ethics of alternately emphasizing different
aspects of my identity. In some ways this is similar to Abu Lughod's
ethical deliberations about her initial feelings of 'inauthenticity'
among the Awlad Ali bedouins, where she was unwilling to stress
her different identity and ideas (Abu Lughod 1986: 18–19). Abu
Lughod eventually resolved it by loosening her ties with her other
life. I did not need to 'pretend to share their values', as I indeed
believe in what I consider to be common values of struggling for a
better future for Egyptian women. Yet my 'compromise' resonates
with Abu Lughod's to some extent. For after sharing many aspects of
their activisms and participating in their discussions, I felt that I
'*became* the person I was with them' (ibid.: 19; emphasis in original).
Moreover, as I grew with them I realized I was not lying about myself,
nor was the information pried out of anyone against her/his will. The

information they kindly provided me with was based on the fact that they knew that, activism apart, I was ultimately to write their narratives.

My 'mastery' of Egyptian colloquial, my mother tongue, was very helpful throughout, since very often particular nuances or words used would reveal more than straightforward statements. The problem of translating these nuances is one that many indigenous researchers face. I have the advantage of being bilingual and mastering both languages (Arabic and English) so that reduces the complications somewhat.

It was also this practitioner situation with its entailing emotional involvements that made the open-ended interviews I had with the feminists very colourful. In most cases what would happen was that, instead of simply answering my questions, we would end up in long – and sometimes intense – discussions. This resulted quite often in unexpected insights coming to the fore which enriched both the content of the discussions (and the research material being gathered) and the relationships being formed between myself and the women interviewees. Nevertheless, I was faced with the dilemma of having to be selective about what would be included in the research – for I could not possibly narrate all the voices or let them speak for themselves. Some form of overall analysis and intervention is necessary I believe, if only to emphasize that what is being said confirms some of the questions being posed in the research.

Certain poststructuralist arguments about representation are relevant in this context, especially when it is argued that the meaning of a subject's statements are always in flux, that there can never be a final accurate representation, but only different textual representations of different experiences (Denzin, in Brown 1995: 40). Since Derrida insists that there is only ever the text, this leads to the issue of the text's authority. Epistemological validity, emphasized for some time, is interpreted by poststructuralists as a text's desire to assert its power over the reader. In fact, the obsession with validity becomes the researcher's mask of authority (Lather 1993: 5), which permits a regime of truth within the text to work its way through to the reader. This implies that the text has a life of its own – something I agree with. Indeed, once the material is written, how it is read by the different readers is beyond the control of the writer, she/he can only guess at the different meanings or interpretations a text can hold.

Poststructural deliberations have unmasked the validity-as-authority arguments and have suggested the renunciation of the desire to produce an authoritative text, since any text can be deconstructed. Alternatives to such arguments, which are also relevant to this study, have been proposed by Lather (ibid.), who suggests five forms of validity: reflexive, ironic, neo-pragmatic, rhizomatic and situated. The reflexive and situated validities are best suited for this study. On the one hand, I am questioning claims as to the validity of what I am representing (i.e. reflexive validity). In discussing gender and Islamisms, for example (Chapters 7 and 8), situated validity is evident in the diversity of feminine voices (Islamist women) opposing the male voices (Islamist men). Situated validity recurs in discussions of the various debates on women taking place in Egypt (in Chapter 5), as well as when discussing the laws that affect women and presenting them only from the perspective of the women activists involved (Chapter 6). I am also arguing for the possibility of the *simultaneity of validities*. For effectively what I am advocating is not that there must be a validity to the text; rather, I am in favour of those aspects of postmodern ethnography which emphasize the reflectiveness and reflexivity throughout the writing process. In doing so I am arguing against and questioning personal authority, as well as taking into account chance and indeterminacy as central to any explanation. In no way do I attempt to resolve the complexities of authorial subjectivity versus textual legitimacy. Neither am I intending to raise expectations of any profound poststructuralist analysis. I am merely pointing out certain uses, relevant to this work, of a poststructuralist deconstruction of *one validity*, as a means by which binarisms can be seen in a more fluid way . It is in the multiplicity of validities I believe, that multiple representations of the aspects described here (feminisms, Islamisms and state laws) can take place.

DETAILS OF FIELDWORK AND PRACTICAL IMPLICATIONS

I went back into the field with a desire to (re)discover the different women activists, observe them and write about them. My intentions were to rely on friends I knew from my college years to (re)connect me to the different activists. My fieldwork turned out to be one of the most formative periods of my life and certainly one of the richest experiences I have had. Not only did I get an opportunity to locate and study the diversity of women activists, but I was able to gain an insight into the issues that are shaping their agendas and mine, and to participate actively with some of them on common issues (e.g. drafting petitions appealing against specific proposed legislation on female circumcision; distributing the written material among other groups; participating in meetings to discuss and compare networks, and so on).

Since I was already[9] familiar with some women's groups it was not difficult to re-establish contact with some friends, and through them to widen the networks. As far as women politicians were concerned, attending many evenings of debates and seminars within the universities (AUC, Cairo University and the University of Alexandria), specific professional syndicates, as well as those arranged by political parties in Cairo, enabled me to meet many more. The 'system' is such, however, that once contact is established with one of these women, the linkages with the others offen come as a matter of course. Having announced my research and purpose – sometimes by being introduced by a mutual friend, and at times by introducing myself, presenting my card and briefly elaborating on my topic of research – I would then be able to request an appointment for an interview. Once the interview was conducted and sometimes even before, I would use the opportunity to ask for names and telephone numbers of colleagues/friends in other groups. Because the circles are anyway quite small, the women tended to know of each other and could help me to get in touch. In fact, most of the women I met were very helpful and were generous with their time and information.

As far as Islamist women were concerned, extensive networks of family friends and friends of friends eventually, and after a considerable period of time (which could well extend to a couple of months), led to contact with the desired person. The more underground the group members felt they had to be, the longer it took to establish contact. On at least two occasions, the meetings did not materialize. I was to learn later that the persons found it unsafe to leave their home – either because of sudden heavy police presence in the area or because of a general increased sense of insecurity or threat. Once direct and personal contact was established however, the length of the interview itself was not fixed in advance. Their time was generously made available to me. Very often I would go to the same women time and again to ask more questions. I also maintained regular telephone contact with some of them (even when I was in The Netherlands).

Apart from open-ended interviews, discussions, debates and the occasional heated arguments, I attended a variety of meetings. These included religious meetings in people's houses and in certain mosques. I also attended and occasionally participated in meetings of the various women's organizations. In addition I attended seminars, lectures and conferences on issues ranging from film-making to the analysis of the functioning of NGOs in the Arab world, to discussions of laws and law-making. Most helpful and dynamic to participate in, though, was the UN International Conference on Population and Development (ICPD, September 1994). On this occasion all the feminists from the different political streams and social strata were literally under one roof. The elation and activism were electrifying and heady – not to mention the fact that I could observe so many interactions among the feminists simultaneously. No less useful and stimulating was the sequel to the ICPD, the Beijing Fourth International Women's Conference (September 1995). The latter highlighted who the Egyptian state had blessed with permission to attend and represent Egyptian women activists in both the official delegation as well as the NGO Forum. In other words, the Beijing conference also served as a Who's Who of the feminists within the officially sanctioned NGOs.

I noticed that one of the best ways to enter the elite feminist secular circles especially was after being invited to a social gathering. Once an invitation to such a party was extended, it signalled an acceptance of the person. I realized that by attending some of these parties, many doors were opened to further contacts, which in effect circumvented a great deal of time and facilitated more personal interactions later on.

In addition, a great deal of data gathering took place in libraries – university and public libraries; private libraries of activist friends; documentation centres of various NGOs; and street vendors.

Both class (upper middle) and family background (rural–urban) meant that I could identify personally and be identified with different classes. In that context, I was accorded the respect of the upper and middle-class group leaders, whilst simultaneously being befriended by the middle and lower echelons of a group. This fluidity was only relevant when interviewing female political party members, since the hierarchies of leader–member seemed to function primarily there.

Fieldwork and writing experiences are as rich as they are varied. What I must say here is that I neither try to present 'the truth' through this text, nor do I claim complete knowledge. I am fully aware that this text as presented has involved and continues to involve much theorizing of the personal. I am also aware that this text may well develop meanings of its own to those who read it. In the following chapters, various aspects of this journey of doing and writing field-work will be referred to.

So, let me now go on with the rest of the narration.

3 The State and Islamists

This chapter traces the development of the relationship between Islamists and the Egyptian state to clarify the political backdrop of Egyptian feminist activism. An historical synopsis is provided first to contextualize the issues being presented. The following sections are devoted to scanning the relationships in the personalized political leadership eras of Sadat and Mubarak. Throughout, the emphasis is on the domestic political scene and the struggle for power and ideological hegemony between Islamists and the state, particularly the shift in the political discourses used by the latter. This is not to undermine the importance of external factors, but rather to sharpen the focus of the issues analysed.

HISTORICAL BACKGROUND

An attempt was made to put democratic processes and institutions into place in monarchic Egypt with the promulgation of the Constitution of 1923. Political parties were formed, a relatively free press was sanctioned, a two-tiered parliament was created and periodic elections were to be held whose theoretical purpose was to allow a significant part of the population to influence policy by choosing political functionaries. In this budding liberal democratic state however, the Constitution gave excess powers to the king who could (and did) dismiss the cabinet, dissolve parliament and appoint and dismiss the prime minister.

Ultimately, Egypt's liberal experience was short-lived, as its budding democracy was abused by both its supposed friends and its enemies. Not only did palace favourites belittle and disregard democratic privileges, but the smaller minority parties breached the spirit of constitutionalism in the country. Even the Wafd, the first nationalist and liberal secular movement/organization/political party in Egypt, shifted some of its positions and loyalties over time in attempts to gain power.

Ideological pluralism did survive, however. In addition to the secular and more traditionally oriented elected political officials, there were militant Islamists, dedicated leftists, evolving feminists and independent nationalists, who reflected a wide spectrum of ideas and whose activity expressed a desire to participate in the political processes.

Egyptian nationalists were actively trying to win complete self-determination from the British (who had effectively occupied the country since 1882), who were still exerting political influence despite nominal independence since 1922. Because of Britain's long-standing presence, Egyptian politics were dominated in the period from 1919 to 1956 by the demands for national independence.

Watershed events such as the two world wars caused an irrevocable change in Egypt, contributing to social, economic, cultural and political transformations. War stimulated industrialization and self-sufficiency and contributed to the growth of new ideas which led to the militancy of a political opposition. The ideological diversity and political and intellectual ferment that characterized the late 1930s and 1940s continued to develop, particularly after the Arab defeat in the 1948 war with Israel (which was blamed on the inefficiency and betrayal of the monarch and his ruling circle). Soon after, a group of military officers, who were sufficiently incensed at the inability of the leadership to address burning issues, plotted the overthrow of the monarchy. As a result of their *coup d'état*, the Free Officers successfully came to power and changed the structure of political, social and economic life in Egypt.

During this period the Muslim Brotherhood played a crucial role in rallying its support base for the cause of national liberation. Co-ordinating closely with the Free Officers, the Brotherhood's tasks included maintaining law and order as well as popular support for the army's role during the 'revolution' of 23 July 1952, itself (cf. Mitchell 1993). It was only after the Free Officers (FO) actually came to power that what had been referred to as the 'honeymoon' ended. Not surprisingly, the various reasons given have to do with the basis and legitimation of power. For, on the one hand, though members of the Brotherhood were invited by the FO's then revolutionary council to take over three ministries, the invitation was contingent on the FO's acceptance of the people put forward by *some* of the Brotherhood members. On the other hand, there was no unanimity among all the Brotherhood on joining this emergent government. In fact, at that stage, there seemed to be a discernible reluctance to 'sully itself with power', and hence lose its popular appeal (ibid.). Whatever the complicated politicking involved, the end result was a legacy of animosity between Nasser and Hodaybi (the Brotherhood's leader), which was to develop further as time went on.

For many Egyptians, the post-colonial state has disappointed the political hopes aroused by the nationalist 'revolution'. Critics charge that a bureaucratic elite was formed during the Nasser years and inherited by Sadat and Mubarak,

> which monopolizes state power in Egypt, and that official politics is about little more than the struggle to maintain this power; the liberation of the nation has not been followed by the political liberation of Egypt's people.
>
> (Baker 1990: xii)

JAMAL ABDUL NASSER (1952–71)

> For some reason it seems to me that within the Arab circle there is a role, wandering aimlessly in search of a hero. And I do not know why it seems to me that this role, exhausted by its wanderings, has at last settled down, tired and weary, near the borders of our country and is beckoning us to move, to take up its lines, to put on its costume, since no one else is qualified to play it.
>
> (Nasser 1955: 87–8)

Acting as deputy premier in the Revolution Command Council (RCC), Nasser first had to fight and win a leadership battle with a fellow Free Officer (then president of the Republic and prime minister), General Muhammad Najib, who was in favour of setting up a civilian constitutional government immediately after the coup. Moreover, the whole military junta was being challenged and politically threatened by the popular and mobilized power of the Muslim Brotherhood, which was frustrated at its exclusion from power.

The junta's power was effectively and often ruthlessly consolidated. Any opposition was crushed, political parties were banned, and members of the *ancien régime* were tried and sentenced. All this was being carried out whilst simultaneously launching campaigns to popularize and mobilize supporters for the ruling junta, which was becoming increasingly militarized and less civilian.

The militarization of the government came at a time when the Muslim Brotherhood's anti-regime activities were at their peak. On 26 October 1954, a member of the Brotherhood allegedly attempted to assassinate Nasser. This gave the regime an opportunity that could not be missed. A revolutionary tribunal was appointed on 1 November 1954 to try those accused of treason. The accused consisted of top leaders of the Brotherhood. All in all, the so-called 'people's court' tried over 875 people, and the military courts tried over 250 officers. By 1955, there were over 3000 political prisoners in the country. During the trials, it was alleged that the then president Najib had been in cahoots with these 'subversive elements', and he was dismissed from the RCC and placed under house arrest (Vatikiotis 1991: 385–7). Thus the regime had 'hit two birds with one stone': the Brotherhood were driven underground and temporarily paralysed by the imprisonment and torture of thousands of its members and supporters, and by deposing Najib and effectively silencing his supporters who were mainly advocates of civilian rule.

The Political Structure under Nasser

In January 1956 a new Constitution was declared. This consisted of 196 articles providing for a presidential republican system of government in which the president appoints and dismisses ministers. It contained two new notions: that Egypt is an Arab nation, and that 'the state is committed to economic planning and social welfare in the interests of social cooperation among members of the nation' (ibid.). The electoral law of 3 March 1956 had provided for universal male suffrage at 18 years of age. Also in 1956, a decree annulled articles 54–80 of the Civil Code dealing with associations. All such associations, as well as political parties and charities, were dissolved and forced to reapply for licensing. Without the empowering legal provisions, relicensing was very much at the whim of the administrative regulation and discretion.

The National Union was formally established in 1957 and was the prelude to the first elections to a National Assembly since the overthrow of the old regime. The elected assembly met from July 1957 to March 1958, mainly as polite listeners to presidential and ministerial speeches. It was dissolved in March 1958 on union with Syria, which was proclaimed on 21 February 1958.

A reorganized government structure took place which was to change again when Syria seceded from the Union in 1961. In June 1962 a National Charter was formed. The Charter provided for the creation of a new state political structure, the Arab Socialist Union which replaced the National Union. The Charter contained the principles of Islam, Arab nationalism and socialism.

On 23 March 1964, Nasser proclaimed a new provisional Constitution which embodied the principles outlined in the Charter. Law no. 32 of 1964, later to become a point of contention between human rights activists, democracy activists and the state, further complicated the process of creating associations and democratic institutions. According to this law, which later became known as the 'Law of Associations', explicit powers were given to the Ministry of Social Affairs and local government and their officials, to license, regulate, monitor and dissolve associations.

Further, the Constitution provided for a very strong presidential form of government. The president is nominated by the National Assembly and is effectively supreme executive head of the state:

> He appoints vice-presidents and dismisses them. Together with his government he lays down the general policy of the State in all fields and supervises its execution (Article 113). The President has the power to initiate and propose laws, approve them, or return them to the National Assembly for reconsideration.
>
> (ibid.: 404)

The Assembly, in turn, is the legislative power in the state, and is elected for five years. All ministers, though appointed by the president, are responsible to it. The Assembly may be convoked, prorogued and dissolved by the president. This basic political structure, with its excessive presidential power, has lasted till the present day. It is not surprising therefore, when state policies are personalized, and much of the anger and political resentment is channelled against the presidents, and their immediate circles.

Nasser gradually decreased the military component of his government by instituting many civil servants in leadership positions. Nevertheless, it *was* stipulated in the Constitution (Article 23) that the armed forces continued to be 'entrusted with the duty of protecting the socialist gains of the nation'. In fact, by 1961, the role of the army in internal security was already paramount. More than three-quarters of the people working in the all-important Ministry of Interior Affairs, were either active or retired military officers (Baker 1978: 75).[1] Thus, the military have been given a privileged and protected role within the country ever since.

According to Waterbury (1983: 323–4), Nasser, along with a cadre of aides, advisers and clients, 'developed a political style of preemption'. So that if 'power centres' (i.e. the state's own agencies, enterprises and affiliated party, as well as centres outside the state like the Muslim Brotherhood) threatened Nasser's regime and personal survival, he relied heavily on state repressive powers such as the police and intelligence agencies, to disrupt their cohesion before they could mobilize effectively against him. This policy of pre-emption involved continuous political repression. This set the tone for forthcoming demonstrations of the state's lack of power.

Geared away from the ideals of democracy, the Nasser regime was to continue its repression of opponents in general and the Islamist regime and its activists in particular. The disciplinary techniques thus instilled were designed for all opponents of the regime. It is not surprising to hear Islamist reflections in today's contemporary polarized politics, which refer to Nasser's period as a 'reign of terror' (Ra'ef 1985). The trial and execution of the prominent ideologue of the Muslim Brotherhood, Sayyid Qutb, took place in 1966, on charges of treason for conspiring against the state. After the humiliating defeat in the war of June 1967, there was a round of purges in the armed forces, followed by trials of senior military personnel in the winter of 1968 for allegedly conspiring against the regime, as well as a restructuring of the armed forces and a reconstitution of Nasser's government. In short, an increasing dent in the political legitimacy of Nasser's regime led to a corresponding increase in fortifications of the state's repressive power.

Consequences of Nasser's Regime on Islamisms[2]

The attempted destruction of the Society of Muslim Brothers in 1954 had failed to extinguish the flame lit by its founder, Hasan al-Banna, back in 1928. After 1954 and in the seclusion of the Nasser regime's prisons (or 'concentration camps' as they were generally referred to by opponents of the regime) Islamist thought was reconstructed, in large part thanks to Qutb.

While Qutb was incarcerated and expounding on his state–society worldview which would later become his book *Ma'alim fil-Tariq* (*Signposts on the Road*), the Muslim Brotherhood sympathizers began to regroup. The Society of Muslim Sisters, led by Zayneb al-Ghazali, undertook charitable and humanitarian work for families and released Brotherhood prisoners, and acted as an important link in the covert reconstitution of the organization. Al-Ghazali herself held meetings in her home for purposes of 'Islamic education', to which many young activists flocked. Al-Ghazali's role in the clandestine reconstruction of the Brotherhood and ideological training of some of its militants should not be underestimated. For here was an Islamist woman activist who set the example of struggle and sacrifice for 'Islam' for forthcoming generations of men and women Islamists.[3]

Other more militant groups were held in various parts of the country. The most active nuclei of young militants were in major urban centres like Alexandria, Damietta, Buhayra and Cairo. The leaders of these groupings were seeking an ideologue. And into this set-up Sayyid Qutb was released from prison in May 1964. His book was the manifesto of the 1964 regrouped Brotherhood.

Yet despite the fact that they had come together again, the Brotherhood could not agree on a political strategy. They were thus easy prey for a regime that was looking for a scapegoat to unite the people behind a leader who was facing serious problems in both foreign and domestic policy.[4] What happened was the discovery by one of the secret services (one of the regime's numerous disciplinary mechanisms) of a 'plot' to overthrow the state by the Brotherhood. Kepel (1984: 32) remarks:

> There is also evidence that the discovery of the 'plot' was a by-product of internecine conflicts in the various secret services, which were scrambling to garner maximum authority among the marakiz al-Quwwa, or centres of power (which were in fact no more than warring factions of presidential courtiers): each yearned to reveal to the prince a plot that rival services had been unable to uncover.

Brotherhood members were rounded up, arrested, tortured, given a farcical trial and many executed in 1966. Such was the fate of the Muslim Brotherhood during a decade of Nasser's regime, which ended as it began with persecution. There was, however, a visible and noticeable evolution in the thought of the Brotherhood. Whereas in 1954 they had refrained from analysing the Nasser regime, by 1965 they had the theoretical tool with which to diagnose the state and strategize for a future Muslim state – *Signposts*. This analysis was to be a first step towards outlining a blueprint with which the struggle for ideological hegemony and political power between the regime and Islamists was to be waged. But 1965 itself was too soon for *Signposts* to be interpreted and its theories made practical.

The Nasser regime's policy of creating martyrs was a decisive factor for the future of Islamist thinking and practice. On the one hand, the halo of persecution suffered in defence of a faith and a social ideal gave Islamist discourse status, legitimacy and a sense of purpose and continuity. And on the other hand, within the movement itself, various currents began to be formed according to various readings of *Signposts*.

Some Islamist ideologues were to preach *'uzla* (total withdrawal from society) as a means of avoiding the horror of the prisons. Others decided to collaborate with the regime in an attempt to Islamize it from within, whilst yet others opted to work from within the ranks of the opposition, also hoping to avoid the torture and imprisonment. Still others organized and planned for the forcible seizure of power, hoping themselves to pre-empt any state attacks. This was the view of the group who later went on to assassinate Sadat.

Here, I find the theoretical and practical distinction made between state regimes and 'religious regimes', as presented by Mart Bax (1991: 7–28), helpful. According to Bax, one of the most important differences between the two regimes, or the two 'power constellations', is the *sources* of their power. The state has effective control over the means of violence (army, police and taxation), whereas most religious regimes do not have control over these vital power sources. These means of violence resonate with what Foucault terms techniques of disciplinary power. The latter have been an important mainstay of Egyptian political regimes ever since. The Egyptian Islamists may not have effective control over the state's means of violence, yet they undoubtedly have developed their own alternative sources of power through their disciplinary techniques. In the following chapter I outline some of the disciplinary techniques that Islamists forge. The reason for preferring and using the term 'religious regime' is a tactical one, designed to highlight that both the state and Islamists are effective power constellations. As such, their forms of power, though different, remain central to my argument – that both need to be seen as political foes of equal stature. By referring to both as 'regimes', I am countering the distinction often assumed that one is more 'powerful' than the other.

MUHAMMAD ANWAR AL-SADAT (1971–81)

It is best that governments are not run by religious leaders. This is not to say a religious man should not rule, provided he has the necessary experience...when I came to office in 1970; my own people were living on their emotions. I immediately called for the rule of reason and was faced with fierce resistance from those who had ruled Egypt through slogans. But I learned that the Left loses all its weapons when the rule of reason prevails. This is why they reject logic and organize emotional demonstrations based on slogans.

(Sadat 1984: 39–40)

This quote highlights one of the Sadat regime's hallmarks, and the aspect which brought state discourse closer to those of Islamist or other religious regimes: dichotomizing, or binary thinking (e.g. reason and emotion and correct and unacceptable political practice). In May 1971 Sadat carried out a purge of personnel opposed to him from within the ruling echelons. In other words, he rid himself of the Leftists/Nasserites, as well as the 'centres of power' (*Marākiz al-Quwwa*), which he so hated. Significantly, he referred to it as a 'corrective revolution'.

Political pressure (both internal and external, as Sadat had tactically and in a controversial move shifted political allegiance from the Soviet Union to the United States) for a multi-party system eventually led to the naming and establishment of three parties: The Arab Socialist Union (Centre), The National Progressive Union's Party (Left) and The Free Socialist Party (right). Despite his purge of Nasserites from within the ruling ranks however, Sadat was soon to see that Nasserism still influenced many Egyptians. In 1972 and 1973, when demonstrating students and workers shouted Nasserite slogans, the spectre of a Nasserite Left hostile to Sadat's rule rose again. Also, owing to the continuous criticism of Sadat's policies voiced by opposition party members, and especially after the food riots of January 1977 (which Sadat blamed on Leftist instigation), he introduced emergency measures which severely restricted political activity, and made protest demonstrations, sit-ins and strikes illegal. In other words, to counter Nasserite influence and further his own political power, Sadat actually maintained the same repressive power strategies as his predecessor.

His repressive moves were severely criticized from the right and left, and many argued that they were unconstitutional and unjustified. In June 1977 a bill was passed in the Assembly which stipulated that no party would be allowed to function unless it had 20 parliamentary members – a move obviously meant to silence the opposition. Further, Sadat's visit to Jerusalem in November created a political crisis. Irritated by the criticism his 'peace initiative' provoked, he denounced 'those who had instigated a campaign of doubt' against his policies and resorted to a favourite tactic: asking for support in a referendum.

Invariably through the usual widespread vote-rigging, he obtained this 'people's support', and proceeded to hunt down his leftist opponents. In June of the same year, a law was passed which purged critics of the government from public life.

In July, Sadat announced the formation of his own party, the National Democratic Party (NDP) with the slogan: 'Food for every mouth, a house for every individual and prosperity for all'. This signalled the death knell for the Arab Socialist Union, as well as the final curtain call of the Progressive Union Party, which was replaced with a 'more reliable' left-wing opposition party led by Sadat's brother-in-law! As the situation progressively worsened, Sadat's measures consisted of attempting to create newer disciplinary techniques. An example of the latter was his introduction of a new draft law in 1980: the Law of Shame (*Qanun al-'Ayb*). Nominally this law was to 'protect values against vice'. Effectively, it would forbid any criticism of the regime, labelling it as being against the well-being of the state and unethical. A Socialist Prosecutor had power to charge anyone before a special court for political offences and, if thought necessary, to send them for trial before a 'Court of Value'. As Hopwood (1991: 115–16) writes: 'It was a strange and slightly sinister method of political thought control ... If used to full effect, such a law was not far removed from those of a police state.' The law aroused immediate resistance, and the Lawyers' Syndicate (a forum of open political debate despite the regime's efforts to tow it in line)[5] organized effective opposition to it. This eventually led to some modifications. Despite this, however, it still remained a crime to advocate any doctrine which promoted 'disloyalty to the nation'.

Sadat maintained an elected assembly but could not tolerate criticism of his policies – be they his economic 'open door' policies, or his political peace with Israel. Both aspects of this rather contradictory state of affairs were demonstrated in the amended Constitution of May 1980. In the latter, he was allowed unlimited terms as president, whilst the same Constitution declared Egypt a democratic, socialist state with a mixed economy and a free press.

This is an interesting example of manufactured consent taken literally. Sadat must have been fully aware that any open public referendum on the issue of the peace initiative ran an inordinately high chance of stripping him of legitimacy. Hence, his attempts at creating a semblance of consent. This act continues to take place in contemporary Egyptian politics and is peculiar to situations where disciplinary techniques (here including all forms of laws) are not deemed enough in themselves. The acting out of a semblance of consent brings into question the whole dynamic of power relations at the time. In fact, such acts indicate flaws within the state's developed disciplinary techniques. This is in itself significant to the analysis of power dynamics between the different regimes, as it indicates the important turning points where a shift in the discourse of the state takes place.

Consequences of Sadat's Policies on the Islamist Regimes

It can be said that prior to Sadat, there was only the Muslim Brotherhood, which was actively involved in the politics of power. But as a result of the Islamist experience under Nasser, and Sadat's very own policies, a whole range of Islamist regimes appeared on the Egyptian political scene. These regimes were deemed to change the alliances of the different political parties, were instrumental in the increasing Islamization of political discourse and the congruent binarisms in political thinking.

In many of his public speeches, press interviews and reflections, Sadat tried to portray the Nasser era as one of materialism and unbelief, as compared to his, which was one of devoutness, piety and unselfishness. Nevertheless, he made a distinction, not lightly taken and very significant to his way of operating, that religion and politics should be separate. I remember him saying in one of his speeches to the Egyptian Parliament in 1979 that 'those who wish to practise Islam can go to the mosque, and those who wish to engage in politics may do so through legal institutions.' Yet, from the mid-1970s onwards, and as the political might of Islamism shifted against him, state discourse also changed as the state-controlled media began to refer to the 'believer' or the 'pious' president.

In the beginning of his term, Sadat calculated that since Nasserites and leftists in general were the main thorn in his flesh, the best means of combating them would be ideological – by allowing political Islam to present itself as an alternative way of thinking for those who had succumbed to the lure of the left. He must have sincerely believed, as many in the seats of power are wont to do, that the current of political Islam can be kept in check and in control, through the forces of state power at his disposal.

Thus, he freed more Muslim Brotherhood prisoners, and rehabilitated them personally and professionally.[6] Sadat allowed their journal *al-Da'wa* (the Call), which had been banned in 1954, to resume publication in 1976. It is noteworthy and indicative of Sadat's policy that he allowed the publication of the Brotherhood's journal, but continued to withhold the granting of political status to them. The arrangement that Sadat seems to have made with the Brotherhood, however, which was to give them a privileged position to counter the perceived 'threat' from the left, seems to have suited the Brotherhood itself. Their antagonism towards Nasser (in view of what they suffered under him) and the left (they saw communism as an atheistic ideology which should be officially banned) rendered the whole idea of countering their influence equally attractive to them, and seems to have fitted comfortably into their own long-term plans. In fact, the Brothers saw Nasserism as the greatest political force opposing their own movement, and hence the strongest obstacle to the attainment of Islamic society.

Strategically speaking, the Brotherhood would have used this period of cooperation to gather strength whilst simultaneously highlighting the regime's weakness in dealing with the social, cultural and political challenges it faced as a result of its openness to the West. As Baker (1990: 247) explains:

> By sustained and forceful criticism, they [the Brotherhood] aimed to show the regime's limitations in meeting the civilizational challenge to Islam [from the West] while taking advantage of any opportunities it afforded to build the strength of their movement.

It is not surprising, therefore, that many critics charged that the Brotherhood had made an explicit political deal as the price for their freedom.[7] The deal was that the Brotherhood would bide its time, propagating all the while its own Islamist ideology to counter those of the left.

At the same time, however, a contrary argument has been articulated. Precisely because of this truce, the Brotherhood has taken special care not to resort to violence and confrontation and to make maximum use of the peaceful means that the limited liberalization afforded them to build an Islamic society. The non-violent attitude of the Brotherhood was heavily criticized and rejected by other Islamist regimes, particularly after the tense period following the negotiations and signing of the peace treaty with Israel (see Mustafa 1995).

The rapprochement with Israel was seen as the last straw by the more radical Islamist regimes (e.g. *al-Takfir wal Hijra* and *al-Jihad*) who perceived the president and/or the whole society as moving further away from Islam. These Islamists were themselves divided according to strategy as to the precise means necessary in order to establish an Islamic state. *al-Takfir wal Hijra*, for example, believed in withdrawing from the whole unbelieving society till their own internal strength enabled them to fight the forces of the state. Meanwhile the *Jama'at Islamiyya* in the universities increased their cadres and numbers by preaching within and without the university campuses and rallying opinion against state policies. *The Military Academy Group* also attempted to carry out a coup.[8] *Al-Jihad* worked to infiltrate army and bureaucracy and clashed violently with security forces on several occasions. Having no long-term motivated 'truce' with the regime, heavily critical of the whole set of policies practised by it, and believing in the importance of active and immediate *jihad* against the whole 'unIslamic' structure, these religious regimes were violent in their attempts to capture state power.

Sadat's policy of limited liberalization could not prevent the rise of radical groups, especially when the economic, social and political programmes he adopted were seen by Islamists as Western and thus threatening to Egypt's Islamic cultural heritage, and their results seemed only to benefit a very small segment of the population. According to certain allegations, Sadat seems to have been manipulating the groups one against the other. In an interview with 'Umar Tilmisani, the spokesman for the Brotherhood, he charged that 'someone deliberately encouraged this ideology [of the extremists] in order to undermine the Muslim Brotherhood'.[9] Moreover, Sadat's call for a separation between religion and politics was not only unheeded, but it strengthened the image, held by many Islamists, of Sadat's 'phoney' religiosity, and hence the conviction, on the part of some, that he must be eliminated if any form of Islamic society was to be established. It was this conviction, coupled with his latest 'purge' of over 1000 opponents in September 1981, that eventually led to his assassination on 6 October 1981.

Power in Sadat's era typically fluctuated. Whereas in the beginning the upper hand seemed to be with the president, there was also an undeniable element of power on the Islamists' side as well. Each party was playing its game for ideological hegemony. The irony during Sadat's time is that he allowed and encouraged one form of ideological hegemony to play out against another (namely Islamists to counter socialism), believing it to be to his advantage. However, since power is not a tangible element which can be removed, stored and doled out, the Islamists eventually ended up with the ideological upper hand. The effects of this particular ideological and political encounter have taken on new forms in the contemporary Mubarak era.

MUHAMMAD HUSNI MUBARAK (1981–)

On 7 October 1981, the day after Sadat's assassination, vice-president Husni Mubarak was nominated presidential candidate by the People's Assembly. Elections were held a week later and he was proclaimed president. Meanwhile, between 8 and 10 October, there were bloody clashes between Islamist militants and security forces in Assiut, Upper Egypt which resulted in many deaths and casualties. The militant uprising had been part of the follow-up plan of an insurrection by *Jihad* to complete the takeover of power (i.e. capture of the state regime) and depose the government.

Upon his election as president, Mubarak made it clear that Egypt would adhere to the Camp David peace deal with Israel and left the door open for other Arab nations to re-establish ties with Egypt as long as they made no demands. Further, he warned of his government's determination to suppress all forms of 'religious extremism' and threats to public order. The security forces were ordered to proceed immediately to arrest over 350 suspected members of radical Islamist regimes, and a large number of army officers and enlisted men were dismissed from their posts – probably as a result of the interrogations which were carried out on Sadat's assassins.

Mubarak and his policies seem to be described in the same vein by many observers. His cautious, middle-of-the-road manner and image as 'arbiter between competing forces' (Hopwood 1991: 187) rather than policy-maker, seemed to be his initial characteristics. And yet, by steering a seemingly 'moderate' course, his achievements included managing to ease Egypt back into the Arab fold, normalizing relations with the then Soviet Union, and eventually attempting to play a leading mediating role in the Arab region, this of course on the foreign relations front.

Domestically, Mubarak let the law take care of Sadat's assassins and approved the execution of five of them. Slowly, he allowed the political parties and their newspapers to come back to life as he gradually released the hundreds of political opponents imprisoned by Sadat.

Hopwood (ibid.: 185–7) quotes Mubarak as saying: 'I hope freedom is not used to an extent that would damage national security. If it is I will not be lenient with anybody.' Hopwood then rightly goes on to say that 'this kind of remark demonstrates the difficulty of identifying one man with the state and its policy. Criticism is taken as personal and critics are dealt with personally by the head of state.' This remark, and consequent practices of repression, are also an indication that the struggle for hegemony between the state and Islamists remains one in which the threat of force plays a decisive role. Furthermore, it underlines that the heritage of the regime's disciplinary techniques remains mired in and dependent on repressive forms of power.

In addition to the ruling National Democratic Party (NDP) some five other parties have been allowed to function. Among them is a left-wing opposition party – the National Progressive Union Party, or the Tajammu' – which is led by one of the few remaining Free Officers, Khalid Muhyi al-Din. Also present is the Socialist Labour Party and the Wafd (a party that has pre-1952 roots, and which tried to re-emerge during the Nasser and Sadat eras, but was 'prevented' from doing so by the regimes). Interestingly, one religious party was licensed – the Umma Party – despite the legal stipulation since the 'revolution' that no party can be formed on the basis of religion. The communists, the Brotherhood, and Nasserites (till late 1994) have not been officially represented. Yet Mubarak has allowed the Muslim Brotherhood to form alliances with other political parties during the 1984 and 1987 parliamentary elections, despite the fact that it was technically 'illegal'.

In the 1984 parliamentary elections, a system of proportional representation was established with the proviso that only those parties gaining 8 per cent or more of the votes could be represented in the Assembly. Any votes gained below this percentage would go to the majority party. Not surprisingly, the only two parties to gain seats were the NDP (390 seats) and the Wafd (58), which had made an alliance with the Muslim Brotherhood and fought the election on one ticket.[10] The Tajammu', despite winning 7 per cent, was unable to gain a single seat, and its votes were lost to the NDP. Despite complaints about rigging, it was claimed to be the most open election in years.[11] However, when a court ruled on certain irregularities in nominating candidates in the 1984 elections, Mubarak acted quickly and new elections were called for in April 1987.

During the 1987 elections, 15,000 candidates stood for 448 seats. Despite the majority of the population's normal apathy and distrust of politicians' ability to bring about any real change in their lives, there were many lively debates and electoral meetings. It is interesting to note the difference in the alliances that formed at this time. The Wafd Party decided to go it alone. The Muslim Brotherhood – insisting it was they who broke up the alliance – formed an alliance with the Socialists and Liberals, with the slogan 'Islam is the solution'. The main leftist opposition remained the Tajammu', while nearly 400 independents stood for the 48 seats allotted to them. Again, the results were not unexpected. After all, the ruling party does have the necessary 'resources' such as monopoly over the media and officially-sponsored and funded rallies (and propaganda). There were also accusations that the results were falsified. Only a quarter of those eligible voted and elected 309 members of the ruling National Democratic Party, 56 members of the Alliance and 35 of the Wafd. Tajammu' received 2 per cent of the vote and thus obtained no seats. The independents were not really independent because they were NDP-sponsored candidates. So there was diversity in the opposition of the new parliament but the left still had no voice.

Once again, the courts declared the 1987 elections null and void because the rules regarding independent and women candidates had not been observed. A new electoral law was passed in October with independent and all-party candidates to stand in the various constituencies without restriction. There was a referendum approving the dissolution of the Assembly which was approved by 94 per cent of the votes. In November, the first rounds took place initially with nine parties which were going to put forward candidates. In the end, however, the Wafd and the Alliance decided to boycott the elections after some of their demands (including the lifting of the state of emergency) were refused. The result was a large majority for the NDP, although a few 'truly' independent candidates did get elected, such as Khalid Muhyi al-Din.

Mubarak was elected by the majority NDP Assembly for a second, six-year term in 1987 the sole candidate to be endorsed. In a referendum he received 97 per cent of the votes cast. Yet despite this seemingly overwhelming support, his critics accuse him of not doing much with it, and giving the impression that he still does not quite know how and what to do with the power he has. This is an image that was shattered in 1988/9 however, when the government clamped down severely on so-called 'Islamic investment companies'. The reasons given were that these companies were trading illegally in stocks, that they were siphoning off investors' funds to bank accounts in Europe and that they were a financially profitable front for Islamist organizations. A great many people lost their entire life savings, and many suicides took place. Though the government tried to propagate that they had actually saved people from further losses, I believe that they were made to suffer in a power struggle between the different regimes. There is no written evidence linking the financial investment companies to Islamist regimes, yet that kind of connection is not unlikely. In that case, these companies were enhancing and buttressing the power and ideological hegemony of Islamist regimes. The latter fact renders the government's attempt at thoroughly emasculating these financial sources of power, in order to assert its own, inevitable.

The elections in 1990 were boycotted by most opposition parties. The electoral system was also changed from the slate to the individual candidacy system. The NDP thus had about 417 of the seats, while Tajammu' gained 5 seats and the Independents finally gained 31 seats. The latter actually had managed to amass more than a third of the seats in the National Assembly, but the NDP managed to persuade the bulk of them to rejoin party ranks.

The November 1995 parliamentary elections have been a textbook example of the Islamist–state struggle for power and hegemony. Fearing an Islamist victory, the government cracked down violently on all Islamists, but especially on all Muslim Brotherhood members. Whereas previously there may have been a certain selectivity in who would be arrested and for how long, the period prior to the November elections witnessed a comprehensive and indiscriminate assault on all Islamist regimes by the state security forces, reminiscent of earlier eras of heavy-handed political repression. Muslim Brotherhood members were rounded up and thrown into jail. Many of them were tried later by military courts. The latter are a strong vestige of martial law, which in itself is the most damning evidence of the regime's lack of faith in its own hegemonic enterprise and its refuge within disciplinary techniques and violence.

Islamist Regimes under Mubarak

Mubarak did try to encourage the secular opposition both on the left and the centre-right as a means of preventing the dominance of the religious regimes. Moreover, allowing the Muslim Brotherhood to form these alliances reinforces the view that the moderate Islamist regimes were being encouraged to mobilize members as a means of countering the extremist ones, whilst at the same time not granting full political party status to a potentially overriding political force.[12]

The Brotherhood's success was, to a large extent, the result of the strategic decisions taken in the 1970s for limited cooperation with the state regime. But on the other hand, the state regime did *allow* them, for example, to go ahead with their plans to create an economic base of Islamic companies and banks, and further their political participation through alliances with other political parties. These latter operations proceeded smoothly until the crackdown by the authorities. Much has been written in the press and elsewhere about the 'Saudi connection' with the Islamist regimes. Saudi Arabia is perceived by many Islamist regimes as a donor, rich not only in monetary support but also as an 'ideological backup'.[13]

Frequent armed clashes and violence between the state regime and the Islamist regimes are continuing. The police have reportedly carried out torture and arrests of 'religious extremists', or 'terrorists', and clampdowns on demonstrations of any kind (some of which have been dispersed with live ammunition), resulting in many deaths. Official policy is that the government is trying to contain extremism by 'persuasion' and that the police resort to violence only when attacked. Some of the recent violent acts to be carried out by Islamists include the murder, in October 1990, of the Speaker of Parliament, Rif'at al-Mahjub, by Jihad members. Following that (in 1992) was another murder of a prominent secularist writer and activist, Faraj Fuda, also by a Jihad militant. The regime is cracking down hard on Islamists who have developed strongholds in certain areas in Upper Egypt. These groups often act in defiance of government security, whilst creating their own structures of 'state within state'.

According to Amnesty International (1994), 'suspected' activists of Islamist regimes are subjected to repeated periods of detention without charge or trial, and very often tortured. Amnesty also reported that

individuals [are] arbitrarily detained in recent years under Emergency Law because they were related by family to someone wanted by the authorities. This practice has apparently been employed to obtain information on the suspect's whereabouts and to induce the latter to give themselves up, or to obtain more information on the suspect who may already be detained. Dozens of relatives have reportedly been abused and beaten up while in detention centres or even in their homes when visited by SSI officers. Often they are subject to continued harassment even after their release.

(Amnesty International 1992)

Yet, so-called 'Islamic' associations reportedly enjoy special favours and privileges with ministry officials, wherein the latter are included on the boards of management of many of these societies and paid a 'salary'. In short, 'Islamic' associations are given far greater freedom of decision-making and activities by virtue of the arrangements with ministry officials, and thus with the ministry. Furthermore, the state seems to be willing to concede on certain issues in order to ease the pressure. For example, on 26 January 1994, the BBC World Service reported that President Mubarak had approved the banning and censorship of certain literature and poetry, which did not conform to Islamic [modesty] requirements. This was seen by secularists as a 'coup' for the Islamists, as well as for conservative and traditional religious elements in society, represented by Al-Azhar.

Another example alluding to the ambiguous and complex relationship between Islamisms and the regime occurred in 1995 and involved a Cairo University professor who lectured and wrote about Islam and exegesis. Nasr Hamid Abu Zaid was charged with *ridda* (apostasy from Islam) and was taken to court by Islamist lawyers in order to divorce him from his wife (their logic being an Islamic principle that Muslim women cannot be married to non-Muslim men). To the shock of many Egyptian intellectuals, the court confirmed the charge of apostasy and ordered the couple to divorce. Arguably, this is a case where the judiciary – supposedly autonomous from the regime – simply took a decision based on its own evaluation of Abu Zaid's literary work. However, I maintain that even if the state is free of involvement from this form of judgemental charade, it remains an important landmark in the history of Islamist manipulation of state-formed and state-protected laws. The fact is that *state-appointed members of the judiciary have agreed to and have been convinced by certain perceptions held by Islamist lawyers, and, by implication, certain precepts of Islamist ideology.* The implications of this incident are thus significant for the understanding of the dynamic of Islamist ideological hegemony vis-à-vis state domination.

Islamist sympathizers and especially members of the Muslim Brotherhood today work actively inside ministries, unions, syndicates and the media to get their message across. In so doing, they create networks that work *with* and *through* the apparatuses of the state regime, as well as influential sectors of the population, to mobilize and recruit gradually.

There is no *single* defined policy of the Mubarak regime towards Islamist regimes. On the one hand, there is covert compromise, symbolized by the favouring of its own brand of 'Islamic' NGOs (previously) the establishment of Islamic investment companies and Islamic banks, and the tacit acceptance of Brotherhood participation in elections and the political process. On the other hand, there is severe repression and violence. Particularly since the parliamentary elections of November 1995, the state has appeared to resort to its means of violence (e.g. targeted arrests) in order to crack down on the Muslim Brotherhood, perceiving it (rightly so) as its primary ideological and political opposition. Mubarak's state regime seems to be caught between trying to moderate and control a vaguely defined and border-less 'extremism', whilst at the same time trying not to alienate the generally growing conservatism in the country. Ultimately, trying to maintain this impossible equilibrium can and does lead to enhancing conservatism, and through the state's excessive repression, vindicating extremism.

CONCLUSION: FURTHER DISCUSSION

In sum, the state regime under Nasser attempted a socialist discourse which was radically challenged by Sadat's regime. In doing so, Sadat relied on and encouraged Islamist discourses. These, in turn, eventually became powerful enough in stature and credibility to challenge and expose the vulnerability of the dominance of the Sadat regime. The Mubarak regime, whilst airing the President's pilgrimage to Mecca on television, attempted to maintain disciplinary techniques which oscillated between permission and repression, and fed into the general Islamization of political discourse (see El-Sayed, in Oweiss 1990). The latter was being nurtured by religious regimes such as the Muslim Brotherhood, by constituting themselves as the only popular, articulate and viable political opposition. The relationship between the state and Islamists therefore can be characterized as one in which the power of one led to a form of counter-power, or resistance, by the other. And whereas the disciplinary techniques used by the state may have failed to accentuate its dominance, they have succeeded in enhancing the hegemony of Islamist discourse. In the following sec-tion and by way of an unorthodox conclusion, I look at the theoretical and terminological deliberations that this relationship between the two regimes has engendered, whilst clarifying the reasons behind my choice of certain ideas of Bax, Foucault and Gramsci.

Bax argues that a religious regime can be defined as 'a formalized and institutionalized constellation of human interdependencies of variable strength, which is legitimized by religious ideas and propag-ated by religious specialists' (Bax, in Wolf 1991: 9). According to Bax, religious regimes are 'power constellations', and as such they can be compared with other social constellations. Religious regimes are also 'political constellations' which implies the preparation of ideologies and setting out of tactics and strategies concerning 'how to fight and how to win' confrontations, collusion, and so on. He also argues that the term 'regime' implies dynamics as well as an open concept, which can be used for all kinds of religious phenomena and at various levels of societal integration (ibid.: 10).

Bax claims that religious 'regimes' play an important role in the process of state formation and state development. Since we have indicated the personalized nature of the Egyptian state, it follows to some extent that one should not talk of 'state formations' without looking specifically at the events that took place during the period of office of each president. Thus we notice that at the time of Nasser, the conflict over political resources (in this case, in terms of followers or membership) between the state and the Brotherhood played a significant role in the formation of the state and its later development. The alleged attempt to assassinate Nasser in 1954 was one of the events that contributed to the tightening of the politically repressive security apparatus under Nasser's government.

Prior to 1952, when the discussions and strategies of toppling one form of rule by another were rife, the Free Officers not only co-operated with, but had members who were themselves of the Brotherhood. Further, the pressure of these religious regimes plays a large part in altering the discourse of the state itself as well as the discourse of the whole political opposition. An example was the discussion surrounding the writing of Islam and Islamic shari'a into the Constitution, and the Islamization of daily language when addressing followers, party members and the populace at large.

Sadat used religious symbolism (e.g. praying publicly on Fridays on national television, having state media refer to and portray him as 'the pious president') to legitimize his regime and his leadership openly, even though he claimed that religion and politics should be separate. Moreover, he structured his state as soon as he became president by relying on and supporting these religious regimes to counter his then political opponents, the leftists.

Mubarak's official political opposition in the People's Assembly was and is composed of active members and adherents of religious regimes (i.e. the Brotherhood). His unofficial opposition *is* almost wholly made up by religious regimes *per se* (such as Jihad, Al-Jama'a, and countless other Islamist groupings). In some cases, appointments to the post of the Ministry of Interior depend on how well the appointee would be able to counter, if not eradicate, the existence and power of these religious regimes. It is interesting to note that one of the Ministers of Interior was sacked after it was revealed that he had carried out several clandestine attempts at dialogue with certain Islamists. The government's official stand was that the minister had no authorization to do so. Yet, it remains doubtful to what extent such a move could have been carried out whilst unauthorized in a country riddled by martial laws.

The concept of 'religious regimes' is also useful since it ties in with the Foucauldian–Gramscian power paradigms used thus far. I find that the ubiquitousness of power relations – with both the state and Islamists – on which both Gramsci and Foucualt agree is largely congruent with Bax's perceptions of religious regimes as 'power constellations'. Bax's concept, when applied to Islamists in particular, serves to highlight the potential for *political organization* inherent within such movements, whereas Islamism as a term would tend to emphasize the religious or 'Islam' aspect more than the schematic and strategized political approaches.

Further, there is an interesting and relevant interrelatedness between religious regimes and processes of state formation – religious regimes themselves are dependent on the state for their expansion. Bax calls this a feature of the 'antagonistic interdependencies' that exist between religious regimes and secular ones. He explains that such interdependencies are far from harmonious as each tries to take over certain functions or institutions from the other but never fully succeeds. The example of the professional syndicates which the Muslim Brotherhood almost succeeded in winning from state control is relevant in this regard. Equally significant examples are the Islamic investment companies, which the state clampdown has not managed to obliterate totally. Foucault's arguments come to mind here, as the interplay of antagonistic interdependencies highlights the power-resistance paradigms evident in the following statement:

> as soon as there's a relation of power there's a possibility of resistance. We're never trapped by power: it's always possible to modify its hold, in determined conditions and following a precise strategy.
> (Foucault 1980: 13)

Religious states and regimes have similarities as well as important differences. Among their similarities, as Bax explains, are the following:

> Both fulfil important functions in the spheres of social organisation and cultural orientation. Both of them develop policies toward

nation-building and community-building. Both contain structures
for internal control and external defence: they are defence-and-
attack units. Both types of regime are confronted with problems
of internal cohesion and external confrontation; and both try to
solve these problems by attracting resources which they attempt to
monopolize... Finally, like secular regimes (states), religious
regimes are also characterized by their expansionist tendencies:
both strive to extend their territories and to exert their influence
over other sectors of society.

(Bax, in Wolf 1991: 11)

The Egyptian state is not and should not, however, be listed under the
category of a 'secular regime'. It is on this point that I differ from Bax.
A religious regime need not stand in opposition to a secular one; in
fact, as the above case indicates, religious regimes also battle with
each other. The Egyptian state has always argued along the lines of a
'holier than thou' discourse vis-à-vis Islamists in general. The religious
discourse has thus featured in, developed and constituted the main site
of the ongoing power struggles. Bax does indicate that one of the
important differences between religious regimes and states lies in their
sources of power. But he nevertheless fails to elaborate that the
legitimacy of both, and thus to some extent their power base, can be
based on a similar discourse.

Moreover, the idea that the interdependencies are continuously
antagonistic supposes that there can be no points of potential – if
rather tacit – consensus. The latter is a point hotly disputed not only
by many Egyptian feminists, who will argue that when it comes to 'the
women's issue' Islamists and state ideas differ little.[14] Thus a more
adequate conceptualization of the relationship between Islamists and
the state is to be found in Abd Al-baki Hermassi's description of
'conflictual participation' (in Zartman 1990: 203). In the latter process, conflict arises in the process of participating, but the participation itself allows for occasional common ground. This has occurred
during all three presidencies.

My contention is, therefore, that *when arguments are based on the
same discourse, the potential for agreement is also validated.* As long as
the discourse revolves around 'who is the better Muslim' of the two
powers, then within that discourse itself both points of tacit accord
and of supposedly glaring differences can be found – depending on the
situation and the balance of power between the different actors. The
fact is that the closer the grounds of legitimation, the more it becomes

crucial to delegitimize the opponents' discourses, primarily by ignoring it – unless it suits a particular political purpose. This is an
important aspect which is ignored in analyses (Bax's included) that
tend to perceive dynamics only in binarisms. This vestige of modernist
thought influences many contemporary analyses of ideological struggles between different 'contenders to the throne' of power. But the
binarisms blur the fact that there are many important grey areas of
similarities and/or consensus. By viewing Islamist groupings as well as
the state as regimes, I am attempting a move beyond clearly outlined
dichotomies and boundaries. In so doing, I am suggesting a shift in
discussions over state and Islamists to a terrain in which these contentions for power may be perceived as equally dangerous as far as
women's issues are concerned.

The emergence and activisms of Islamist regimes in resistance to
state regimes, is a central backdrop to the power struggles which
Egyptian feminists are part of, and which invariably influence their
debates and activisms. In the following chapter, the Islamist struggle
for ideological hegemony will be analysed by surveying the emergence
and ideas of some Islamist regimes.

4 Islamisms and the Seeds of Disciplinary Power

In the previous chapter, the struggle for ideological hegemony was analysed primarily via looking at the Egyptian regime through the office of the three presidents. In this chapter, a further important part of the historical jigsaw composing the backdrops to women's activism is disscussed. The *raison d'être* and the consequent hegemonic ambitions of some of the Islamist regimes are analysed. The predominance of women's activism during the early times is not comparable to the contemporary landscape. Though undoubtedly women would have played important roles,[1] documentation of this is scarce, with the exception of Zaynab al-Ghazali's own autobiography. Hence, this chapter is concerned mainly with the early period, the narratives of which are dominated by men.

In fitting this jigsaw together, seminal works of some of the ideologues of contemporary Islamist regimes are examined. I begin with an analysis of the prominent book of Sayyid Qutb, whose influence is felt by men and women activists alike. Other works examined are those of Shukri Mustafa and Abd al-Salam Faraj. In many ways, Qutb's work pinpointed the *direction* to be taken, Mustafa's ideology and activities clarified the practical implications and difficulties involved, and Faraj's texts expounded on the necessary *means of action*.

SAYYID QUTB

On Social Relations

Qutb's work is, with few exceptions, based on a clear-cut dichotomy between Islamic (good) and non-Islamic (bad). This binarism is not only pertinent to Qutb's thought, but to much of the conceptualizations formulated within Islamist regimes. Concerned with the setting up of alternative state and society structures, the continuous comparison with existing socio-political entities (i.e. the Egyptian state, 'the West'), is inevitable in almost all the writings and proposals. Furthermore, the following has to be read whilst keeping in mind that what is

80

being prepared and presented as Islamic teachings are part and parcel of the creation of a body of knowledge. The latter is then the focus of Islamist disciplinary power, which is meant simultaneously to elicit obedience and instil a feeling of empowerment in its adherents.

Signposts on the Road

As mentioned previously, this book by Sayyid Qutb was perceived by Islamists as an outstanding work of ideology which set out the main signposts along the road to an Islamic state. Islamist regimes either used it as their guide and based their own strategies on it (like the Society of Muslims and Jihad); or shunned it completely and attempted to distance themselves from it (like some, though by no means all, within the Muslim Brotherhood).

Signposts was an excellent indicator of Qutb's overall attitude towards, and perceptions of, authority and the state. As Kepel (1985: 46) lucidly put it: 'the book aspires to be both an instrument for the analysis of contemporary society and a guide for a vanguard whose task is to inaugurate the resurrection of the *umma*. In short, it is a manifesto.'

On Society and State

In a chapter entitled 'Islam is the Real Civilisation', Sayyid Qutb expounds his views on societies that call themselves Muslim but are in fact in *jahiliyya* (ignorance). Qutb's *jahiliyya* was a society ruled by an evil prince who had made himself an object of worship in God's place and who governed according to his own caprice instead of ruling on the basis of principles by the Qur'an and the *Hadith* (sayings of the prophet). *Jahiliyya*, then, is 'a combination of infidelity, decadence, and oblivious ignorance, similar to that prevailing in pre-Islamic Arabia' (Ibrahim 1980: 431). According to Qutb, there are only two distinct kinds of society within Islam: a Muslim one and a *jahiliyya*. Needless to say, the Muslim one is governed by Islam (which, to him, is faith, legislation, worship, social organization, theory of creation and behaviour). *Jahiliyya*, on the other hand, 'lacks Islam', in other words, lacks civilization:

> Thus, a society whose legislation does not rest on divine law (shari'a) is not Muslim, however ardently its individuals may

proclaim themselves Muslim, even if they pray, fast, and make the pilgrimage... A society that creates a made-to-measure Islam other than that laid down by the Lord and expounded by his messenger... cannot be considered Muslim either.

(Qutb 1991: 12–13)

In similar vein, Qutb considered the only legitimate sovereignty in a well-governed (i.e. Muslim) polity to be that of God. Likewise, he is the sole object of worship (*'ubudiyya*). Thus, a regime can exercise sovereignty only in God's name, by applying the prescriptions of revelation. According to Qutb, the principle of divine sovereignty is a guarantee against the discretionary power of the ruler: only that which bears the divine seal is just. Only legislation governed by the book is immune from being transformed into mere judicial machinery in the service of a despot.

Qutb also explains that *jahiliyya* society confers sovereignty upon other than God and turns these sovereigns into objects of worship. It is characterized by the idealization of the power-holder (whether it be man, caste or party) and by the people's worship of him. Further, Qutb distinguished two faces of *jahiliyya* society. One phase negates the existence of God in favour of explaining history in a materialist manner, attempting to apply a system of so-called scientific socialism. Another system recognises the existence of God whilst limiting the practice of worship to a personal arena, away from the organization of everyday life. In outlining these features of *jahiliyya*, Qutb was in fact declaring that the Nasser regime, despite its claims, was Islamicly illegitimate as far as he was concerned.

On Solutions

The restoration of Islam, wrote Qutb, requires a genuine revolution, under a leadership of a 'vanguard of the *umma*' which must take as its example 'the sole Quranic generation' (i.e. the companions of the prophet). Today's vanguard must contemplate the Qur'an and must turn its back on non-Muslim culture. The vanguard must begin by purging its own consciousness of *jahiliyya*:

> What characterises both Islamic credo and the society inspired by it is that they become a movement (haraka) that will allow no one to stand apart... the battle is constant and the sacred combat (jihad) lasts until judgement day.

(Qutb 1991: 14)

Qutb held that faced by the totalitarian state being created by Nasser-ism, Islamist regimes must not limit themselves to words alone. The mode of action had to be adapted to the form of state repression: against *jahiliyya* Islamists – the 'vanguard of the umma' (Kepel 1985: 129). – and had to resort to a movement, to a struggle that would not be purely verbal.

Interestingly enough, it was the Supreme Guide of the Muslim Brotherhood, Hasan al-Hodaybi, who refuted Qutb's work. In his book *Preachers not Judges*, al-Hodaybi states that the task of the Brotherhood was to *preach* Islam in the society in which they lived. He did not characterize the society as *jahiliyya*, but merely noted that many Muslims remained in a state of ignorance.

Hodaybi also argued against Qutb's position that no one is a Muslim simply by virtue of saying so. Herein lies the crux of the problem that divided Islamist regimes among themselves from that time onwards. The radicals believed that Egyptian society was *jahiliyya* in the strong sense, meaning that the (Islamist) movement was the proper instrument for the propagation of Islam. Moder-ates held that preaching alone would lead Muslim society, now ignorant of the universal validity of the Qur'anic rules, back to Islam.

The problems assumed a more practical form in their divergent assessments of the nature of the Egyptian political system under Nasser and his successor. Would the Brotherhood be permitted to preach or not? Hodaybi, followed by al-Tilmisani,[2] responded in the affirmative. The latter group held that the Nasserite state was not structurally different from its predecessor. Sayyid Qutb and his radic-alist followers disagreed, however. They believed that the independent state represented the reign of *jahiliyya* and of barbarism, under the aegis of an iniquitous prince. To them, words were of no use against such a regime. Islam could only be propagated by action (ibid.: 63).

THE SOCIETY OF MUSLIMS

Between 4 July and 1 December 1977, the Egyptian press – otherwise preoccupied with praising Sadat (the 'peace president') for his visit to Jerusalem in November – offered its readers daily photographs of bearded young men accused of belonging to a group called *al-Takfir wal Hijra*.[3] A long list of offences and crimes was attributed to the group, not the least of which was the kidnapping and assassination of the former minister of Waqfs,[4] Sheikh Muhammad al-Dhahabi.

Hostage-taking was unprecedented in Egyptian political life and the fatal outcome of this violence was inexplicable to Egyptian society. Moreover, a revelation of the sect's practices and mores, the ideology of its leader (an agronomist named Shukri Mustafa) and the scope of its recruitment only added to the anomaly of the situation.

The confrontation between the regime and the Society of Muslims came at a time between the January riots against price increases and the president's speech to the Israeli Knesset in November. It was to prefigure the battle the government would later wage against Islamists, who refused to accept the 'shameful peace with the Jews'.

Before the onset of the peace process, Islamist regimes were accorded a tolerance tempered by discreet police infiltration, the regime's undisclosed aim being to offer an outlet for Islamists other than planning the overthrow of the regime. In 1977, however, this mutual tolerance soured into antagonism as the enmity provoked by Sadat's trip to Jerusalem mounted steadily until it reached its climax in the conflagration of summer 1981 and Sadat's assassination.

The aspirations for a Muslim society, the qualification of the present one as *jahiliyya* and the belief that it had to be destroyed (and a Muslim society erected on its ruins) lay at the root of Shukri Mustafa's thought. Sadat's Egypt – nominally at least – no longer punished 'crimes of opinion' as Nasser's had, but the *jahiliyya* model persisted. As far as these Islamists were concerned, the 'worship of man by man' and the 'sovereignty of man over man' still prevailed, albeit in an altered form.

In accordance with this view, Shukri Mustafa undertook to destroy the instruments of legitimation of the Egyptian regime one by one. His first target was the religious institutions. Shukri regarded *'uzla* (withdrawal from society) as a necessary stage during which the group could build on its strength, until it shifted from a so-called 'phase of weakness' to a 'position of power' (cf. Kepel 1985: 82).

Shukri held that the period of *'uzla* should be the only one in which extensive preaching is to be carried out. But this was not to be performed by today's ulama of al-Azhar, for whom Shukri held little more than disdain:

Islam has been in decline ever since men have ceased to draw their lessons directly from the Qur'an and the Sunna, and have instead followed the tradition of other men, those who call themselves imams.

(ibid.: 79)

In attempting to build a counter-society, the Society of Muslims attracted a number of Muslim youth. Through some of its practices,[5] the Society of Muslims was already attempting to implement its policy of rejecting the *jahiliyya* society and erecting its version of a Muslim one. The sect thereby reminded its adherents of its objectives, developed its own forms of disciplinary power and represented a constant danger to the established order.

Shukri perceived that even though the doors of *ijtihad* (independent reasoning) had been closed to the people since the thirteenth century, they had been held wide open for the 'ulama of the princes'. These ulama issued *fatwas*[6] tailored to fit the views of the sovereign – whoever he was and whatever his views – in order to 'spread sin' and to declare the 'illicit legal in the name of Islam'.

In support of his contentions, Shukri cited several examples, among whom was Sheikh Shaltut (Sheikh al-Azhar during Nasser's period), who had delivered a *fatwa* declaring banking interest legal, even though the Muslims consider it usury. He also cited Sheikh Al-Sha'rawi,[7] who stated that Treasury bonds do not contravene divine law.

After the corrupt religious institutions and personae, Shukri's next target was the army. One of the major reasons for the omnipotence of military officers within the Egyptian regime was the state of war with Israel that existed until 1977. In the vocabulary of Arab nationalism, the Jewish state is an enclave of imperialism on occupied Arab land. In Islamic categories, it becomes a land usurped from *Dar al-Islam*[8] by the infidel, and therefore part of *Dar al-harb*, which must be attacked continuously through *jihad*, which is proclaimed and commanded by 'the commander of the faithful'.

Whilst the first affirmation formed the heart of the discourse of the Nasserite state, the second was the favourite theme of the monthly magazine *al-Da'wa* between 1976 and 1981. Shukri openly opposed both these stances. Struggle against religious legitimation of the state; indifference to anti-Zionist struggle lead by an immoral leader (president); and later, radical rejection of any collaboration with the 'institutions of *jahiliyya*' (including public empowerment and the educational system) – all of these factors led Shukri to place himself on the margins of society, flouting established custom. He challenged the social conventions of daily life. One such social convention was marriage, which the Society practised in a very particular manner. It was the 'Muslim marriage' for which all that was required was the presence of witnesses and the couple's consent. This was regarded as 'leading women astray' and served to outrage public opinion. In the Egyptian press, the scenarios of such events hardly varied: seduced by the captivating words of Shukri or one of his disciples, a young girl deserts her family home, abandons her studies and goes to live among the group. Apart from the total denial of social agency that such one-sided portrayals invoke, the interesting point to keep in mind is that *women went to join this group, being subject to considerable social risk as they did so.* They were not dragged or abducted; they willingly went to participate in the activism of an Islamist regime. This is both relevant and valid for our later analysis on Islamist women's activism.

Shukri argued that in Egyptian cities today, marriage takes place very late and young people suffer as a consequence. He thus re-established early marriage for his members, and undertook to decide and arrange these marriages. By challenging such basic social practices, Shukri was also including them, thereby reifying them as part of a political discourse.

Shukri's Society is an example of how inner disciplinary practices are created and maintained, and the extent to which they are perceived as different and thus 'dangerous' by the rest of society. Foucault's (1977) contention that disciplinary practices may involve the literal dividing off of segments of the population (through incarceration or institutionalization) is relevant in this regard. Shukri clearly divided himself and his disciples from the rest of society by *willingly* marginalizing his group and creating alternative forms of institutions within which his disciples functioned. There is no subtlety in the stark divisions that he made between the Society of Muslims (good) and the rest of society (bad).

What is interesting is that the labelling process, which Foucault expounds, is being carried out in this instance not only by the government (via its own disciplinary mechanisms such as the security forces, media, and so on), but simultaneously by Shukri himself. In this case, the labels circulating demarcate between normal and abnormal, the devout Muslims and the heretics. Here an important aspect emerges: those who are different themselves make the distinction, not so much in defence, but as calculated strategy. This is, therefore, a division in which all parties participate and duplicate exclusionary practices of 'the Other'. The policy of *takfir*, for example, labelling enemies as *kafir* or *murtadd*, is a disciplinary practice which aims at dividing people, i.e. literally those who believe/those who do not, Muslims/non-Muslims. This effectively becomes a disciplinary technique and a form and source of power. The creation of divisions is also a form of social control which marginalizes 'the Others' and simultaneously denies them any form of socio-political legitimacy.

Shukri's language expressed demands that arouse deep feelings among Muslims. The state, therefore, perceived it as imperative to silence him – a task that was to prove far from easy. Moreover, other underground Islamist regimes were emerging – presenting the society with political rivals. One such rival was the Muslim Brotherhood.[9] Each typically denied 'the Other' the right to speak in the name of Islam, a fact consistent with the point raised in the previous chapter, which is that the need to delegitimize the opponent's discourse increases in direct proportion to the similarity of the sources drawn upon for legitimacy. Shukri's group and the editors of *al-Da'wa* encountered one another only sporadically. For one lived on the fringes of society whilst the latter manoeuvred within it. There were, however, clashes between the Society of Muslims and other less well-known Islamist groups, reminiscent of Bax's reference to confrontations with other religious regimes (Bax, in Wolf 1991: 3). These clashes, and the so-called 'physical elimination of apostates' (i.e. members who deserted to other groups), were the first signs of the Society of Muslims' violent tendencies.

In November 1976, Shukri carried out these punitive expeditions, believing them to be an internal matter which was necessary to assert his authority in the face of challenges from other groups. This was the chance the police were waiting for, as 14 members of the society were arrested. The police action took the leaders of the society unawares. For, despite realising that the Egyptian state was in *jahiliyya*, they had not yet developed any clear tactics in their relation to this state, particularly since they were misled into trusting the 'tolerance' of the Sadat regime. After several futile attempts at countering the allegations of the state and 'correcting' the negative image formed of him by the media, Shukri decided on a master stroke which would restore his authority and present a direct challenge to the state. That was when the society kidnapped the former minister of Waqfs. Since the state refused to meet their demands, they killed him. And within a few days, most of the sect's members had been charged in a military tribunal and executed.

The Society of Muslims was a unique phenomenon in Sadat's Egypt. By organising a counter-society in which much of the dominant social practices were inverted, it allowed the Islamist youth who followed Shukri Mustafa to live out their own utopia. This tendency of Islamist regimes eventually sank into oblivion. But its achievements and errors left many a lesson for others, particularly the group that was later to assassinate Sadat. The confrontation between the state and the Society of Muslims and the latter's destruction, invalidated the 'phase of weakness' strategy – one of the bases in the analysis and strategies of Sayyid Qutb. In fact, the young Islamists who were to come after Shukri no longer availed themselves of it.

THE MILITARY ACADEMY GROUP

In 1974, a group led by a Palestinian tried to ferment an uprising in the Heliopolis Military Academy (in a Cairo suburb) and assassinate the head of state. The facts of the case remain murky even now, but nevertheless, the incidents are interesting for several reasons. First, the abortive attempt was a dress rehearsal for the frontal assault later to take place by *al-Jihad* in October 1981. Secondly, it was the work of a tendency of Islamists whose analysis of the state and society differed from Shukri's.

The leader of this group, Salih Sirriya, was thought to be a member of the Islamic Liberation Party.[10] When he arrived in Cairo in 1971, Sirriya began frequenting the Muslim Brotherhood and holding lengthy discussions with both Hasan al-Hodaybi and Zaynab al-Ghazali. At the same time, he began to assemble a group of young people, most of whom were students in Cairo and Alexandria.

Unlike Shukri, Sirriya did not attempt to create a counter-society and organise any *hijra* (migration). In fact, his disciples continued to lead normal lives so as not to attract the attention of the authorities. Further, they did not agree that all society represented *jahiliyya* and anti-Islamic barbarism, but held instead that the head of state alone blocked the spread of an Islamic mode of society. Here, the labelling is limited and the exclusionary tactics are selective. Nevertheless, the delineation between the religious regime and the worldly regime is quite clear.

After organising a group of conspirators, Sirriya and his disciples attempted their *coup d'état* on 18 April 1974. They failed. But the government was nevertheless caught unawares. Consequently, great efforts were made to implicate foreigners.

It must be recalled that this sudden eruption of 'violence' against the state came at a time when all the members of Islamist regimes imprisoned under Nasser were being released, and another such movement was growing on the university campuses, with state sanctioning. Thus it was that as soon as Egyptian prisons were emptied of Nasser's Islamist prisoners, they were filled once again with Sadat's. Inside the prisons, some of the inmates 'changed sects' and exchanged information and knowledge. Moreover, they formed links or enmities which were to continue outside the prison walls.

THE *JAMA'AT ISLAMIYYA*

The *Jama'at* were the Islamist student associations which became a dominant force on the university campuses during Sadat's presidency. To understand better the reasons for the growth and popularity of such movements among students, an appreciation of the latter's background is necessary.

After Nasser declared that higher education would be free in 1960, and with the phenomenal population increase since the early 1970s, universities in Egypt have become cramped and overcrowded. In fact, a nickname for today's universities is 'the university of large numbers', and this terminology is also used in official discourse.

Another feature of the 1970s was the migration of teachers and lecturers out of Egypt and to the Gulf states, thereby depriving the country of an important educational resource. Thus, university students were faced with overcrowded lecture halls, in which it was a rare privilege to follow all the lectures. It became common practice to learn the lecturer's paper by heart (often sold by them at a profit), and enrol in a 'private tuition' course (provided by these same lecturers outside the university regulations), in order to pass the examinations. The majority of students could afford neither manuscript nor tuition. Consequently, anger and frustration at the whole system were rife.

In addition, problems like transport to and from the university added to the hassle and irritability experienced by the students – particularly the women. It is not surprising, therefore, that when the leaders of the *Jama'at* managed to come up with viable solutions, a large majority of the students – men and women – were at least willing to listen.

Nevertheless, to believe that it was these material concerns only that prompted the students to join the cadres of the *Jama'at Islamiyya* is to oversimplify matters. For one thing, the *Jama'at* started (after the 1967 defeat) as a minority within a student body dominated by the Nasserite left and Marxist currents. It was only after 1972 that their fortunes took a turn for the better, for they had finally found the key to success: discreet, tactical collaboration with the regime to break the left's dominance on the campuses (Abdalla 1985). After all, it was ultimately in the state's interest to eliminate this opposition from the ranks of the students.

With discreet state support, this Islamist group made its breakthrough during the period of relative calm that prevailed on the campuses after the October war of 1973. A mere four years later, they were in complete control of the universities and had driven the leftist organizations underground.

The *Jama'at* managed to create an intricate, efficient and well-organized infrastructure within the universities. The establishment of summer camps served as recruiting and training mechanisms, and generally prepared the cadres of the *Jama'at* for the possibility of taking on tasks other than smashing the Nasserite and communist left for the benefit of the ruling group (Rubin 1990; Mustafa 1995). In their view, Nasserism constituted an intense period of *jahiliyya*, yet the Sadat era was scarcely any better. The internal contradictions of the latter period had, however, enabled the *Jama'at* to grow in the shadow of the state.

After managing to dominate the Student Union, the *Jama'at* attempted to spread their activities outside the campuses.[11] Their rationale was their aspiration to become the motor force of the process of transformation of *jahiliyya* into Muslim society. In any event, the *Jama'at* did succeed in becoming quite effective and influential outside the university sphere.

Two events were to open a chasm between the *Jama'at Islamiyya* and the state in 1977. The first event concerned the Society of Muslims affair, and the second was Sadat's trip to Jerusalem. The former forced the *Jama'at* (owing to the pressure of public opinion) to denounce the activities of Shukri. This was despite the fact that the *Jama'at* disagreed with the manner in which he had been tried and subsequently dealt with by the state.

As to Sadat's trip to Jerusalem, it is necessary to point out that Israel was as much an enemy of the *Jama'at* as it was to other Islamist groups. And no amount of convincing is ever likely to penetrate the deep ideology of animosity towards Israel inherent in Islamist thinking as a whole. The *Jama'at*, therefore, began to exploit opposition to the policy of peace with Israel, on which Sadat had gambled much of his legitimacy and political survival.

From then on, the *Jama'at* suffered administrative harassment and later police repression. There was a striking change in the tone of *al-Da'wa*'s column on 'News of the Youth and Universities'.[12] As early as January 1978, articles were describing persecution and injustices suffered by the *Jama'at* at the hands of 'them' (i.e. the regime). In other words, the distinction between 'us' and 'them' resurfaced, as the undeclared truce between the state and these Islamists ended.

The *Jama'at* thus came to win recognition as an opposition force. From then on, their numbers rose steadily. The university years 1979/80 and 1980/1 saw repeated incidents and commando actions involving the *Jama'at* and deviants, at the two universities of Middle and Upper Egypt (al-Minya and Asyut). However, tension ultimately crystallized around the confessional problem, i.e. sectarian conflicts. In the opinion of the *Jama'at*, the 'people of the Book' (Jews and Christians) may peacefully enjoy their status of *dhimmi*[13] until the inevitable day they become convinced of Islam and adopt it. They are not supposed to be too ostentatious in their rejection of this process. This way of thinking was counter to the Coptic demand for cultural identity. Young generations of Copts suffer the same social, cultural, economic and political tensions as do all Muslim Egyptians, and many have lately manifested a tendency to turn to the Church.

The *Jama'at* claim that Western Christians and Lebanese Christians have led the Copts astray, inciting them to reject their status as tributaries, to propagate their faith to build new churches, and thus to provoke Muslims (Kepel 1985: 158; Abdel Fattah 1984). It is the duty of all 'good Muslims', according to the *Jama'at*, to oppose these sinister enterprises. This is the general line of argument underlying most conflicts between Islamists and Copts. It is interesting to note that actual conflicts between the two take place after a particular state decision or action that inflames the Islamists, but that is rarely connected to the Copts at all. In the spring of 1980, for example, the violence between the two sects began with the presentation to Sadat of the Israeli ambassador's credentials and the asylum offered to the ex-Shah of Iran.

In sum, the *Jama'at* do not hesitate to fan the flames of sectarian tension in order to wrongfoot the state and indirectly demonstrate their capacity to supplant it.[14] The Islamists challenge the state because it 'does not keep the Christians in their rightful place' (i.e. as tributaries) and 'uses them to persecute the Muslim people'.

In June 1981, immediately after Islamist–Coptic clashes in an area of Cairo named *al-Zawiya al-Hamra*, the regime attacked and liquidated the *Jama'at* on the pretext that they were inciting sedition. In order to establish a confessional balance in the repression and thus to disarm any potential Muslim solidarity, the regime also dealt heavy blows to the Coptic Church and hierarchy, which were cast as the Christian equivalent not of al-Azhar, but of the *Jama'at* (ibid.: 165). Thus the era of the *Jama'at* had effectively come to an end – but only after Muslim–Christian conflict had become a lurking devil in every district, town and dwelling of Egypt.

AL-JIHAD[15]

> I am Khalid al-Islambuli, I have killed Pharaoh, and I do not fear death!

Khalid al-Islambuli, a lieutenant in the army, killed Sadat at the peak of the president's unpopularity, after a year marked by *al-Zawiya al-Hamra* troubles in June, and the sweeping repression carried out by the regime against the religious and secular opposition (in which 1500 people were arrested).

The group to which Islambuli belonged is somewhat more widely known than the other Islamist movements described so far. A pamphlet by the group's ideologue 'Abd al-Salam Faraj, is available. The title of the book *Al-Farida Al-Gha'iba* (The Hidden Imperative), is a reference to *jihad* (holy struggle) which Faraj perceives as imperative to wage against the Pharaoh,[16] but which the *ulama* have striven to obscure. 'The Hidden Imperative' became the constitution of *al-Jihad*.

The ideology and action of the *Jihad* group mark a shift in the line of thinking followed by the Islamist movement since the publication of *Signposts*. 'The Hidden Imperative' represents the group's theory and practice in the form of a negative assessment of the various components of the Islamist movement in general. Al-Jihad, Faraj explains, is seeking to overcome the record of failure (Guenena 1986).

In Faraj's view, all the varieties of the transitional strategy conceived by Shukri Mustafa, the *Jama'at Islamiyya*, the neo-Muslim Brotherhood and everyone else – each designed to avoid harsh repression whilst simultaneously training militants had ultimately failed. Faraj contends that despite all his precautions, Shukri Mustafa died on the gallows in 1978. Moreover, the anti-Islamic nature of the state had not changed since the inauguration of the Islamist movement, a fact which is in itself a sign of failure.

Faraj ignored any analysis of society in his book and instead devoted it to the question of power and the state. In examining what had been the weak point of Islamist thought since the time of Hasan al-Banna – namely, how to seize power – he ascribed absolute priority to *jihad* against the Pharaoh (or despotic ruler); to holy combat in the form of an uprising against the regime, and the assassination of the head of state. In fact, Faraj ordered a holy war against a regime that did not govern according to the shari'a alone, but instead applied a legal system adulterated by Western legislation.

In effect, Faraj's tract presents a programme of action for the establishment of an Islamic state. Within the *al-Jihad* group[17] the leaders of the Middle Egypt branch (i.e. Karam Zuhdi) seem not to have held Faraj's text in high esteem. According to Zuhdi, *jihad* was an imperative upheld by all consistent preachers. Zuhdi also felt that *jihad* had to be waged first and foremost against the Copts, and only later against the president (whom he considered their hostage) (cf. Kepel 1985).

Thus the *al-Jihad* militants of Middle Egypt and Cairo did not view the Copts in the same way. The Cairo group held that the prime objective of *al-Jihad* was the destruction of the infidel state. The 'problem of the Copts' would somehow be dealt with in the process. Zuhdi and his friends, on the other hand, considered Christian proselytism the major obstacle to the propagation of Islam, and therefore merited priority in all their strategies (ibid.: 207).

The two groups, however, held regular meetings and in June 1980 they decided to coordinate their activities, each retaining the freedom of action within his own region. To seal their agreement they asked Sheikh 'Umar 'Abd al-Rahman[18] to become their Mufti. So whilst Faraj and Zuhdi represented the executive power, their mufti issued *fatwas* legitimizing all their actions. He was their al-Azhar. When they heard the *fatwas*, the young militants were assured of their entry to paradise when they joined the armed *jihad*.[19]

Al-Jihad members clamoured to accept the responsibility for the decision to assassinate Sadat. According to Khalid al-Islambuli's testimony, the assassination was the logical consequence of Faraj's thinking. In addition, the opportunity[20] made it a feasible idea.

After the assassination plan was presented to the leaders of the two branches, a heated argument broke out between Karam Zuhdi and Abbud al-Zummur (a 35-year-old air force officer trained in problems of military security) about whether or not the organization was capable of moving directly from the assassination of Sadat to the 'popular revolution' that was supposed to bring about the Islamic state. While Zuhdi declared he could take control of Asyut,[21] Abbud had justified doubts about the ability of the Cairo branch to neutralize the nerve centres of the capital.

The failure of the Islamist movement cautioned against by Faraj, claimed *al-Jihad* itself when the state system did not change and was in fact continued under the presidency of Husni Mubarak. Despite Zuhdi and his group's attempts at gaining power in Middle Egypt (they had in fact managed to paralyse the security forces of the region) their uprising was crushed by paratroopers flown in from Cairo. In sum, the attempt to seize power had failed, and the mode of government was to remain, according to their understandings, as un-Islamic as it had always been – i.e. the apostates of Islam were still ruling.

Yet despite the crackdown carried out by the state on the *al-Jihad* organization in its entirety, it still remains an active thorn in the flesh of the state. 'Terrorist' attacks are carried out in its name, the latest being the murder of an Egyptian diplomat in Geneva in November 1995. The branch in Middle Egypt in particular – because of its deeply rooted character and solidarity network – is still the headquarters of much of the planning carried out by today's *al-Jihad* members. And from their various activities[22] it is clear that the group are still bent on the same ideology: *jihad* against the Christians and against the state, as the legitimate way to gain power.

The *al-Jihad* group, along with other Islamists, apparently propagates a varied discourse of protest that will remain a striking aspect of the Egyptian political scene as long as the legitimacy of the state structure is equated with religious subordination. As Bertrand Badie (in Kazancigil 1986: 256) sums it up:

> The coexistence of these formulae for protest thus constitutes another mark of Islamic culture. *The absence within it of political*

legitimacy in the strict sense contributes to the tendency for such formulae to seek religious legitimacy.

(emphasis added)

Badie also points out that this phenomenon has two consequences. First, it strikes fiercely at the political power in office, for in this manner protest establishes its own legitimacy, which will challenge that of the established power. And second, this simultaneity of protest formulae tends to place the protest beyond the reach of the institutionalized political system. This latter aspect would best suit the *al-Jihad* group since the others, like the Muslim Brotherhood and the *Jama'at*, were, in the beginning at least, placing themselves more or less within the institutionalized political system.

COMMONALITIES AND DIFFERENCES

In his study on the anatomy of Egypt's Islamic militants, Saad Eddin Ibrahim (1980) concluded that all four comparable Islamic movements have grown primarily out of the middle and lower sectors of the new middle class. These groups are of recent rural background, experiencing for the first time life in huge metropolitan areas where 'foreign influence is most apparent and where impersonal forces are at maximum strength' (Ibrahim 1980: 446). All these factors play a crucial role in managing to attract members to the Islamic movements.

All four militant groups perceive the adherence to Islam as providing a complete and righteous vision for a healthy society on earth and a heavenly paradise hereafter. In fact, part of the attraction of Islamisms lies in their promise of double salvation. Some Islamist groups like the Muslim Brotherhood have demonstrated their capacity to create successful social institutions for the needy (e.g. schools and clinics), whilst filling the political vacuum with a holy purpose. In other words, they have in a sense sanctified and made successful this life and the next.

All groups are religious regimes in that their structure and formation are formalized: they appoint spiritual leaders and various forms of political representatives, economic spokesmen and public relations people; in general, they run themselves on a well-defined and clear hierarchical basis. Also, they are institutionalized to a great extent: as a political, religious, social and economic set-up which often provides practical alternatives to Egyptian Muslims, both in their daily lives as well as on the ideological level.

Moreover, their *raison d'être* is based on religion and religious symbolism, significance, etc. Islam, or their interpretation of it to be more precise, is their ideological creed, their sense of identity, their purpose in life, if not their livelihood. Their whole structure, internal or external, is based on, if not derived from, 'Islam'. The Brotherhood's motto, first articulated during the 1987 elections when they formed the Alliance, was 'Islam is the solution'. Indeed, their main political demand, and the main aim of the other Islamist groups, is the implementation of the shari'a, or Islamic law as the constitutional law of the country.

It is undeniable that these groups have formed, at one time or another, by their mere existence and function, a very noticeable 'power constellation'. Further, their *modus operandi*, makes it very clear that the working out of strategies and tactics to overcome opposition is an integral aspect of their mode of functioning. Hence their political alliances, social policies and economic alternatives.[23]

Within each group, a body of knowledge was created. This was based on some form of 'Islamic teachings' and was used as a disciplinary practice to elicit control – obedience – from individuals. The latter feel empowered because 'Islam is the solution', whilst at the same time are more docile because they are not questioning the teachings as such but using them. This body of knowledge in its diversity serves the purpose of creating divisions between individuals, labelling them as Muslims/Copts, believers/non-believers, with us/against us, etc.

Islamist regimes in general share a low opinion of al-Azhar's corps of *ulama*, whom they refer to as the 'pulpit parrots' (Ibrahim 1980: 434). Some of the members regard the *ulama* with outright hostility; others regard them with indifference. Underlying both negative attitudes is the militants' belief that the *ulama* have abdicated their responsibility towards Islam, have emptied the religion of its socioeconomic component and are no longer qualified to lead the community of believers. Worse still, the *ulama* supposedly stand in the way of rebuilding a true Islamic social order (ibid.).

All groups agree that the political system is corrupt and inefficient, and that evidence for this is abundant. External evidence includes the defeat of the system by the 'enemies of Islam' (i.e. the Copts, the Christian West, Jewish Zionism and atheist communism). From some of the Islamists' point of view, the regime has made humiliating concessions to those enemies.[24] The system, by deviating from the straight path, has failed to prepare sufficiently to repel external assaults on *Dar al-Islam* (Ibrahim 1980: 430). Internally, almost all Islamists agree that the most obvious signs of corruption and inefficiency are demonstrated in the regime's oblivion to the shari'a *and its adoption and enforcement of man-made, Western, imported legal codes.* It is this latter perception of the regime's point of weakness which constitutes the main reason why personal status laws, for example, remain the bargaining chip, conceded by the state, to appease conservative Muslim opinion. In other words, they are the only laws which are based on the shari'a, as opposed to the other laws, which are civil laws.

The groups believe that the leaders of the present system (i.e. Nasser, Sadat and Mubarak) have not set an Islamic example in behaviour and life-style; nor have they any intention of reinstating Muslim institutions. The majority of these Islamists believe that the deviation from the shari'a is the core explanation of why Egypt is suffering from internal decay and external 'humiliation'. It follows, then, that the solution to all this lies in a system that commits itself and begins to implement the shari'a (see Kepel 1985; Burgat 1995).

One of the major differences between Islamist groups as a whole exists between the Muslim Brotherhood and the rest of the Islamists. Whereas the former believe that the proper Muslim state will come about gradually through preaching to the masses, the latter believe that violent action (whether withdrawal or some form of *jihad*) has to be resorted to in order to arrive at an Islamic state.

Among the militants themselves, however, each group perceived the state and society differently. The Military Academy group (MA) condemned the political system in the main. The society at large (though described as decaying and riddled with problems) was not blamed. In fact, it was viewed as a victim of the iniquitous prince at the top of the political system. As one of the surviving leaders of the attack on the Military Academy stated:

> We believe that the Egyptians are basically the most religious of all Islamic peoples. They were so even before Islam... They have continued to be very religious. Egypt would therefore be a very good base to start the world Muslim revival. All that the country needs is a sincere Muslim leadership.
>
> (anonymous, as quoted in Ibrahim 1980: 431)

This way of thinking decisively affected the strategy of the MA group. Their aim was a direct hit at the leader. And despite knowing that their strength could not possibly take on the whole state structure, their ideology was to commit an action as an 'outrage for God'.

The Society of Muslims, on the other hand, does not make that distinction between the political system and the society at large. They see both as equitable and as mirrors of one another. According to them, a corrupt society breeds a corrupt political system, and vice versa. Furthermore, they perceive the present political system in Egypt and Egyptian society as beyond redemption – thus remaining in a state of *jahiliyya*.

Their strategy, therefore, was a patient and long-range one. Owing to the state of *jahiliyya*, society had to undergo moral reconstruction from the ground up. To achieve this, a nucleus community was built, with a micro-society of believers who were supposed to act out the true life of Islam. By withdrawing from the rest of the *jahiliyya*, the Society of Muslims was implementing the *hijra* and renewing themselves during a phase of weakness. Their aim was gradually to grow in strength and then emerge to bring about a radical change in both society and state structures.

The *Jama'at Islamiyya* were largely inspired by the works of Sayyid Qutb, but had no clear strategy of their own. Their actions tended to be a mixture of ideas from both 'camps', reformists and militants. With the former, they believed in preaching to society as the means of achieving a gradual transformation to a 'Muslim Society'. From the militants they accepted the idea of the basic corruptibility of the state structures, and of the leader.

Al-Jihad's main ideologue did not dwell much on society, although it was agreed that the latter was still in *jahiliyya*. But the most striking point in *al-Jihad*'s ideology, was their insistence on armed *jihad* as a basic tenet of their strategy. To them, *jihad* was the only means to topple the present state structure. Among themselves they differed in deciding whether to attack the state directly or indirectly (e.g. through the Copts).

In sum, it may be said that whilst some Islamic militants aim at changing the individual as a means of reforming society, others aim primarily at society as the locus of change. Some movements seek partial change, whilst others seek a total change in whatever locus they believe to be most significant.

Through the formation of what may be called the 'community counter-culture', however, the Islamists have given rise to new forms of protests directly concerned with protecting the *identity* of Islam – against immorality, corruption and inefficiency. It is specifically in the context of protecting the Islamic identity that one sees hostile opposition to the development of a new family code or the adoption of a new status on women.

The 'women's issue' is the next important and major difference between Islamist regimes and hence needs to be mentioned in this context.[25] The women and men argued that there was no such thing as a 'women's issue', and that in fact there is a broader issue of 'society'. There were nevertheless both inter- as well as intra-group differences, and it is with a great deal of difficulty that such opinions can be summarized or in any way generalized. The Society of Muslims, for example, had women as active members (though ranked as second-class and subservient to men).

Jihad also had some women members, some of whom I interviewed. What was interesting about *Jihad*, however, was the discrepancy between what the male members said (or did not say) about the women activists, and the image thereby portrayed, and what some of the women themselves had to say. Male members of *Jihad* portrayed women as occupying the sole functions of mother and wife, as they believe ordained by the shari'a. Interestingly, I did not need to go through the men to reach some of the women activists, but was taken to them through a mutual woman friend. These women told me of assignments to carry and deliver explosives, messages and act in many cases as links between different members of the organization. Apart from these roles, some of the women were involved in searching for and procuring and educating future wives. Taking all this into account, I am left to wonder exactly how the male members defined 'wives' and 'mothers'.

Moreover, on meeting these women, I was myself plied with questions as to the who, where, when and why of my research. All the women *Jihad* activists I came across left me with a strong impression of self-confidence and a burning sense of purpose. Finally, none of the *Jihad* women I met let the opportunity of our meeting pass without referring bluntly to the fact that I ought to be veiled myself, so that in many instances the power relations between researcher and researched seemed to be at best ambiguous, for I felt both researched and a subject of admonition. I was also left with a feeling that I owed them something for their consenting to meet me – in some cases despite personal danger.

The Muslim Brotherhood members differed among themselves a great deal in their views of women, so a generalized position is inappropriate. However, the writings of some of their most prominent members leave little room for ambiguity. Although the primacy of motherhood and the role of spouse is certainly stressed, *these roles are seen as themselves political roles, and not domestic ones.*

In sum, there are important differences and commonalities between the diverse Islamist regimes herein portrayed. These range from their *raison d'être* to their disciplinary techniques, to their *modus operandi* vis-à-vis the state. What is important to note is the inevitable ideological challenge they pose to the state – especially when the legitimacy of the latter is shaky and its most effective source of power is repressive. Islamist regimes have proved by their political existence and socio-economic practice that they are an effective ideological and economic alternative to the existing state structure. Whether they operate from within existing state structures or attack violently from the margins, Islamists have made their presence at all levels of life keenly felt. Effectively, there are no other political opponents of the Egyptian state that carry as much political weight, economic clout and social support. That these forms of power have repercussions on how women's issues are perceived, and consequent levels of feminist activisms, is undeniable. As such a political, economic and cultural factor, Islamism is bound to affect all discourses taking place within Egypt.

The following chapters will trace the diverse sites and voices of women's activisms.

5 Feminist Voices and Women's Organizations

The different feminisms mentioned in Chapter 1 are herein presented and analysed, both by giving voice to the activists from the different currents, as well as clarifying their perspectives on the issues dealt with in this research: Islamism, feminism and the state. In the last section, an analysis of the material is made in light of hegemonic power relations.

The first Egyptian Women's Union was set up by Huda Sha'rawi in 1923. Feminist activity in Egypt, however, had started in the late 1880s – a time of great national turbulence as a result of British colonial domination. Egyptian feminism thus goes back more than a century. Not new to the politics of arguing and fighting for women's rights, therefore, Egyptian women have successful and illustrious historical precedents, which have provided the basic groundwork for subsequent struggles.[1]

Soon after the establishment of the Women's Union, the differences and divergence in strategies and ways of thinking between activist women members became apparent. These differences were ideological and religiously based. There were those, like Inji Aflatoun for example, who felt that a more radical (relatively speaking) leftist agenda, 'closer to the people', was needed. On the other hand, there was the notable example of Zaynab Al-Ghazali who felt that Sha'rawi's example was too Western and thus inauthentic, and left the EFU to form the first Islamic women's association in 1936.[2] Such differences, and the consequent split among groups of women, more or less set the tone for the ideological and strategic differences adopted by today's feminists.

Despite fighting and winning the struggle for active participation in Egyptian political life, many Egyptian women feel that the 1980s and 1990s mark the beginning of their 'endangered rights'. Boasting no unified women's union, they participate in an abundance of non-governmental women's associations, women's groups which are formed around varying issues, political parties, as well as state-sponsored 'women's organizations'. The various NGOs are hampered by certain state-imposed laws (e.g. Law 32 of 1964) which govern them and specifically prohibit 'any involvement in politics, or political activity'. It seems that even in our present times, the most acceptable and less 'harassed' forms of women's organizations are still those that deal with the 'traditional occupations of women', that is, occupations that are mainly concerned with charitable work for the poor and underprivileged, or with organizing women's projects that remain as politically innocent as possible.

Trying to list all the active women's groups and all the different activists within the country today is not feasible in this context, for this is not a Who's Who project, nor is it an attempt to create an encylopaedia of women's NGOs in Egypt.[3] Instead, the aim is to highlight the diversity of forms taken and ideas espoused by the different groups and individuals, and then analyse the resulting power dynamics.

What is intended is a survey of particular groups and women activists who are concerned with working towards *effecting a fundamental change in society by altering existing gender relations*. From its inception, Egyptian feminist activism has been grounded in charitable activities, or what I refer to as traditional help. By traditional help I mean those activities that have come to be seen as 'women's work'. As mentioned above, this means charitable work as well as literacy, healthcare and various other domestic 'womanly chores' like sewing, cooking and child care. Groups which come together specifically and only for these purposes are not considered here. This condition is, however, 'dropped' when looking at Islamist women, the reason being that the paucity of information available about them and their organization does not permit the luxury of being selective. Moreover, for a great many of them, doing political work for the 'Islamic community' cannot be separated from doing work for women.

Issues which involve marriage and the divorce laws (the Family or Personal Status Laws – PSL) have been extremely controversial since the very beginning of a women's movement in Egypt, and still continue to be some of the most urgent points on the various agendas of women's groups. Other issues have emerged in the past 10–20 years, namely, fighting conservative pressures that attempt to keep women in the home and out of the labour market; rape and punishment for rape; veiling, or a variety of issues relating to 'women in Islam', which include fierce debates on 'the proper roles and attire of Muslim women'. These and other issues are among some of the non-traditional work that has been taken up by women's groups and independent activists alike.

There is no such thing as a single, homogeneous women's movement. There are many extremely active women's groups and associations, who know of each other and whose members may have worked on an individual basis with each other at some point in time on certain projects and issues – the environment, health care, family planning or campaigns involving Personal Status/Family Laws, citizenship and labour laws. In general, however, these groups and individuals often work separately and without consistent coordination or cooperation.

Further, the groups cover the whole political spectrum, from leftists (such as those in the Tajammu' Party and the Nasserist Party), to the centre (like some of the independent women's associations, as well as the ruling party's own 'women's committee'), to the right (as in the Islamist women's groups). The situation is such that the polarization among the left and right is intense. To expect some form of collective movement on women's issues, which would bring together the supporters of the Islamists with leftists, is presently asking too much.

The following section deals with the process of broadly mapping out the various groups, which will be organized in the order of political parties, private voluntary organizations or non-governmental organizations and independent women activists. Throughout, I leave space for the women's own words and thus the polyvocality of their discourses. In the last section I analyse the power dynamics the different discourses narrate.

WOMEN IN POLITICAL PARTIES

Parties limit their activism and interests only to within the sphere of contesting political power, or the carrying out of political opposition, and not as a matter of changing society. If it were to be broadened to an activism concerned with changing societies, then the women's issue would necessarily occupy a much better position than at present, since it is a focal axis of changing society.

(Amal Mahmud, Nasserist Party)

There are thirteen political parties in Egypt. The five main ones are the centrist ruling National Democratic Party (NDP), the Tajammu' Party (leftist), the Wafd Party, the Liberals, the Labour Party (which is allied with the Muslim Brotherhood and is therefore more to the right of the political spectrum) and the Nasserist Party (leftist). All have some form of a *lajnat al- mar'a* ('Women's Committee')[4] which is actively involved in organizing plenaries, discussions, seminars, setting up and working on women's projects, lobbying for women's issues and distributing publications of relevant studies or seminars.

I have chosen to write about the political parties which, in my opinion, best represent the different feminisms advocated. Hence I concentrate on the women's committees of the NDP as the ambiguous ruling party; the Tajammu' as a leftist and largely (though by no means exclusively and homogeneously) secular-oriented feminism; the Nasserist Party as indicative of Muslim feminism, and the Labour Party as a manifestation of Islamist feminism. None of these classifications is in any way absolute or universal. In fact, within one party, the range of opinions may well encompass the whole range of feminisms. However, I have taken the feminism of the elected (or, in the NDP's case the appointed) head of the women's committee to be at least acceptable by the majority of members of the party.

The Ruling National Democratic Party (NDP) – Farkhanda Hasan

> I do not believe in calling for some rights. I do my job first and prove that I am doing it and that I can do it well.
>
> (Farkhanda Hasan)

The ruling NDP has a women's secretariat with networks and branches throughout the country. The NDP also has tentacles in many other nationwide women's associations organized around certain themes (health, labour, etc.). These associations either come directly under the control of the party (the members and/or participants are linked with the party structurally), or are indirectly controlled via the Law of Associations (Law 32 of 1964) in one way or another. These associations are all registered with the General Department of Women's Affairs of the Ministry of Social Affairs, which supervises their activities and deals with the implementation of the above-mentioned law.

Other than setting up and working on a variety of economic and social projects for women (which usually are concerned with literacy, health and income-generation), the various women's groups are concerned with organizing workshops, seminars, discussions and lectures on a variety of social and political issues relating to women.

Farkhanda Hasan was appointed by the president as head of the Women's Secretariat (WS) in the NDP. Hasan is a professor of geology at the American University in Cairo, a member of the

Shura Assembly (Egypt's equivalent to the House of Lords), and was a member of the General Assembly (equivalent to the House of Commons). She insists that

> I was not a part of any movement. I worked my way through men ... I was elected by fellow colleagues to the chairmanship [of the geology department]. I am not asking for women's rights as much as I am proving what women are capable of.[5]

In fact, she asserts this through describing the work of the WS in the NDP:

> What we do in the party is to prove to the society that women are just carrying on with the process of development. This is a way of deserving [women's] political participation in the decision-making levels. We are few in numbers because men started earlier so they are ahead. The percentage of women is small, so that is what we are working on.

When asked about the aims of the WS, Hasan insists that there is only one aim – that of increasing the participation of women in political life and decision-making. How the Secretariat goes about this is by attempting to raise the awareness of society and the women themselves. This is through conferences, seminars, various media and other channels.

The WS has 26 women secretaries in the 26 governorates; each governorate is in turn divided into sectors (urban) and centres (rural). For each sector or centre there is an under-secretary, and each has tens of basic units, and for each basic unit there is a woman. In total there are more than 1500 women in the various sectors.

One of the projects that Hasan describes enthusiastically is related to the creation of a database of working women, which will then be studied, added to and improved. This database is to be used as a document in attempts to prove women's existing effective participation: 'Such gender analysis is our way of proving to society what women are doing and who is doing what.'

In response to a question on the relationship between the WS and the rest of the party, Hasan, not surprisingly, indicated that things ran very smoothly. Do men party leaders interfere in the decision-making process or the allocation of resources to the WS? Hasan emphatically replied: 'No way, no way, no way'. In fact, it was her emphasis which made me wonder whether she was reacting to the question itself, or to my posing of it. For in this interview, the power dynamics between researcher and researched seemed rather one-sided. On the one hand, hers had been a very difficult schedule to squeeze into. And once I had secured an appointment with her, she was the only woman with whom I felt a sense of urgency and lack of adequate conversational time. In our first telephone conversation, Hasan had caught me completely off-guard by asking me to specify the time I needed. 'Half an hour?' was her leading question. Immediately, I felt at a multiplicity of disadvantages. I was forced not only to circumscribe the time I would want, but I also realized that this was a take-it-or-leave-it situation. I immediately asked for 45 minutes. Once we started the interview, Hasan was interrupted at least five times. In total, I had about 25 minutes of her time. During the interview, Hasan did answer my questions, but it was equally clear that the 'party line' was being reeled out. In itself, of course, that is also part of what I was after.

Hasan's views on the feminist groups in Egypt are interesting in that they mirror not only her opinion, but in all likelihood that of the government itself. According to Hasan, feminist and women's groups are to be classified and seen according to those who are 'very active, moderately active, and those who had better not exist'. However, she makes a distinction between the 'women's movement' (which she sees as the old feminists) and 'women's societies and organizations'. As far as the latter are concerned, she 'cannot see that women's contribution to life in Egypt is much affected by women's groups. What helped women is education, not these groups. As to the reasons for this supposed ineffectiveness, Hasan emphasized that 'their work is limited, they did not effect women going to school and were not instrumental in any way on such important issues'.

To further her criticisms, Hasan declares that 'I am against having separate things for women, it is over, we needed it before, not now'. The question that inevitably comes to mind is, if Hasan believes that separate women's 'things' are unnecessary, why does she not propose the dissolution of the Women's Secretariat within the NDP?

As far as Islamisms are concerned, Hasan reiterates the official view that 'they are terrorists using Islam as a political toy. [Islamists] are moved by higher political movements.' According to Hasan, Islamism 'will fade away. It will take some time, give it four years, five years.'

The Tajammu' Party – Laila Al-Shall

I was calling for the overthrow of the British colonialists along with the throngs at 'Abdin Palace in 1940s. I was 15. I did not realize then that this was politics.[6]

Out of the various political parties mentioned, the leftist Tajammu'
are well organized, have clear and known aims, membership conditions, rules and regulations, and present and future agendas. After the
Labour Party (strengthened by the Muslim Brotherhood connection),
Tajammu' is the second largest opposition party in Egypt. Both
women and men members have a history of involvement in some
form of labour activism from an early age. The aspect of labour
involvement runs consistently throughout their careers, and the
sense of commitment to effecting political change comes across very
strongly.

Al-Shall worked in the Women's Secretariat of the early *Ittihad
Ishtiraki* or Socialist Union of Nasser's times, before its division into
parties.[7] Her involvement in labour unions and women's issues was
simultaneous. Al-Shall was elected to her post as Assistant Leader of
the Progressive Women's Union (PWU) and a member of the Central
Committee of the party. She has also worked in a public sector
company for the past 30 years and now occupies the highest public
service position within it.

The meeting with Al-Shall is itself of fieldwork experience interest.
My first attempt was to try to meet – again – the head of the PWU.[8]
But after making two appointments, which she did not attend, I
decided to see her colleague, Ms. Al-Shall, instead. This worked out
rather well, for Al-Shall was not only an interesting and enriching
person, but she was easy to get along with – I did not feel disadvant-
aged or unequal in any way. Her approach was to discuss and
exchange views, so that I did not feel that I was receiving the party
line only, but the sum of long and serious reflections and experiences.
Al-Shall was obliging to all my queries, never once looked at her
watch and seemed to enjoy the opportunity of recollection. 'Please
feel free to contact me at any time,' was her parting comment.

The PWU of the Tajammu' was formed in 1984. They have
branches in various governorates and a pyramidical organizational
hierarchical structure. Top members of the PWU are key members of
the Central Committee of the Tajammu'. The PWU's general political
framework falls within that of the Tajammu' Party. However, 'the
PWU is independent, and there is no interference from the party in
the work of the PWU'. So far, Al-Shall claims, there is no tension with
men members. On the contrary, the men in the party are 'very supportive and many attend the monthly seminars organized in Cairo,
and participate – though not as members of the PWU, but as members of the [Tajammu'] Party'. According to Al-Shall, the PWU is

totally against feminist ideas. And we have been fighting people with such ideas for some time. Men and women are not separate in their fights in society. Men are our companions in the struggle. We think women's issues however, have a specificity which needs to be addressed.

Tajammu''s main stated aims, according to Al-Shall, are raising women's consciousness and increasing literacy, defending women's rights and increasing women's public participation in order to improve their lot. Al-Tajammu' attempts to carry out their aims through organizing lectures and seminars. These lectures are usually in response to issues of importance in society, e.g. 'women and Islam' and 'women and the media'. Also, they mobilize on issues and projects of social urgency, e.g. for the flooding that took place in November 1994. In such cases, Al-Tajammu' will set up bazaars and organize exhibitions to raise money for the victims as well as carrying out projects in Cairo and rural areas.

The PWU works on four main issues: Citizenship Laws; Law of Associations no. 32 of 1964; Personal Status Laws; and the Labour Laws. On all of these, the PWU, in conjunction with the Tajammu' Party, contributed to the debates on the laws, carried out studies on their effects, proposed alternative amendments and, in some cases, called for the abolition of the law. The latter is especially the case with respect to the Citizenship Laws (for which the party has sponsored many court cases of women) and the Law of Associations.

Al-Shall reiterated that the PWU works with other women's committees, NGOs and democratic organizations. In fact, 'a continuous coordinating committee to coordinate the activities with these democratic associations' exists. However, attempts to organize such a committee on a large scale are, according to Al- Shall, 'unwanted by the government'. Not unlike other NGOs and political parties, the PWU also organizes and runs literacy classes and income-generating projects, through which 'we try to join women to us – we are not a social organization so there is a difference. Our social work has to be done with a political dose.'

As far as both Al-Shall and Al-Tajammu' Party are concerned,

Islamism is not representative of Islam proper. They are against democracy and freedom of discussion and ideas. The murder of Faraj Fuda clearly indicated this. [They have led us to the state where] we are working to establish ideas that were already established years ago, e.g. women's right to work in the 1960s was a right, and now we are asking for it all over again. These ideas have taken us back many years.

According to Al-Shall, the Islamist success is interpreted in terms of their easy access to abundant sources of funding. 'Foreign support', a term favoured by the government, was one I often heard in secular circles. Al-Shall went on to give the example of the Islamist large presence during the ICPD (International Conference on Population and Development).

They must have had a great deal of funds to go to that. The registration was already some large amount in dollars, and we could not afford to send many of our representatives because of that expense.

When asked her opinion about women who joined these Islamist groups, Al-Shall said that youth in general find Islamic preaching persuasive at a time of economic hardship. This economic essentialism on Islamism is consistent with the views held by leftists, since to acknowledge the political vacuum that Islamism appears to have occupied is simultaneously to concede the ineffectiveness of the ideologies they are upholding. Moreover, Al-Shall had this to say:

People are attracted because of the poor social conditions. The Egyptian people are by nature very religious, so it is easy to get convinced by religious arguments. Egyptian women are by nature followers, so they follow their husbands into these groups. If you see these groups, they have no women leaders like Huda Sha'rawi. Egyptian women are by nature followers, and have no independent personality.

Al-Shall's arguments tend to be essentialist. This form of response, however, is common to most secular feminists when an understanding and an opinion on Islamism is asked for. Al-Shall, like others, makes little distinction between Islamists, and lumps them all together under the rubric of political Islam. The latter is seen as misguided at best, and knows only violence at worst. In fact, Al-Shall's terminology for these groups is both telling and interesting: she refers to them in Arabic, as the *'muta'aslimin'* [sic], or 'those who put on Islam'. This term is opposed to the Arabic *'Muslimin'* [sic] which means Muslims. The term is interesting because it indicates that Islamists are thus denied the legitimacy and validity of their claims to the religion.

Al-Shall predicts that a great deal of work has to be done in order to counter Islamist ideas and influence on women's issues. Her opinion is that

> These *muta'aslimin* will decrease the opportunities for success on women's issues, so we as political parties and organizations have to work very hard and very much and productively to improve conditions.

Further, Al-Shall maintains that because of Islamism on the one hand and government pressures on the other, Egypt cannot boast a 'women's movement':

> We have no women's movement, but we have women's work. This is because there is a lack of coordination between all the different women's organizations. This is one of our aims to create such a coordination. Until now we cannot face the increase of influence of these *muta'aslimin*. The Union [of different women] can help collect such activism.

Later on, however, Al-Shall retracted and said that such a Union or collective would be in essence, a matter of appearance; it is the ability to come together as united women and take a united stance that is the crux of any positive development.

The Nasserist Party – Amal Mahmud

Owing to the fact that the Nasserist Party had only recently (in 1990) acquired its right to exist and act as a political party,[9] the organization as a whole is still very much in the formative stage. This is especially apparent in the women's committee of the party which has yet to publish its own agendas and participants' work, as has been done by the Tajammu', for example.

The Nasserist Party women maintain that there is no political activism relevant or exclusive to women. Like Tajammu' and the Islamists, theirs is an issue of social activism. As Amal Mahmud, head of the Women's Committee in the Nasserist Party, put it:

> When we joined political activism, we did so out of a social awareness and not out of any [gender] awareness. We understood from our experiences during the student movement in the early 1970s, that political activism is not just talking but taking action.[10]

Throughout our meeting, which lasted almost four hours, Mahmud was enthusiastic, serious and friendly. She was different from the first two women, in her open support for my research. She made sure that I felt at ease with her, and though we met in her office during working hours in the company she works in (her third or fourth – and only paying – job), her attitude reflected her concern with giving me all the time I needed. Mahmud's calm manner, her persistence and sense of strength belie her manner and her activism. She was one of the few with whom my identities as researcher and activist were mirrored, respected and understood. Our conversations were precisely a give-and-take. It was not only an interview, we discussed issues.

Mahmud's experiences are derived from her first and earlier activism in the labour movement. Her awareness of her gender identity, she asserts, goes back to the same experience. Mahmud recounts how, when she was fighting for workers' rights and was nominated for a post in the Labour Union, her nomination was rejected on the basis of her sex:

> The rumours went flying to ridicule men who would vote for and come under the leadership of a woman. But *Alhamdulillah* [thank God] I was able to overcome this barrier through the support of the male labourers who insisted that I as a woman, was better than many men. Nevertheless, many other barriers were installed. It was through this experience however, that I realized what it meant to be a woman. I also realized that the Egyptian society, once they find real leadership, do not consider the gender issue or the ideological issue – communist or otherwise. They follow those who are capable of presenting their concerns.

In describing the development of the women's committee, Mahmud mentions participation in diverse women's conferences internationally and nationally. By 1985, Mahmud said, the serious confrontation with Islamist influences had already reached its peak. She cited the example of a conference organized by the Union of Arab Lawyers (in which Mahmud as member of the Nasserist Party-under-construction, participated), in which Islamists insisted that the women's section within the Union of Arab Lawyers should be dissolved. This claim was made on the basis that women should be at home anyway, and that the only matter to be discussed was the correct implementation of the shari'a:

> Our confrontation with them at this point was very severe and decisive. We answered their claims to speak in the name of Islam

by proving to them that Islam gave women the same rights they were attempting to abolish. We also told them that as far as child-rearing is concerned, it is not only the responsibility of the women, but of men and of the society.

The Nasserist Party Women's Committee's (NPWC) aims differ little from the Tajammu's: combating illiteracy, providing adequate health-care, setting up projects for the poor and rural women, consciousness-raising, and so on. Not unlike the Tajammu' and NDP structures (in fact, all the political parties share the same hierarchical organizational structure), each governorate has representative offices and these are expanding into rural centres.

The NPWC publish a magazine from time to time as part of their awareness raising and spreading the faith campaign, as it were. The magazine's name is suggestive of the global ideas being determined and propagated locally. *Umm al-Dunya* (mother of the world) also means, in local parlance, Egypt the nation. The NPWC goals were determined by a general discussion of a larger proposal put forward by Mahmud. The proposal was discussed not only by the women's committee in the Cairo headquarters but all the various committees' members (men and women) of the party and of the different governorates.

Asked if all matters relevant to the women's committee went through a similar process, Mahmud answered, 'The rest of the issues are no one else's business but our own in the committee'.

Mahmud was the only political party member who was prepared to seriously consider and honestly answer my question on the intra-party gender balance of power. Instead of the traditional party solidarity line, Mahmud echoed and elaborated her Tajammu' colleague's concerns (expressed a year earlier) on this matter. Where the activism of men and women members of the party is concerned, Mahmud maintains that:

> there is no equality in the interest given to women's issues, I do not think this problem is just an aspect of our political party, but of party politics – and of the society as a whole. Because the handling of women's issues, in my opinion is still rather backward – even among those who are progressive and dealing with societal issues. They deal with societal issues without dealing with the particularities which will take over the change in society. I see that changing the position of women will change that of society, so I deal with it not as a peculiar issue, but as a [general] political issue. Many men,

or many party leaders perceive women's activism in their parties as though it were a peculiar activism, meaning an activism that is carried out by women members of their parties.

Mahmud claims that since she herself does not make that distinction between women and the rest of society, she sees no difference between her work in the gender arena and public work:

> I do not deal with women's issues as gender issues, but as social issues, and as such, since we work with the people anyway, then we [women] are basically carrying out our work anyway. Woman is the key to development, to family, to society. How can we go into society as political parties, with the erroneous idea that women are only a problem of sex, a problem of certain laws, a problem of abortion rights or any of these various compartments?

The prioritization of women's concerns in the party itself, therefore, is, Mahmud clarifies, an issue not yet worked on. Women in top leadership positions within the party are still few and far between. Mahmud admits that they have a long way to go.

Indicating her standpoint on women's activism and her opinions on Islamism, Mahmud had the following to say:

> I see that from within Islam Islamist ideas can be countered, since I am a Muslim. I do not deny that others have different ideas but I do not see them possible on the basis of my faith, and I also do not see the feasibility of the implementation of such ideas [which are not from within Islam] from a situation in which Islam is the religion of the state.

Basically, Mahmud's argument is that Islamism can be countered only by another Islamic discourse. In referring to the 'different ideas' of others, she means secularist discourse, which she sees as incapable of being accepted as long as Islam remains the meta-narrative – grounding reality – of the whole society. Mahmud, whilst acknowledging that women's issues have their own particularities, nevertheless refuses to identify herself as a feminist. She understands that 'it is not an issue of woman against man. Feminism is not social, *it is not political enough*. Even if you broaden its definition, it may well be relevant to NGOs but not to a political party.' Islamism's effects are felt, according to Mahmud, through *ishtibakat hiwariyya* (or discursive clashes). The NPWC is thus actively engaged in organizing seminars to promote and explain the 'correct' views on Islam. But Mahmud does not see Islamism as a woman's issue.

This extremism is not a woman's issue. Its concern with women is aimed as a diversion from the real issue at hand. Extremism is a phenomenon which has developed in the Egyptian reality, and in a backward reality, as a result of economic and social problems. And at the heart of these problems in which youth feel a loss of hope in the future, where a specific national project is missing. So youth look to a continuity with the past. Those who have no economic problem have an ideological vacuum – the absence of a project.

Mahmud contrasts the political situation of the 1980s and 1990s with that of the 1960s in which enthusiasm for a project was occupying the mind of youth. According to Mahmud, the future course leaves no choice but to effect radical change worldwide. Islamism therefore has to be a passing phase, since 'Islamism is an expression of the bankruptcy of any real concept of change'. As far as Mahmud can determine, Islamists have no programme of action on politics, education, the economy or health: 'they are hiding behind slogans'. Moreover, Mahmud maintains that the present government's approach elicits more sympathy for Islamism than Islamism itself. In other words, her opinion strengthens the idea that the government's own mediocrity of discourse and inefficiency of action count in the Islamists' favour.

Mahmud points out that women will be the first to pay the price for any social, economic and political change. In order to organize against this, she reiterates the necessity of a women's united front. According to her, this form of women's union is discouraged by Egyptian law. Nevertheless, a group was formed from a variety of women's organizations (political parties and NGOs) which has met since the mid-1980s to set up just such a committee. This group is busy attempting to study and find points of commonality between the different groups.

Mahmud referred to another, similar initiative which the Egyptian government was taking an interest in. The reason for this sudden concern on the part of the government is linked to their suspicion that such a coalition, if allowed to form on its own, would comprise mainly those in opposition to them. Thus, to try to counter that independent initiative and to attempt to hegemonize and control such forums, the state created its own structure.

The main drawbacks of such initiatives are, as Mahmud described, that they are 'not genuine'. Part of their ineffectiveness relates to their

goal of trying to pre-empt and limit the women's NGOs activities –
except those registered with the Ministry of Social Affairs (MoSA)
under the notorious law 32 of 1969. The name of the government-
sponsored initiative is *lajnat al-tansiq al-sha'biyya lil-tahdir li mu'ta-
mar pekin'* (The Popular Coordinating Committee for the Preparation
for the Beijing Conference). As with the other initiative, this is also
exclusive of the Labour Party women's committee. Mahmud predicts
that such an initiative will, in all likelihood, grind to a halt after the
Beijing Conference, since it 'is not rooted in genuine activism'.

It was Mahmud who first brought my attention to the fact that
some form of cohesion and coordination does take place between the
different women's committees of the apparently non-reconcilable
parties. Such coordination relates to issues of social crisis (e.g. during
earthquakes, floods and international issues such as lobbying on
behalf of the Iraqi or Palestinian causes):

> We work together and can agree on certain social programmes but
> not on many internal political [women's] issues. Generally coordin-
> ation possibilities are open between us and other political parties.

When asked about her expectations for women's activism in the near
future, Mahmud maintains:

> I am not optimistic. The situation is not conducive to group work.
> We are still mired in individual and petty grievances. The situation
> is not mature enough for group political participation.

She also contends that this situation is part and parcel of the New
World Order's agenda to break up groupings. According to her,

> The New World Order brings up all forms of struggles in order to
> effect the hegemony of the USA on the whole world and to promote
> its ideas, weapons and its international police role. Look at the
> former Yugoslavia, the former Soviet Union – it is a scenario of
> differences [which prevails].

In Egypt, Mahmud maintains, this global scenario is mirrored in the
break-up of political parties 'so as to block the possibilities of the
emergence of cohesive action and real alternatives'.

The Labour Party – Asmahan Shukri

With a background and ten years' experience in the field of antiquit-
ies, Shukri is a perfect example of how many Egyptian women entered

the field of politics. After finishing her first degree, Shukri, who comes from a family with a long and distinguished history of involvement in national politics, married and had children. It was only after her youngest herself went to university, that Shukri decided to get actively involved in public forums. Her father is Ibrahim Shukri, who has a long and distinguished political career, which includes founding the Labour Party in the mid-1970s and being its current leader. Shukri's first political involvement was joining the party, not only in the Women's Secretariat, but also as member of the Executive Committee.

Shukri wears a head cover consisting of a scarf which covers her hair. With a quiet, efficient and concerned manner about her, she invited me to interview her at her home. Despite her generosity with her time and information, I felt somewhat uncomfortable with her. Shukri is approximately my mother's age and my respect for her, even if only on the basis of age, is substantial. Hence my intense unease when she used the linguistic form of respect in referring to me (*hadritik*). Shukri was merely acknowledging the researcher in me, and acting in a very dignified polite manner towards me for that reason. Still, her open/deliberate respect was unexpected and left me feeling uncomfortable, since I felt that it was more natural that, with the difference in age especially, the respect (and its consequent power implications) should flow from me to her. Despite, or maybe because of this I very much appreciated her making time and taking the trouble to see me. The power relations in our case, I believe, would be interpreted differently by each of us, for in her respect, there was a sense of my having the upper hand in some way. Yet I felt that I was (and am) indebted to her throughout. I recall one particular incident when I had an appointment with her at a set time in the Labour Party headquarters. I waited for approximately 20 minutes, at the end of which I believed that I had been stood up, so to speak. This would not by any means have been the first time during my fieldwork experience.

Yet, just as I was about to leave in frustration, Shukri came running in looking tired, flustered and out of breath. She apologized profusely – another unexpected and deliberate gesture of respect. She had good reason for not coming to the appointment at all. And yet, because she did not have my telephone number, she was unable to cancel the appointment, and had thus gone to considerable trouble to show up. I was touched. This kind of treatment was precious indeed.

Shukri maintains that the reasons for women's relatively scarce participation in Egyptian public life have to do with the political atmosphere, and some of our social values, as well as the exigencies of everyday life – 'being mother and wife and running around'.

Women have so much to do and so little time to do it all. That is why women's political participation is in the main among the very young (teens and early twenties) and much later in life (in the forties and fifties).

Shukri puts some of the blame for women's non-participation on educated women themselves. The aims of the Women's Committee of the Labour Party are to work towards increasing the participation of as many women as possible in the activism of the party itself, as well as to develop women's capacities to help themselves first and society second. Also, the aim is to encourage women to register on the electoral roll and to take part in elections, since 'women are half the society and the law allows it'.

The means used by the Women's Committee include cultural seminars. Several such seminars were held by the Women's Committee around the theme of 'women's liberation'. According to Shukri, these were held to 'answer those who say that Islam is a cause of women's backwardness'. Other means include giving economic aid through organizing markets, bazaars, expositions (e.g. of second-hand clothes) and literacy classes. Also uniquely provided by the Women's Committee of the Labour Party, and indicating a very deep awareness of a serious social-educational need, is organizing classes to offer extra tuition to children. Moreover, the policy implementation begins with social and interpersonal relations and depends on men:

If every man member were to allow his daughter(s) and wife (wives), and sister(s) to participate, that would make a lot of difference. So I think the key to the problem is still with the man and not so much the woman.

Shukri also emphasized the role of their weekly newspaper, *Al-Sha'b*, in forming public opinion.

The women's committee is not, it seems, in itself the highest priority for the Labour Party. The manifestation of this is to be found in Shukri's admission that despite having many party branches in several governorates, 'they do not all have all sorts of committees'.

Shukri has no problem in saying that as far as the relationship between the Women's Committee and the rest of the party is concerned,

> We see ourselves as an inseparable part of the party and do not have a special policy, but a general policy which everyone tries to implement in their areas. Our priorities are put forward to the General Secretary and the best gets chosen. We are always consulting them [the male members of the Party] in all our movements. We are not independent but one of the many secretariats.

As for the decision-making process within the party on issues planned and carried out by the women's committee members on their own affairs, Shukri maintains that 'whatever decision has to be submitted to the General Secretary. He has the final say.'

According to Shukri, achieving their aims is difficult due to the fact that

> our presence as an opposition party complicates matters because people want to be safe so they join NDP. This has to do with the government's role because the opposition is looked at with suspicion and not as an acknowledged part of the national opposition. The opposition is viewed as a challenger and treated with wariness and punishments. [Male] members are subjected to pressures for their membership.

Shukri had this to say on Islamism as a terminology:

> I think it should be Islamists, moderates and extremists. The mix between Islam and extremism is unfair and intentional. Yet not all these terrorist attacks are Islamist – but extremist.

Shukri described herself as 'an Egyptian moderate Muslim'. Yet, when I asked her about the difference between being a Muslim and an Islamist in her case, a long period of silence followed in which she seemed at a loss for words. To avoid the embarrassment, I eventually changed the subject.

Shukri spoke of veiling as a personal decision *par excellence*. Any government interference or influence on the debate surrounding veiling is unfair and will lead to a counter-reaction:

> The veil is an indication of religious revival – this is throughout the Arab and Islamic world. There is no need for the government to carry out a war against this, for what purpose? The government

also should not attack those who are propagating a moderate religious teaching.

Shukri, not unlike her colleagues on other political parties, contends that the

> Women's movement needs serious development and a gathering of strength. [Present] efforts are uncoordinated and contradictory. Everyone feels in opposition to the other. We need to return to some form of a Women's Union to unify these strengths – but one that is removed from state control.

Yet, I asked her whether she thought that such a Union would be inclusive of the Labour Party women – especially in view of the fact that secularists would form an important element. Shukri responded:

> We agree with other women activists and organizations on issues like Bosnia and Iraq. So why not be able to have a general agreement? There is no separation between religion and the rest of life. There are broad lines on women we can all agree on: if we start with women and non-participation, and work against this; [this would mean] more participation of women in politics to vote and give their voices. A [women's] union I think, would be able to coordinate and encourage such movements.

As far as feminism is concerned, Shukri declares that she does 'not like this term because I feel that separation between men and women in society is not to the benefit of women'. In other words, Shukri too understands feminism in terms of a split between men and women, whereas the ideal and the reality for her would mean society working together to better itself. In other words, the two sexes should not work against each other. This is consistent with Shukri's earlier references to the responsibility that educated women have to become politically active, whilst alluding to the fact that men, by not giving permission to the female members of their family, were impeding such developments.

What is striking is the fact that each women's committee in all the parties is responsible for carrying out traditional charitable and social activities. Laila Al-Shall explained this to me by saying that just as men had longer experience in the political process, women had longer experience in social work.

The NDP is an agenda that will rationalize, justify and laud the status quo, and stress women's achievements in much the same way as it praises the accomplishments of the present regime's policies, as though the former was merely a sign of the latter. The Tajammu' agenda is essentially a socialist one, which also belongs to an opposition party. Hence, they are critical of the regime, and call primarily for more, 'real' democracy and a more equitable redistribution of wealth. Similarly, the Nasserites are also deeply critical of the current government on many issues, democracy and economic policy being some of their main points of contention. Both the leftist parties find the economic policies of the Mubarak government – not to mention his foreign policy – a series of ongoing errors, which are destroying the country and increasing the rich–poor divide with drastic social, economic and political results.

The women's agendas in the different political parties discussed do not differ to any radical extent from each other. Each of them ultimately aims to improve the lot of Egyptian women: through increasing their literacy rates and their socio-economic position, as well as attempting to eradicate forms of ignorance and discrimination in general. These are all basic concerns.

The means through which these aims are being carried out are sometimes different in nuance, but the creation and execution out of educative, productive and other projects, each aimed at solving the various problems, is a process that is carried out by each party and group again and again. Because of this similarity in processes, there is an immense duplication of effort. In fact, this is a problem that women from across the political parties are aware of and complained about. As indicated above, all reiterated the necessity of some form of cohesion between women's committees and other independent groups and individuals in order to avoid wasteful repetition, and to try to unify efforts to become more effective.

What is different is the political indoctrination that lies either openly, or behind and in between the lines of each of the projects that are being carried out. Each group, representing the different parties, tries to propagate the ideology of that party, with the not uncommon view that their projects are also sites of future members and activists.

Only a few of the women interviewed from the different parties were willing to admit that getting their message through to male members of the party was an unending uphill struggle. This would ostensibly translate into difficulties in making the women question come at the head of the party priorities list. This was attributed, as Farida Al-Naqqash from Tajammu' indicated, to 'the predominance of certain cultural perceptions, as well as the fact that political activity in itself is still hazardous'. The latter is due to the ever-present risk of arrest or harassment by the authorities, and hence the discouragement for women's participation. Consequently, there is still a male monopoly over the political process which is both difficult to overcome and makes effective political say for women complicated.[11]

What appears quite clearly from the above discourses is the almost unanimous rejection of the term and identity of feminism *based on the fact that it is understood as an opposition between men and women*. This rejection makes sense in light of the extreme reluctance to separate women's issues from those of the larger society. However, these women activists, by their mere activism, are maintaining a position that underlines the need to change society through women's issues. In that light, feminism is rejected because it is 'not political enough'. Hence, it seems a calculated strategy to deny the term because of the belief that it does not serve their purposes.

The opinions on Islamist regimes were consistent with the overall political orientations of the different parties. Homogenized and essentialized perceptions of Islamism/Islamist movements are true of all but the Labour Party. Yet even in the latter, the attempts at distinguishing between the different Islamist currents seem rather limited, one of the reasons being, I believe, that the Labour Party itself is allied with the Muslim Brotherhood. The latter portrays itself – despite many internal differences – as the moderate group, as opposed to 'the other extremists'. The different standpoints on the government were also in line with the positions of the different parties, either as the ruling one itself or as those in political opposition.

As a site of political power, the women's committees in the different political parties do not come without their problems. The insistence of each of them to view the 'particularities' of women's issues from the perspective of the broader societal context has its pros and cons. On the one hand, such an approach is also an understandable tactic in a situation where, as Amal Mahmud clarified, women's issues are seen as marginal to 'more important' societal concerns. In consenting and insisting on arguing from within that framework, women are carving out a necessary space to legitimize their own issues. On the other hand, however, the risk of repeating the same oppressive and marginalizing discourse is also imminent. In replicating the hegemonic discourses – even if for reasons of altering the power dynamics – the balance of power itself risks perpetuation.

In the following section, we encounter women who work in NGOs and whose attitudes and activisms around Islamism and feminism show both continuities and breaks with the above narratives.

NON-GOVERNMENTAL ORGANIZATIONS (NGOS)

NGOs are of two kinds: those that are registered under the Law of Associations and therefore in some way or another come under the control of the Ministry of Social Affairs (in which case they are listed as PVOs – Private Voluntary Associations); and those that have attempted to avoid that control completely and have either registered as research centres of some form or another,[12] or have no legal registration at all and work in an unofficial capacity as discussion groups, or otherwise.

Avoiding ministry control involves constant battles, extreme ingenuity or contacts with the right people in government – or all three. The basic 'tool' used by the ministry in its attempts to organize and monitor the activities of these 'independent associations' is the Law of Associations, more commonly known as Law 32 of 1964. Among the main stipulations of this law is that PVOs should not be political, nor contravene existing cultural and religious norms and practices. The parameters of political involvement and 'transgression' can be somewhat loosely defined – by ministry officials themselves more often than not. It has been *alleged* that in many cases, when top ministry officials are personally involved as chairpersons or honourary members of such associations (as indeed can be stipulated on the NGO), then the 'freedom' or leeway becomes more pronounced. However, any overt criticism of the government is out of bounds, and therefore when said or implied, it is often in the most veiled and diplomatic manner.

Women's NGOs are also diversified. I adopt the classification provided in a study carried out by the New Woman Research Centre (NWRC) in Cairo. The latter is also one of the NGOs which will be discussed here.

Women's NGOs are classified as follows:

1. Those organized around promoting all women's issues mainly through research.
2. Those organized around particular concerns (e.g. reproductive and health rights) and whose aim is to empower women through certain projects.

3. Those who work from within different organizations in special women's committees.
4. Those formed on a temporary basis to follow or study a particular issue (e.g. preparing for the Beijing Conference).
5. Those who concern themselves with women's interests as part of their overall programmes.

In the following section, examples of the three different sorts of women's activism (secular, Muslim and Islamist) are analysed. These would fall into the above classification of women's research centres (1) and general organizations (5). To be more specific, the New Woman Research Centre (NWRC) is the site of secular feminism. *Bint Al-Ard* (Daughter of the Earth), also a research centre, is in some ways the site of Muslim feminism. A group such as the women's committee within the Committee on Islamic Jurisprudence (itself a part of the Doctors' Syndicate) is chosen as a site for a form of Islamist feminism.

New Woman Research Centre (NWRC) – Ayida Saif Al-Dawla

Islamists are not coming – they are here.

Before I start this subsection, it is important to stress the point made earlier about the contacts and the fluid nature of membership among like-minded groups. To give but one example, Dr Amal Abd Al-Hadi (a physician) is a member of the NWRC, as well as a member of the Association for Health and Environment Development (AHED),[13] and has previously worked on diverse issues with women members of both Tajammu', the Nasserist Party and the NDP. She is also in touch with members of the Association of the Egyptian Women's Writers, and so on.

Not only does simultaneous membership in more than one group mean increased cooperation when necessary, it also means that there is a continuous and on-going process of networking among women from political parties and NGOs alike. Nevertheless, this process of networking has yet to overcome the unnecessary duplication and doubling of effort that take place on many women's issues. In other words, networking has yet to prevent the disintegration and enable the work towards cohesiveness and unity among the diverse women's groups and women activists.

One of the associations which has consciously and deliberately distanced itself from getting entangled and obstructed by Law 32 of 1964 and the MoSA, is the New Woman Research Centre (NWRC). They registered themselves in 1991 in the Office of Property Registration and Accreditation as the New Woman Study and Research Centre. The group originally came together to learn about and discuss feminism in Egypt and the issues and problems that women were facing in the 1980s. Gradually, as the problems they met to discuss seemed to increase in frequency and severity, and as their own formulations of a 'new feminism' and 'a new feminist discourse' began to take shape, a number of issues emerged. First, that working in isolation leads only to doubling of efforts and decreasing effectiveness, a realization which prompted them to seek contacts and start networking with other women's groups. Second, that one of the main ways of reaching a broad base of women has to start at the grassroots. This would have to be carried out in unison with other like-minded women and women's groups, via projects which enable women to develop services to help themselves;[14] as well as organizing debates, seminars, workshops, and the like on themes and issues that are important and relevant to women.

The objectives of the New Woman Research Centre include supporting and training women researchers interested in women's issues; coordinating similar activities and sharing experiences with like-minded NGOs; publishing and distributing literature relevant to women's issues and setting up a resource centre; holding seminars and workshops with various specialists on women's issues and providing legal and medical consultation to women on a voluntary basis. The NWRC describes itself in its leaflet as:

> concerned with research and exchange of information, as well as experience in issues that concern women's equality and rights, with emphasis on Egyptian women in particular and Arab women in general. This centre represents a new step in our struggle against the subordination and suppression of women. (ibid.)

Meeting Saif Al-Dawla is akin to a strong shot of adrenaline. She seems to be bursting with energy, even when she is sitting down. Being a member of the NWRC myself, I have a strong sense of involvement with the group. Yet despite my feeling at home with them, there was no question of being 'in control' during the interviews/conversations with Saif Al-Dawla – arguably because of her own overwhelming and contagious enthusiasm. I perceive in our conversations a constant process of reflection, challenging thoughts and stimulating ideas. Even though her experience in activism exceeds my own, Saif Al-Dawla and other NWRC members try to avoid hierarchy in their inter- and intra-personal dealings.

Saif Al-Dawla describes herself openly as a feminist – and she does not mince the words. Proud to be a feminist, she argues that religious discourses should remain in the domain of private life, and should not structure any feminist discourse:

> We [the NWRC] have a distinct approach which we have aired in Egypt and out of Egypt...Our position is *a position of feminist political distinctiveness*. The ICPD[15] has shown this. In fact, the ICPD proved our point that the attempt to separate feminist work from political work is futile and artificial.[16]
>
> (emphasis added)

Further, she explains that in Egypt,

> we cannot talk of a women's movement as long as we as organizations can be denied our legal existence with the movement of a pen. Without a public, without extensions into the neighbourhoods, the factories, we cannot talk about a women's movement. We can talk about a women's NGO movement which is developing. There is an NGO movement which is still very shaky.

The absence of a movement, she elaborates, explains what is happening on the feminist scene:

> So many splits. No movement is able to lay its conditions and say 'we are legitimate, let us change the conditions that bind us'. Change does not happen with consensus or compromise from the part of any organization. Only a movement can effect change. There is already so much compromise, so much opportunism which flourishes in this atmosphere of no democracy.

As far as the relationship with the state is concerned, Saif Al-Dawla maintains that the further the NWRC moves away from government control the more the attempts at control vary and increase in intensity. '[The attempts at control] will continue and we will continue to slip away. Till when and how it will end is difficult to say now.' And Saif Al-Dawla had this to say for the NWRC:

> From 1984 till today [1994] we existed as 'hippies' without any [legal] registration. Now we exist as a civil company and we will use this to the end, if we are banned as a civil company we will try

to register as something else, if we cannot register as something else we shall exist – in more difficult conditions. But since my [NWRC] criteria for continuation are not the availability of funding or a mailing box, but the condition of my continuing is that I have a target/direction, then the compromises [made] change according to these conditions.

When asked to specify the extent to which the current political situation had caused any compromise, she said:

The compromise [for us as NWRC] was the capabilities of the group. When we started working with other organizations, our compromise decreased, since we could do more things. Similarly, when we started to work with more individuals – not necessarily as members of our groups, but as interested people – again our compromises diminished.

Saif Al-Dawla was equally clear about the impact of Islamism. She upholds that

Islamist discourses do not create fear, but anger. It is so much political abuse of religion that it leaves one fuming. It is the Islamism which comes cloaked in liberalism – such as those who speak to appease Islamism from the podiums of supposedly liberal institutions – this is what leads to anger and provocation.

Thus, Islamism *per se* does not, in Saif Al-Dawla's opinion, structure their activism or their discourse; it is the fear of arrest by the authorities which does: 'It is the wariness from going to prison which is what is taken into consideration in all our activism, not Islamist discourse'.

As to the countering of the Islamist discourse, 'the best forms of counter-attack are precisely to speak out openly'. Saif Al-Dawla also implies that women who are attracted by Islamism and become active in its name do so not out of a sense of liberation, but as a form of false consciousness. Moreover, she argues, Islamists have both financial and moralizing means:

These people [Islamists] have newspapers, they have facilities. In each country which suffers from moral degradation, a great deal of talk on morals starts circulating as if morals never existed – as if inventing cold water. So one is given a sense of direction by being told how to do all these moral things: how to pray, do one's ablutions, do this, do that.

In a fit of anger at what she perceives as an injustice – that the NWRC is roundly attacked and criticized, and yet Islamists are seen as a desirable and normal aspect of political life – Saif Al-Dawla says,

> Islamist [women] cannot forget their bodies, and they present an idea on a plate of gold for Western stereotypes. They nourish Western ideas that these Muslim women are out there looking for a lost identity. Besides, Islamists also have corruption and hierarchy just like the government, but no one remembers to ask them about that!

Mentioning the multiple shifts in the government's positions on female circumcision before, during and after the ICPD, Saif Al-Dawla rhetorically asks: 'Who is really in charge here?' The government's position indicated a dependence on and wariness of Sheikh Al-Azhar's views on the matter. The latter, it appeared, dictated the direction the government was to take (or not take) on banning circumcision. Ultimately, despite promises from the Minister of Health, the practice was not banned, but was to continue subject to certain conditions.[17] As far as Saif Al-Dawla is concerned, it indicates that Islamism is already the government ideology.

Hence, Saif Al-Dawla does not distinguish between official Islam (as propagated by Al-Azhar) and the Islamism of the Muslim Brotherhood. She states:

> I do not see a minister saying something that indicates that he is influenced by Islamists, but what I do see and read is Sheikh Al-Azhar says this, Sheikh Al-Azhar maintains that. And that is what is quoted by the government, as well as what is followed.

She further maintains that 'the government we have today is already Islamist. Even if there are no Islamists in person, the governing ideology is Islamist.' In fact, she predicts, the situation 'will get quantitatively worse, but it won't get qualitatively different. Space is getting more and more tight depending on the political allies that the government takes.'

Saif Al-Dawla's future outlook concerning the challenges that women in Egypt face was grim. The greatest challenge, she perceives, is poverty and what will come from it. Saif Al-Dawla, not unlike many others engaged with civil society, believes that structural adjustment policies will leave society in turmoil. This will, she contends, create fertile grounds for 'Islamist terrorism, non-Islamist terrorism and state terrorism'.

In line with her ideas on 'state terrorism', Saif Al-Dawla emphasizes that democracy (or the lack of it) is the immediate challenge facing Egyptian women's groups. Referring to the initiatives Mahmud talks of earlier, Saif Al-Dawla maintains that in its preparations for the Beijing Women's Conference, the government is putting on a face-lift. She argues that 'there are attempts to make the laws and their implementation look better while maintaining the same constraints – this is the challenge to us [NGOs]'. Further, the situation becomes more complicated, in Saif Al-Dawla's opinion, because there is no clear dividing line between the different camps:

> It is not a clear-cut structure between ideologies, there are those who have eyes on both camps, and as long as this stays the case, it will be difficult [to find a solution]. The police state will become more forceful. Islamists are not one thing [and hence] there are many dangerous compromises that can be made. The state will and can negotiate with liberals and with Islamists – sometimes they have the same benefits, the same possible advantages, and the same enemies. Voices which call for radical change have no room in this space of negotiation. Radical means those who suggest change, not reform, but change.

Bint Al-Ard – Jihan Abu Zaid

Having heard a great deal of positive comments about Jihan Abu Zaid, who, for all intents and purposes is the main activist and spokesperson for the Bint Al-Ard Association, I finally met her during the ICPD in September 1994. At a later date, Abu Zaid was to confide to me that she sometimes wondered if people knew her real last name. This was because she is often referred to by other women activists as 'Jihan Bint Al-Ard'. So synonymous is her person with her activism that some activists are not aware that she has another career as journalist and writer.

In her early thirties, Abu Zaid is active and eloquent. She is one of those who was not only helpful in telling me about her organization, but in introducing me to a great many other people. Such is her popularity among the networks of women's NGOs, that often just to introduce myself as her friend ensured me a warm reception from other women activists.

Our sessions rarely took the form of an interview (though I did tape her once), but many of our discussions took place informally. As a person who grew to be a good friend, Abu Zaid was also my fieldwork mentor. In that respect, our discussions always left me with the impression of having learned a great deal, not just about women's activism in Cairo, but about the multiple facets to being a woman in contemporary Egypt.

Bint Al-Ard's beginnings were in 1982 as part of a larger solidarity movement set up for the Palestinians after the Israeli invasion of South Lebanon. Their functions revolved around consciousness-raising and fund-raising for the victims of Israeli aggression. The movement's original branch (and headquarters) in Mansoura (Nile Delta) included a women's committee. Despite the near annihilation of the solidarity movement after the oppositions' departure from Lebanon, the women's committees in Mansoura continued working, and decided to broaden the scope of their activism. Bint Al-Ard's national political activism has gained it the respect of many Egyptian NGOs in general.

Despite years of activism, Bint Al-Ard is still technically 'under construction' as an NGO. Having repeatedly presented their papers to be considered for registration as an NGO under Law 32 of 1964 with the MoSA, they were consistently refused. Not surprisingly, the reasons for their refusal are precisely those that distinguish their activism: their openly political inclinations.

Bint Al-Ard's aims, as clarified by Abu Zaid and printed in their magazines, are similar to the NWRC's. These goals include legal and general consciousness-raising, with an emphasis on young girls (and boys) and rural women; issuing ad hoc publications which in themselves aim to 'highlight women's creativity in a realistic and free manner'; organizing lectures and workshops in cooperation with other like-minded NGOs; as well as carrying out relevant fieldwork especially in the area of the groups' origin (in the Delta). Interestingly, Bint Al-Ard specifically state that they are aiming at raising the consciousness of Egyptian men as well as the women, and lobbying 'important people...who can influence and actively contribute to women's social and political issues'.

Abu Zaid sees her activism as 'imbedded in a feminist consciousness which includes a harmony of Islamic values with principles of human rights and justice':

I do not see any problem with, or relevance, as an activist, of being called a feminist. To be referred to as such will not affect my ideas or convictions. I am an Egyptian woman fighting against the oppression of women and of our society. Our whole society is oppressed by a great many injustices, women are very often worst affected by injustices, but they can also be, and are, very capable of identifying and fighting injustice.

The problems with women's NGOs in Egypt, according to Abu Zaid, lie with restrictive laws which lead to the nurturing and conflating of petty differences among different women, groups, and organizations:

Just as there are many dedicated and hard-working women, there are also many women interested only in power – either for themselves or their groups. These people want to be the only 'real representatives' of women. We have to struggle very hard to learn how to work with each other and for each other as women. Too much backbiting, criticising, petty fighting, so much great talent wasted on shining and trying to be *the* woman of society.

She sees no option but to continue struggling and not work in isolation. Bint Al-Ard's inception lay in the idea and practice of working with others and participating in groups. This continues to be the *modus operandi* of Abu Zaid today and for the near future:

One person in this field [of women's struggles] cannot do it on her own. We have to work together. We have so many capabilities, so many brilliant and sincere people, we have achieved so much already, but the way ahead is still long.

Abu Zaid sees Islamisms as important and significant socio-political phenomena. She explains their impact by describing them as

part and parcel of the general wave of religious conservatism in our society. It is difficult to determine which encouraged the other, political Islam, or religious conservatism. Both complicate fighting for women's issues because both look at women in a very one-sided manner. Women are the 'vitrine' of their ideas. Some women are attracted to them because they are disillusioned with everything else and attracted by the capacity of some of the leaders of the Islamist movement to speak well and convincingly. They provide them with a sense of purpose, a tool to fight injustices.

She shares Saif Al-Dawla's opinion that the influence of some clergy is prevailing, encouraged by the government:

If only they were the nice Sheikhs who know and can talk about how Islam is tolerant of differences and just towards women and men. But no, they [the government] choose the ones who perpetuate ideas of backwardness and so increase the difficulty of an already explosive situation. The thing is that it seems that the government tries to be more Muslim than the Islamists themselves, so the moves are all in one tight circle that only gets tighter.

Abu Zaid believes that women's groups are perhaps the most important sections of society which can determine future outcomes. She shares Mahmud's (Nasserist Party) point of view that to speak of women's issues in a vacuum is meaningless. However, she further maintains that to subsume women's issues into wider societal problems is equally unhelpful since 'it has already been tried and it is not enough'.

According to her it is all very well to consider women's rights as inseparable from society issues, but to speak only within that context risks losing political meaning. She argues for a two-pronged approach that acknowledges the woman–society political axis whilst creating a space for women's concerns.

As an example of Muslim feminism, Abu Zaid and Bint Al-Ard share many points in common with both the Muslim feminism of the Nasserist Party activists, as well as the secular feminism of the NWRC. I believe that such a feminism has the potential to act as a bridge of understanding between secular activism and Islamist activism. In the following section, we look at certain forms of Islamist women's activism.

Islamist Women and Islamist Women's Groups

> I consider our work a form of *jihad*, it is volunteer work dedicated to God.
>
> (Muslim Brotherhood woman member)

When discussing Islamist NGOs it is difficult to draw a line between Islamic and Islamist NGOs. The one point of distinction is, arguably, that the former are supported by the government (by listing them as 'general benefit societies' which are accorded privileges over other NGOs according to Law 32 of 1964), and the latter tend to remain unregistered. As to Islamic NGOs, out of 330 associations registered as 'general benefit' ones, 128 of them are Islamic (Ben Nafissa, in Qandil and Ben Nafissa 1994: 273). That is, almost 40 per cent of these associations are professing to work in the name of Islam, and are given special status by the government.

What this status effectively means is that in case of dissolution, the government cannot take over the assets of the association. This might seem rather unimportant at first, until the comparison with the case of the secular feminist Arab Women's Solidarity Association (AWSA) is made.[18] After creating some pretext of financial mismanagement to dissolve AWSA, its assets were promptly seized and given to another previously unheard of NGO with the name of 'Women in Islam'. If assets are power-bases, then the government response is a clear indication of the reallocation of power in some peculiar manner to its own favour. Moreover, if the process of denying power to some and bestowing it upon others is an indication of political favour, then the state has openly discriminated against a secular feminist group, and favoured its own creation, an 'Islamic' one. In other words, the state has silenced the discourse of secular feminism, whilst furthering its own 'Muslim' discourse.

These government-supported women's NGOs are not overtly political and dare not challenge government policies or guidelines. Their job, generally, is concentrated on charitable work for Muslim women. The Islamic ideology espoused by these groups is more often than not a reflection of the 'acceptable' and official Islamic line. Some of these organizations may well be sympathetic to the Islamist cause and their line of thinking, but any open support for anti-regime rhetoric or activities would be counterproductive to their existence. Illicit or 'underground' support for Islamist causes would be very difficult to determine – particularly since the activities these groups carry out are kept strictly within the sphere of charity and are not political. Some of these organizations also have Quran-teaching classes, but these are not used as overt recruitment and indoctrination forums.

At their request, and because of the politically tense situation between Islamists and the state, the names and specific position of most of the Islamist women interviewed will not be given or detailed. They are thus given fictitious names. Suffice it to say that as with the other women, there is no homogeneity among them. Some are involved in a variety of activities within several gatherings simultaneously, whilst others concentrate their efforts within one particular group or cluster. They range in age from the twenties to the sixties; some are in their late teens. Some are 'theorists' involved in drawing up blueprints for the future, whilst others are active outside of academia. The women interviewed seemed to agree on the fact that the origins of many of the groups today were neither organized nor planned. Many started as Quran teaching and analysis 'classes'.

Today, in the words of one of them, they are 'people interested in working towards more Islamization'. Theirs is a form of 'structural *jihad* in which they 'participate in all spheres of life and spread the *Da'wa* [message] in all spheres of life'.[19]

My experience with these women was as confusing as it was enriching. Enriching because I approached them with the predominant idea (based on my earlier notions) that they were basically suffering from a serious case of false consciousness. I must admit that I approached them with an inherent sense of almost superior pity mixed with trepidation – for surely they were also terrorist sympathizers? I spoke with many women from the Muslim Brotherhood and a handful from *Jihad*.[20] By the end of my interviews I was humbled, and angry at allowing myself, the activist-researcher, to have judged them before studying.

My sense of confusion, however, has to do with the unavoidable realization that these women were not only kind, humorous, strong and self-confident, but they also made a great deal of sense in their argumentation. I was torn between understanding the logic of their Islamic argumentation and rejecting what I considered the absurdities of some of their conclusions. Their logic is a familiar and acceptable discourse of Islam as all-encompassing justice which was part of my own upbringing. Yet their conclusions, regarding, for example, the absolute necessity of the veil – and the extreme form of it as well – left me cold. This argument ran as follows. Verses from the Quran were read and then interpreted in such a way that the only recourse to counter it was to say something along the lines of: that is not how I understand it; or these old interpretations need serious revision – both of which they consider equivalent to blasphemy. It was a classic catch-22 situation: I was unable, as a Muslim woman who grew up with Islamic convictions, to deny the legitimacy of their Islamic basis (e.g. the Quran), whilst I could not accept the interpretations they used with their consequent social implications. Using the example of the veil as an illustration, the relevant verses were read from the Quran and interpreted as ordering all women believers to cover themselves. My understanding, however, was that these same verses were basically cautioning women to dress modestly. Moreover, I believe that 'modesty' can be interpreted and practised differently. Unlike the Islamist women I spoke to, I do not believe that these verses impose one particular style of dress upon me. Yet, attempting to argue with them on this point is futile, as they believe in their interpretations, which have the legitimacy and authenticity accorded to older and

'more learned' interpreters of Quranic text. Besides, the voice of
authority over the authentic meaning of God's words is a closely
guarded domain. It was not for me, a mere mortal unversed in the
intricacies and complexities of the science of interpretation, to dare to
voice an alternative meaning to God's words. Herein lie the seeds of a
further disciplinary mechanism of power which not only Islamists, but
all conservative adherents of religion, follow. It was then that I
realized just how easy it is to fall into the trap of attacking them by
shouting: 'Absolutism!' 'Fundamentalism!' 'Terrorism!'

From my very first encounter with the women, the power relations
between interviewer and interviewee were almost immediately determined. For to gain access 'to a hearing' in the first place, and since I
was not a foreigner who could be forgiven for not knowing and not
practising 'properly', I had to succumb to being the listening student. I
may have been asking the questions, but they were not answering
them, they were teaching them.

Despite the differences, there are threads of commonalities among
their respective endeavours. None, for example, is willing or prepared
to concede that issues pertaining to women are a separate dimension
to the overall struggle for a 'truly' Islamic society – a position by now
not unfamiliar. Women do, however, have an important capacity for
empathy. This in turn is used to participate actively in changing
society to create an Islamic one. As one told me:

> As a Muslim woman I feel all the pain that goes on internally and
> externally – the pains of all the Muslim nations are a part of me.
> That does not mean I remain encased at home. I go out to treat
> these pains. Or I teach my child to grow up to do so, then particip-
> ate in doing so myself when they are old enough to take care of
> themselves. (J)

The practical implications of this outlook are manifested in the fact
that, along with their male counterparts, the Islamist women groups
are organized around many sites: from charity to syndicates to university. The main centres of these activities are usually the mosques,
and a point is made of training women to teach, help and otherwise
provide advice and assistance to other women. I remember attending
one meeting – composed of the older, middle-class women leaders and
organizers of a Muslim Brotherhood-affiliated group. During this
meeting, there was genuine concern over the fact that despite devising
and having the facilities for a project to teach girls living in rural areas
skills with which they could earn an income, they could not find

women who could teach or train them. The whole project almost fell through (rather than let a man teach the girls) had it not been for a last-minute location of a suitable woman.

Another commonality among Islamist women is a visual, symbolic one – the veil. As one woman put it: 'The appearance [of the Islamist woman] is crucial because it is an external message and an internal commitment'. The veil takes many forms and shapes in present-day Egypt, each form symbolic of the different motivations and purposes of its wear. One form is the *hijab* which of itself has many variations. The most common is a scarf that covers the hair and neck, with any body wear mostly covering the arms and legs. As long as the skirt covers to the ankles or the trousers are loose enough and themselves covering the hips and thighs, the wearer of this is a *muhajjaba*.

Another form of veiling is the *khimar* which is a much wider, round scarf covering the whole breast and chest area. The length of the *khimar* scarf varies, some women wear the scarf itself all the way down to the thighs while others wear it down to the waist. The front of the scarf is usually pulled down to conceal the forehead. The rest of the clothing for the *khimar* centres on a shapeless one-piece, one-colour garment, usually a dull grey, blue, brown or black. Sometimes, gloves are worn.

The third form of veiling, with less variation than the other two, is the *niqab*, which consists mainly of a complete face cover with a narrow opening (the opening may be simply two slits for the eyes), so that forehead, nose, mouth and chin are totally concealed. The scarf in this case may fall just short of the dress worn underneath, which is long, shapeless and black, worn to the ground. The *munaq-qaba* usually wears black gloves as well. Needless to say, the *niqab* is the most advanced stage of commitment to a version of 'Islam'. Supposedly, the symbolism implies that the more pious a Muslim woman, the longer the headscarf and the less colourful and fitted the dress, so that less of the female contours or body shape is visible. To many women, the type of veil they wear symbolizes how far they are prepared to go to demonstrate their loyalty and adherence to the cause of Islam.

There is no unveiled Islamist woman. All of them wear one type of veil or another. Whatever the kind of headscarf, the veil *per se* is a prerequisite to being considered an *Islamist* woman, since the basic understanding is that the veil is the *essential symbol* of a *Muslim* woman – a basic requirement of Islam. It is the adoption of the veil which indicates a particular consciousness or awareness, which in turn is an indicator of a change – in orientation, outlook, religious observance; in short, it is a *sign* and a message.

The original activity that continues to prosper and be a focal point is what is referred to as 'Islamic discussion groups' in which explanations, teachings, interpretations of the Islamic heritage (particularly the Quran, *Sunna* and *Sira*) take place. These sessions are intended as helpful guidance and enlightenment of the seekers, and in some ways, they *may* be used as recruitment techniques – depending on the aims of the organizers, and the intentions of the larger group if it exists. For many of the participants, however, these discussion groups are the focal meeting points where there is an exchange of information and knowledge about Islam. The general feeling among some participants in these discussions is that 'proper' dissemination of the 'true' Islamic teachings and principles is lacking in ordinary state-controlled systems (i.e. schools, universities and other state-run institutions, as well as the media). Many of the members feel that the state is an illegitimate entity, which is wilfully *subverting* the 'proper' teachings for its own corrupt needs and thereby misconstruing, if not polluting, the very essence of Islam. These discussion groups are meant as collective counter-attempts to re-educate and disseminate the 'true' Islam among the people.

It is not possible to generalize about the different group tactics and ideologies in gaining adherents. For example, I have been told by one informant who attended lessons in a mosque that when she asked one too many questions, she was told: 'You come to receive learning and obedience, no discussion is expected from you' (MB). Another informant told me that discussion was encouraged, 'as long as the basics of what was being taught was not denied' (J). Yet another informed me that she never felt the need to question what was being taught, and the group 'teacher' on one occasion got very irritated with her and almost shouted: 'Have you no mind?!' (MB). This woman in particular stopped going to the meetings because she felt pressured to perform by asking questions. So, clearly, there are no set rules, and hence no generalizations, to describe these processes.

Some of these discussion groups in theory are open to anyone interested in gaining enlightenment on Islam. Because of the existing tensions, new applicants are usually friends and/or acquaintances of members of the group. Those who are not directly known to the members, and considered too distant, go through a screening process in which the intentions and seriousness of the applicant is assessed. Their criteria for choosing and the manner of attracting new entrants differ from one group to the next. In principle, no one is denied admission to a discussion group. However, if the applicant-cum-new member is not fully trusted, then she is excluded from certain activities. This is done by not informing her of meeting times and places, or in some cases, by being told she/he is not welcome.

For the Islamist women interviewed, the emphasis was placed on a better *understanding* of the position and role of women within Islam, not only for themselves, but for society as a whole. For them, being Muslim women is seen as a personal identity, a way of living in the modern world, which includes an awareness of the extent of the challenge faced as such. For many of them, it was the sense of loss of this Islamic identity, vis-à-vis the predominance of Western norms and cultures, that pushed them to seek their Islamic heritage. For others there seemed to be a more vehement feeling that it was not just the loss of their Islamic identity, but the feeling that they were *made to* ignore this sense *on purpose* by an overriding Western hegemony over all aspects of their lives – a hegemony that they felt was intended to make them feel inferior.[21] In fact, some of the generally anti-Western sentiments and rallying calls for joining some of these movements run like this: 'Israel is from the Euphrates to the Nile' (J); and 'What is happening in Bosnia to the Muslims there is written on the walls of the Knesset' (J).

As Islamist women, they are aware of a certain dependency on the part of the men, on them, for electing and encouraging an Islamist movement against an illegitimate state. Among other things, they are aware that theirs is a multifaceted role not only as supportive wives and mothers, but as politicians, teachers, theorists, and much more. One woman described herself as a 'soldier of God and of his prophet' (J), another maintained that 'When you work for God, you are at once everything in this life and nothing in front of God' (MB). Along the same lines, another said, 'We are fighters in a war' (J).

Oppressed women? I think not. But women who, like their counterparts described above, actively struggle for what they believe in.

BY WAY OF CONCLUSION

The roads to power are not the same, but the struggle for power among feminists is as fierce, if not a mirror of, the struggles that men wage. By presenting the parties and NGOs through the voices of one of their members, the intention is not to homogenize the voices within each group, but on the contrary to reveal some of them. For as I stated at the outset, what is attempted is but a small segment of an enormous kaleidoscope. I have not argued that these women are the only voices within these groups, but I have presented some of the many, many circulating. The diversity of the voices of secular, Muslim and Islamist activisms cannot yield to one research. Their numbers alone, let alone their diverse arguments and programmes, would warrant a great many books.

This chapter has looked at three streams of feminist thinking – secular, Muslim and Islamist – through presenting their activism within political parties and NGOs. Rarely did these women describe themselves as feminists, or uphold their activism in the name of a particular stream of feminism. On the contrary, most of the women activists (with the exception of the secularists) were against the term 'feminism', believing it to be divisive and irrelevant. Yet, I maintain that their specific concern with women's issues, and their activism in that regard – even when done from a standpoint of negation of the necessity for such specificity (e.g. Farkhanda Hasan from the NDP) – speak volumes for their feminist convictions. The varied perspectives of these feminists on feminisms, Islamisms and the state play an important role in determining their own feminist orientations. Secular feminists, for example, tend to perceive Islamism as an increasingly powerful and frustrating threat; muslim feminists argue for some form of a dialogue with Islamism and secularists from within an Islamic framework; whilst Islamist feminists live, act and preach Islamist ideals, the basis of which are antagonistic to and dismissive of 'Westernism' and its secularist vestiges.

The diversity within one group of feminists as I have identified them is substantial. What can be surmised from their voices is that secular feminists see no middle road – either one is religious or one is not. There does not seem to be an awareness that there are shades of both secularism and religious observance. The polarization among the groups is such that it reinforces the exclusivity each group intentionally or inadvertently maintains. Also, even when certain women claimed secularism as the basis of their activism (e.g. Nasserist women), that indicated not that they work outside religious frameworks, but rather that they see these frameworks as part of an 'Arab heritage'. The latter is defining for both identity and work, and these activists are selective in their appropriation of what it is they wish to maintain from this framework. In other words, though they claim that their agendas are free of religious argument and rationalization, these

women cannot avoid the more pervasive political situation around
them, which is one of a general Islamization of discourse. It is all very
well to utter 'Religion is for God and the nation is for everyone',[22] but
when special attention and time are devoted in agendas to 'highlighting the correct Islam and its implications for women', then what is at
stake is more than simply contributing to a topical subject. More
likely, the issue of religion and women's roles within religious conceptualizations is paramount to any propagation of a message. What
differs is the extent to which religion is said to and actually does
feature openly in different argumentations.

We have also seen that Islamisms are as diverse in their manifesta-
tions as they are in the way they are interpreted by others. From its
fiercest opponents to its strongest adherents, essentializations of 'the
Other' are very much part of the discourses taking place by all manner
of feminists. Whether they are secular, Muslim or Islamist feminists,
there is a general tendency to perceive 'the Other' as either suffering
from a false consciousness, delusion or as being altogether misled by
the men. Despite the many statements to the contrary, each featured
in the discourse of 'the Other'. The secularism of some, for example,
was highlighted in relation to Islamist convictions of 'the Other', and
vice versa.

The perceptions of the government indicated that whether secular,
Muslim or Islamist, feminists feel the disadvantage in power relations
that the law buttresses. No one had much to say in praise of the
government (except of course, its representative). In fact, the latter is
seen as in many cases being the partner of Islamist thought (by secular
and Muslim feminists) or downright anti-Islamic (by Islamist feminists). In short, a relationship of power between the government and
Islamisms was acknowledged, either directly or indirectly, by all
women activists.

Having surveyed the different sites of activism, the following chapter will look at the main debates around which different women
activists mobilize.

6 Current Debates on Women's Legal Rights in Theory and Practice

> As the twentieth century draws to a close, there is a very real danger that the momentum of the Egyptian women's movement may have been halted or even reversed. Enormous pressure is being brought to bear on the women of Egypt by forces actively working to create a general climate in the country that could eventually deprive them of their rights or impede their exercise of these rights, whether by invoking antiquated habits and customs or by wilfully misinterpreting both man-made laws and divine teachings to suit their purpose.
>
> (The Communication Group for the Enhancement of the Status of Women in Egypt[1] 1992: 4)

This chapter will look at the various laws from the perspectives of different women activists. Only those laws – and those aspects of the laws – which have been mentioned by activists from the NGO and political parties as problematic will be discussed. These are the PSL (Personal Status/Family Laws), Citizenship/Nationality Laws, laws dealing with women's political rights and Labour Laws. The reason why I look at both laws and current debates is because many of the debates are about these laws, whilst others are carried out in conjunction with or around the laws.

The first section of this chapter is a brief introduction to the relationship between the state and laws, which forms the framework for this presentation. The second part is a summary of a number of Egyptian laws concerning women and the debates surrounding them. In the third section, the remaining debates which occupy women's groups and around which they mobilize will be viewed.

WOMEN, STATE AND LAW

The legal dimension of the power relationship involving women activists and women's issues vis-à-vis the state cannot be understated, for no survey of the power dynamics can afford to ignore the form of power that the state wields via its laws. The laws of a state are the written codes of conduct that define part of the state's power and are a reflection of the state's ideological, cultural and social determination. In many cases, the laws of the state are the most important standard to which individuals look for protection and try to conform to. As Migdal says, 'The major struggles in many societies... are over who has the right and ability to make the countless rules that guide people's social behaviour' (Migdal 1988: 31).

Most definitions of the state, as Moore points out, include some reference to it as a bureaucratic/legal/coercive order:

> Administrative, legal and coercive systems are the main means through which the state structures relationships between society and state, and they are also involved in the structuring of many crucial social relationships within society as well – for example, family relationships.
>
> (Moore 1988: 135)

Also on the same theme of the law and its regulatory significance, an analysis of Stanton's work by Eisenstein shows how the former believed that the law can regulate inequalities, whilst Eisenstein herself points out that very often the purpose of the law in liberal and patriarchal society is to define certain relations of power outside the law (Eisenstein 1984).

The relations of power being defined in this case are those between the state and women through the broader relations between state, Islam and society. Debates that concern women and the law in Egypt are numerous, as there are various legal issues that need to be tackled if demands of women's groups are to be met on the one hand, and Islamist political agendas are to be satisfied on the other. An important aspect of these laws, and one that indeed reflects the Egyptian state's ideological and cultural convictions (and manipulations), has to do with the Islamic character of certain laws – namely the Personal Status Law (PSL). Even though all other Egyptian laws are civil laws – styled after French civil laws – the only law that is quite explicitly based on the shari'a is the PSL. Keeping this fact in mind, it is also worthwhile mentioning that Egypt is a signatory to the UN's CEDAW (Convention on the Elimination of all Forms of Discrimination against Women). Whilst maintaining a whole host of reservations on cultural and religious grounds,[2] the mere fact that it has ratified the CEDAW is potentially useful for secular and Muslim feminists alike. However, discussions on CEDAW are not widespread partly because as an international law which the Egyptian state ratified only with reservations, it is perceived as less critical to day-to-day concerns of Egyptian women. Only a limited number of secular feminists – inevitably lawyers – have taken up the issue and are carrying out discussions and lobbying for its infiltration into national laws.

Women and the Law

A debate that takes place between the secular and Muslim-oriented women's groups concerns the vast difference between the word of the law and its implementation. The reasons given for this include the lack of awareness among many women of their rights, hence the concerted effort and emphasis within the different programmes on legal consciousness-raising to be included within literacy and all other women's projects. Another reason was that even for those who were aware there still seemed to be a lack of knowledge about *how* such rights were to be implemented. Tied to this was the observation that many women were not encouraged to practise their legal rights owing to a variety of social-cultural influences that created value-systems which put such practising in an unfavourable light.

As part of the campaign to raise women's awareness of their legal rights, a group of women (labelling themselves the Group of Seven, or the Group of Women Concerned with the Affairs of the Egyptian Woman) came together to set up a project of producing a booklet that would bring together and explain all the laws that pertain to women, a 'revolutionary' task that was both crucial, and involved much research and effort. So on 17 October 1987, a seminar was held which brought together 80 of Egypt's most prominent intellectuals, journalists, lawyers, social workers, people from universities, research centres, international organizations, parliamentarians, politicians, youth representatives, bankers and businessmen. As a result of the comments and suggestions that emerged during this seminar, a booklet was indeed produced in 1988 entitled *The Legal Rights of the Egyptian Woman: Between Theory and Practice*. Owing to the favourable reception of this work, and the important discussions it raised, the first edition was revised by a prominent Muslim feminist lawyer, Mona Dhul-fiqar (one of the Group of Seven), and a second edition was published in 1992.

Another legal debate within the secular women's circles centres on equality and the extent to which the constitutional statements are being adhered to by the law. Within this general debate various other issues are brought up, such as the right to judgeship.

Egyptian women's struggles revolve around 'attempting to understand the law', as the secular feminist lawyer Amira Bahiy al-Din puts it, not only because of its complicated nature, but also in the sense of trying to understand the rationale behind its male-centred and woman-unfriendly phraseology. The frustration of some feminists is such that the secular activist Bahiy al-Din almost argues *against* the legal awareness of women:

> I am not for raising legal awareness of women ... because if we look carefully at the texts (*nusus*) of Egyptian laws, we will find that these dictates treat women's issues – in my opinion – in an unsuitable manner ... so that knowing these unpalatable facts will lead to widespread depression. I want to remove this depression off women, and thus I am for the dominance of ignorance of the law and not the awareness raising of women of these laws!
>
> (Bahiy al-Din 1995: 102)

Those who know Bahiy al-Din will understand that this was meant half-jokingly and said with a great deal of sarcasm. Her sentiments with respect to the inherent ambiguity and male bias within the law is not unique, however. It must be stated at the outset that since the laws being debated are presented from the point of view of women activists, usually the less palatable aspects are what will be outlined and highlighted. The laws in their totality are thus not reviewed here. Moreover, the critiques surrounding the laws are divided into two kinds: those that lament women's lack of legal awareness, and those that take issue with the laws themselves. Some of the former do imply that awareness leads to a possible avoidance of the legal pitfalls. Yet not all who bemoan legal ignorance do so because they see the laws themselves as necessarily flawed or lacking. On the contrary, the implication of the latter approach often is that if only women were to be more aware of their legal rights, the problems being faced by them would be substantially mitigated. Hence, the acceptance or relative tolerance of these groups (who come from diverse feminist strands) for some of the laws as they stand. This is particularly the case with reference to some aspects of the Labour Law, and the Social Security Laws.

Women's groups, within the NDP, Tajammu' and Nasserist parties, as well as NGOs all seem to feel that the Family Law/Personal Status Laws (PSL) – those dealing with marriage, divorce and custody of children – were at the top of the most problematic list. The main complaints centred on the details of the laws, whilst fewer argued for an effective means to apply them. Too many women were suffering from the difficulties involved with petitioning for a divorce, claiming alimony and contesting custody of children. Among the complaints mentioned was that the decision on whether women should be granted a divorce or not rested with a male judge.

Consequently, one of the main calls of the women's groups is that the ban on promoting women to the position of judges be lifted. Highly qualified women, it is argued, are refused a judgeship purely because of their sex and because of certain cultural influences which maintain that women should not be holding positions which require 'male' characteristics like rationality and lack of emotion. Others uphold that enabling women to become judges would be a step towards eliminating the excessive male domination of the judicial system as a whole, and provide an ambience in which women filing for divorce receive more sympathy and understanding through the judgments.

Almost all groups – whether secular, Muslim or Islamist – have a host of criticisms of the PSL. The secular feminists find it abhorrently male-biased and unjust. Some argue it is unconstitutional and contrary to the principles of human rights, as well as the CEDAW. Muslim feminists share the secularists' basis for concerns, whilst also arguing that the PSL actually contravenes the spirit of the shari'a on which it is supposedly based. Islamist feminists maintain that the PSLs would be redundant if proper and all-encompassing shari'a laws were applied, since the latter would provide total justice and cannot be equalled by any man-made laws. What follows is a brief overview of the PSL.

The Personal Status Law (PSL)[3]

> I do not understand the philosophy behind the production of [these] clauses... I have worked for fifteen years on these cases and I do not understand... I implement all that is possible to implement from these stipulations but I do not understand their philosophy!
> (Bahiy al-Din 1995: 107)

This Family Law is ostensibly based on and derived from the Islamic shari'a, a fact which influences (and in some cases causes) many of the debates raging around it. The PSL is intended to set down the basic regulations for interactions between men and women in marriage (the contract, respective duties of the spouses towards each other and towards their children), through to divorce or death. The PSL does not apply to non-Muslims, except in cases where the spouses do not follow the same religion or the same sect. The Inheritance Laws incorporated within the PSL are applicable to all Egyptians irrespective of their religion.

The latest history of the development of the present Personal Status Law is significant to this research. It was proclaimed as law in 1920. In 1925 it was amended by Law No. 25/1929. These laws dealt principally with divorce and alimony. The other domains of family law continued to be governed by the shari'a. This continued to be valid for the next 50 years until Law No. 44/1979, which amended the above two laws, was passed. The latter law was cause for much controversy and dissent – especially, but not solely by Islamists – with the main charge being the claim that it went against the shari'a. The main amendments introduced included the right of the wife to keep the family home after divorce, the right of the first wife to be informed in case of the husband's marriage to another, as well as her right to demand a divorce on that basis. As a significant way of demeaning the law, it was termed 'Jihan's Law'.[4] Eventually, it was abrogated on procedural grounds in 1985. In June of that year however, a similar law (Law No. 100) amending the 1925 and 1929 laws was enacted and is now the law in force. It is important to note that all amendments to the PSL were piecemeal, and mostly passed outside Parliament. This underlines the extent to which debates on aspects of a law that regulates interactions between men and women, and has direct influence on the family, are volatile and sensitive.

The Marriage Contract

The main condition for a marriage contract to be declared valid is that both parties (man and woman) should consent to it. Other conditions are the setting of the minimum age for marriage at 18 for men and 16 for women.[5] Technically speaking, both parties are entitled to include any conditions they deem necessary for the settlement of their relationship – as long as both consent to them. Practically, however, few women avail themselves of the opportunity to stipulate any conditions in the marriage contract. These conditions may include that the husband cannot take another wife and if he does so, this would give her (the present wife) the right to seek divorce automatically. Another condition may be that the wife shares in the *'isma* or the right to divorce. A wife-to-be may also stipulate that she be allowed to study, to work, to travel, and so on. Yet in Egyptian society, for a woman at the outset of her marriage to set conditions (some of which may entail divorce) is at best a bad omen, and at worst simply not done. Realizing this, a group of women activists (secular and Muslim), along with lawyers, religious jurists and academics, drafted a New Marriage Contract (NMC). The NMC makes possible the stipulation of conditions by listing some of them in a manner similar to multiple-choice formats. The aim is to simplify the process involving formulations of conditions and to make them readily available. The signatories to the contract need only indicate the appropriate sections. The NMC is drafted with the intention that it replace the old marriage contract.

Though the NMC was drafted with the cooperation of religious jurists (representing the official religious establishment of al-Azhar), it raised a great deal of controversy. Only in the days prior to the departure of the Egyptian delegation to attend the Beijing Fourth International Women's Conference, in September 1995, did the government announce that the draft NMC had been accepted by the ruling NDP to be 'discussed' by Parliament. This is reminiscent of the government's earlier decision to pass the 1985 amendments to the PSL in 1985, immediately before the Nairobi Women's Conference. Considering the great lengths the government went to secure their majority in the parliamentary elections of November 1995,[6] the passing of this marriage contract as law is, ironically, a real possibility.

'Urfi (unofficial) marriages are non-notarized, but are still valid. There are drawbacks to *'urfi* marriage, however. Although they give the same rights (alimony, husband's pension and judicial protection of the relationship itself) as in the notarized/registered marriages, these rights cannot be enforced in the courts. Moreover, parentage of the children can be established only through the wife's institution of legal proceedings.

Repudiation

A husband may and can exercise his right to divorce (repudiation) without being required to prove fault or declare any grounds for it. Moreover, he can do so simply by pronouncing the statement – even in the absence of witnesses – 'Go, you are divorced', or something to that effect. To make it official the husband must then register this divorce within 30 days.

There are two forms of divorce: the irrevocable divorce and the revocable one. The former is effective on its occurrence irrespective of the *'idda*[7] time. With revocable divorce, on the other hand, the marriage is not dissolved until the lapse of *'idda*, during which time the husband may reinstate his wife with or without her consent. This, however, can only occur up to three times, with the third time rendering the divorce irrevocable.

Women's Rights in the Event of Divorce

Law No. 100/1985 requires a husband who intends to divorce to inform his wife through the Notary Public and to deliver a copy of the divorce papers to her or to her attorney. (Her divorce is not effective until her knowledge of it.) Moreover, the divorced wife is entitled to *'idda* maintenance for one year. Law No. 62/1976 gives priority to alimony as the most important debt, and penalizes a husband who fails to pay alimony to his wife by a fine and/or imprisonment for a maximum period of up to one year. In addition, a divorced wife is entitled to *al-mut'a* alimony for at least two years, depending on the husband's financial and social standing, the length of the marriage and the reasons for the divorce. The wife is also legally entitled to a deferred dowry which is agreed upon in the marriage contract and is paid at the time of the divorce or on the husband's death.

As far as the custody of children is concerned, mothers have custody of boys until they reach the age of 10 (which a judge may extend to 15) whilst girls remain in their mother's custody until the age of 12 (which the judge, at his discretion, may extend until marriage). Either parent is entitled to see their children whilst in the other's custody. If visiting rights cannot be agreed amicably, then it is up to the judge to organize a schedule of visits in a suitable place.

Moreover, a husband who divorces his wife is held responsible for providing her and their children with a home. If the conjugal home is the only one available, then the wife is the one who has the right to live there with the children until the period of her custody of them expires. It should be noted that in the so-called 'Jihan's Law' of 1979, the wife automatically retained the marital home in the event of divorce, regardless of her custody of the children.

If the divorced mother remarries she loses custody of her children, who then should be placed in the custody of their maternal grandmother. If that is not feasible, then they should go to the paternal grandmother, until they reach the statutory age at which custody reverts to the father. The point is though, that if the mother is for some reason unable to fulfil her function, the first preference is always given to maternal relatives before paternal ones. Nowhere is a male member assigned this kind of care. The underlying logic is that this is meant to be to the benefit of the child. In fact, this is a firm gendered basis of the law implying that only women (mothers and/or grandmothers) should look after young children.

Grounds on which Wives may Apply for Divorce

These are six grounds in all, which are as follows:[8]

1. If the husband is imprisoned for three years, in which case she can apply for divorce after one year.
2. If the husband stops supporting her.
3. If the husband deserts her for more than one year.
4. If the husband is suffering from an incurable disease (e.g. insanity or leprosy) which the wife was unaware of at the time of marriage.
5. Sexual deficiency (i.e. husband's impotence and sterility).
6. Abuse or harm which renders living together intolerable from a social or cultural point of view, such as husband's mistreatment or his taking a second wife. The determination of the validity of the harm is left to the discretion of a judge.

All these conditions have to be proved and/or witnessed.

REACTIONS AND RECOMMENDATIONS

A blatant inequality exists between men and women when it comes to divorce. Husbands need give no explanation for their divorce, whereas women have to have recourse to a variety of conditions, some of which are difficult to prove in court. This situation is often justified by claiming that women are more emotional than men and therefore they may well seek divorce (and social ruin by implication) on 'irrational' grounds. The feminist lawyer Bahiy al-Din argues that the way the conditions themselves are phrased is 'very dangerous'. As an example she cites condition 6, which states that a wife has to have suffered 'abuse or harm which renders living together intolerable from a social or cultural point of view'. The questions Bahiy al-Din raises are most relevant to women from the lower social classes. How can these women, she asks, who come from a social milieu in which it is acceptable for men to beat their wives, claim that this practice is 'socially intolerable'? Moreover, Bahiy al-Din questions the validity of these conditions when the harm inflicted by a husband on his wife is usually done in private. Yet, according to the PSL, it must be witnessed by others to be proved in a court of law.

Bahiy al-Din also maintains that despite society's glorification of motherhood, mothers are treated as 'foreigners' to their children after divorce. According to the law they are paid to nurture the children as divorced women. This critique, however, is not shared by many other feminists, some of whom maintain that the 'alimony' received by women after divorce, ostensibly to care for the children, remains important and is a right for every woman. Bahiy al-Din provides a comprehensive critique of almost every aspect of the PSL – far beyond the scope of this chapter. Her views on the various forms of 'alimony' are somewhat unique.

Going back to the issue of the absence of women judges in Egypt, there is no written law that requires this, but there are more entrenched patriarchal reasons why it continues to be the case, despite the outstanding qualifications and experience of many women lawyers. When it comes to determining the general harm inflicted on a woman by her husband in court, many problematic issues arise. First, ultimately it is up to a male judge to empathize with and verify a woman's pain. The question then arises, how just can such an assessment be in a patriarchal society? Moreover, in an environment in which family relations are supposed to be kept secret by the women, and are generally a cultural taboo in public, it is immensely difficult for women to narrate all the details of the harm or abuse they feel, in front of men – be they judges or anyone else. Cases abound wherein women invoking harm in general and psychological harm (mental cruelty) in particular as grounds for divorce rarely succeed in proving their case to the court's satisfaction. Protracted litigation and an aggravation of the tensions between the spouses is thus the outcome.

The length of the legal procedures required (for example to claim alimony or determine custody) is another major concern and not only to activists. The necessary follow-up is also a costly and long-term process. One of the attempts to respond to this occurred at the end of January 1994. A new law was drafted by Ministry of Justice experts which is intended to simplify and speed up litigation procedures in divorce cases. Some of the tenets of the draft apparently entitle women to sue their current or ex-husbands for maintenance without the services of a lawyer, as well as empowering judges to inform litigants of the correct legal course they should take, instead of leaving them completely dependent on the advice of lawyers. Not everyone is happy with this draft however, as many women lawyers in particular uphold that it is not so much the *procedure* that needs amendment, as the legal text *governing* such cases itself. What is also criticized is the expectation that plaintiffs need not go through a lawyer but can petition the court directly. This could, critics say, cost the plaintiffs their case if as women they have no legal background and present a weak case.[9]

Feminists agree that though the present PSL grants women more rights than the 1929 Law, much still needs to be done in terms of amendments to correct deficiencies and overcome practical difficulties in its application. Meanwhile, the Communication Group is calling for two urgent amendments to the law, the first being that the legal age for marriage be extended to 18 for females and 20 for males whilst increasing the penalty for violating this provision:

> This would help solve the population problem and would also assist in decreasing cases of divorce resulting from early marriage, particularly according to a study carried out by the Central Agency for Mobilization and Statistics published in 1983. 25% approximately, of the total married females have been married at an age below 15.
>
> (The Communication Group 1992: 26)

The second amendment they called for is that the age of maternal custody of children be increased to 12 for boys and 15 for girls, 'as this is more compatible with the children's needs for their mother's care and is in line with the court precedents in this respect' (ibid.).

It is notable that none of the feminists in this group have called for the lifting of the conditions for divorce imposed on women, nor have they urged a revision of the gender discrimination underlying these conditions. The amendments they consider lie within the broader cultural and religious framework of the PSL as it stands today. Moreover, in the comprehensiveness of their listing of the various laws, this group seems to have 'missed' the blatant discrimination that is found in the Criminal Code (*Qanun al-'uqubat*).[10] Bahiy al-Din, in describing this law, distinguishes between the clauses as follows: 'Clauses which discriminate between men and women in the same action, clauses which are not to women's benefits, clauses which do not discriminate but their application is discriminating'.

As far as punishments for adultery go, discrimination is shown by setting a condition for the punishment for adulterous men: they must have committed the adultery in the marital home. But in the case of adulterous women, they are punished no matter where the act was committed. Moreover, men who murder their adulterous wives are viewed sympathetically by the court and hence are given a maximum of six months' imprisonment. Women who murder their adulterous husbands are not viewed with any sympathy and are given the two-year maximum sentence. So even the maximum sentences for the sexes is different. And further, the partner of an adulterous woman is punishable, but not so the partner of a male adulterer.

Another odd aspect of the Criminal Code has to do with the form of punishment allotted to men who abduct a woman (either with the woman/girl's consent or against her will). Basically the abductor is faced with a choice: either legally marry the girl/woman, or face death by hanging. Though there is no specific mention of rape in this instance, it is sometimes the case that kidnapped girls/women do not consent to being kidnapped and certainly not to being raped. Hence Bahiy al-Din's credulous question 'Which idiot is going to choose being hanged?' In a society where women's virginity is very highly valued, and where a family's main function is to protect that virginity till the woman is handed to her husband intact, the proposal of marrying the man who spoils this process is a face-saving option which cannot easily be refused:

> Virtually then, such a law is encouraging any man to go out on the street, choose any woman he pleases, kidnap and rape her, then get married to her so he escapes any punishment and so she can then get legally raped. Then divorce her at any time he pleases. In fact, he can keep doing this any number of times![11]

Punishment for prostitution contains another discriminatory aspect. Male clients of women prostitutes are not punishable if caught. Not only that, but *these men themselves are used as credible witnesses in court against the same prostitute they have bedded.* This is a very blatant and important example of the extent to which this aspect of the laws is gender biased as to border thinly on the lines of injustice.

POLITICAL RIGHTS

An historical perspective

Egyptian women were the first Arab women to acquire political rights. Article 32 of the 1956 Constitution guarantees the political rights of Egyptian women, and article 4 of Law No. 73, promulgated that same year to regulate the exercise of political rights, rules the following:

> Those entitled to exercise political rights must be enroled in the electoral registers. Women who personally submit applications to this effect must also be enroled therein.

In an explanatory note to this law, the legislature observed the principle of equal rights for all citizens – men and women. However, it was observed that 'in deference to Egypt's cultural traditions', the law did not make women's registering in the electoral roll mandatory as is the case with men, but left it optional for women wishing to exercise their political rights and duties.

The 1971 Constitution affirmed the political rights of women and their role in society, providing in Article 11 that *the state guaranteed the compatibility of a woman's duties toward her family with her role in society*. This was followed by Law No. 41 of the same year wherein for the first time women were guaranteed 30 seats as a minimum representation in parliament. This law also made it compulsory on all citizens entitled to exercise political rights, to enrol themselves in the electoral registers. In effect, this meant that the registering of women ceased to be optional. Under the new law a Voter's Registration Committee set up in each police station automatically enters the names of all females upon their reaching the age of 18, in the roll of eligible voters.

However, 1986 figures show that only 18 per cent of eligible women voters entered and actually registered in the electoral roll. Moreover, and ironically, despite the higher rate of education in urban than in the rural areas, there are more female voters registered in the rural areas (The Communication Group 1992: 29).

In 1986 the Supreme Constitutional Court ruled the provisions of Law No. 41/1979 allocating one seat for women in each constituency unconstitutional, on the grounds that such a limitation goes against the principle of equality enshrined in the Constitution. Whilst this ruling may be sound in theoretical terms, in practical terms it represented a setback for women. According to the Communication Group:

> When the repealed Law allocated a seat for women in each constituency it was intended to guarantee that women, who constitute half of society, should be represented in the People's Assembly. In this sense it is true to the meaning of the constitutional requirement of equality, while making allowances for the historical and social factors which have deprived women of the ability and self-confidence necessary to play an active part in public life. Moreover, the repealed law was fully consistent with the International Convention for the Elimination of all Forms of Discrimination against women which Egypt ratified and to which it gave the force of law by a Presidential decree in 1981. The said convention stressed the importance of instituting special measures to help raise the status of women in a transitional stage until full equality is achieved.
>
> (ibid.)

Another law which had a negative effect on political life in general, and which affected both men and women was Law No.114/1983, which was an amendment to Law No. 38/1972 on the People's Assembly. This amendment introduced the concept of proportional representation, which did not enhance political participation either by enrolment in the electoral registers or by nomination to public office. This 1983 amendment was challenged in the Supreme Court for breach of the principle of equal opportunity, as it deprived independent candidates, who do not belong to any political party, from standing. In view of the seriousness of the challenge, and in an attempt to pre-empt a judgment for unconstitutionality, President Mubarak passed a decree proclaiming Law No. 188 for 1986, amending the law governing the People's Assembly and providing for a seat in every constituency for independent candidates. This new law was itself challenged on the same basis, and in an unprecedented decision, the Supreme Court ruled it unconstitutional on 19 May 1990. Consequently, the People's Assembly was dissolved in October 1990 after a public referendum. Laws No. 201 and 202 for 1990 (amending Law 38/1972 concerning the People's Assembly, and Law 73/1956 concerning the exercise of political rights) were then passed by the People's Assembly. Together, these new laws cancelled almost all the provisions introduced in 1983 and 1986 regarding proportional representation.

The number of women nominated for membership of the People's Assembly dropped and the number of women elected in 1987 dropped accordingly from 37 (30 elected for the woman's allocated seats, and 7 appointed). In effect, the percentage of female membership dropped from 6.7 per cent to 4 per cent in 1987. In 1990, seven members were elected and three were appointed. Thus the percentage continued to drop in 1990 to around 2 per cent (ibid.: 30).

Channels through which it is Possible to Exercise Political Rights

There are four main channels through which Egyptian women can participate in public life and in the political decision-making process, and these are:

1. registering in the electoral rolls;
2. standing for elections in the People's Assembly and Shura Council;
3. standing for elections to popular and local councils; and
4. joining political parties.

Political apathy, however, is a general feature of the majority of Egyptian voters and potential participants in the democratic process, both women and men. It effectively means that many women prefer to be observers rather than participants in the democratic process. This situation changed dramatically, however, during the preparations for and throughout the ICPD, which was closely followed by the Beijing Women's Conference. The ICPD literally changed many women's ideas and expectations on political participation. The memberships of groups such as the New Woman Research Centre increased almost immediately after the ICPD. As Saif al-Dawla remarked, 'It is the culmination of so much work – like a dream.' In spite of the fact that, because of its openly secularist and unashamedly feminist standpoint, the NWRC was one of the most attacked feminist forums, its membership almost doubled. So it is not surprising that other groups, with far less 'radical' standpoints, also witnessed a boom in membership.

Most of the secular and Muslim feminists interviewed agreed that the ICPD had provided a much needed and unique forum for women and men to meet and discuss interesting and important issues relevant to women. Having participated in the ICPD myself, I was party to the near euphoria brought about by the opportunity to discuss, relatively freely and openly,[12] all manner of ideas.

Despite the obvious polarity in the debates, the fact that the issues were out and being discussed – sometimes shouted and screamed – was in itself an achievement of great significance.

Moreover, as many feminists I spoke to reiterated, the ICPD itself, and preparations for it, had given women – secular and Muslim – the opportunity to work *together* on issues. The experience, and its achievements, was seen as positive in and of itself, as well as a boost to future cooperation between these women. 'We worked so well together' was an often repeated phrase, in many cases closely followed by the exclamation, 'I/we did not expect it to go so well'.

Islamist women I spoke to, who also participated in the ICPD, appreciated the opportunities the ICPD offered. In their case, they were very critical of secular feminists and the topics being discussed. To many the conference was an invitation for all sorts of immoral ideas (e.g. abortion and homosexuality) to be 'forced down our throats'.[13] Yet, their presence was seen as an important counter to the tendencies of 'secularism' and 'Westernism', to 'portray the real Islam'. Many Islamist women who did not participate reiterated the well-worn male propaganda that 'the hosting of this conference is like hosting Satan' and was 'a terrible blow on this land of [the pure and holy] al-Azhar'.[14]

Preparations for Beijing brought the secular and Muslim feminists together again. However, the euphoria of the ICPD gradually evaporated as the government tightened its noose around the 'legal NGOs', i.e. those registered with the Ministry of Social Affairs. The government's policy was thus to pursue a policy of exclusion of those groups who had proved most threatening earlier during the ICPD. To do so, women activists were pitted against each other as those who had government approval were given the money and the resources to distribute accordingly. 'Others' were encouraged to participate in the Beijing Conference not as NGOs, but as 'consultants', hence simultaneously robbing them of legitimacy, independence and representativeness.

Nevertheless, despite and because of these impediments, these international conferences have become an important venue for political participation. Whatever the future may bring, the ICPD remains a landmark in the history of Egyptian feminists' political participation.

The Women and Political Participation Debate

The debates on the political participation of women are still very much at the stage of trying to understand the reasons *why* women's participation is minimal. The 1995 parliamentary elections offer clear evidence of this low level of participation. According to *Al-Ahram*

Weekly, while 87 women nominated themselves, only 43 completed the electoral process. Eventually five of these women won parliamentary seats.[15] Various reasons are suggested and discussed, many of them are almost uniformly agreed upon.

Political participation, it is argued, goes hand in hand with economic participation. Since women's economic participation is itself hindered and declining owing to women's concentration in the 'less developed' service sector, as well as the informal sector with all the exploitation that entails, not to mention the endemic sexual division of labour and the double burden many women have to endure, political participation becomes very difficult and problematic indeed.

Moreover, the domination of particular traditions and cultural ideas, which are both repressive and patriarchal, means that women are discriminated against in various ways. Thus, the value of women's political participation is degraded and remains an ambivalent and highly dangerous activity at best, particularly in situations where a lack of democracy and the proliferation of institutions makes male political participation itself difficult.

In a seminar held at the Tajammu' Party headquarters in May 1993, in which women from various NGOs, other political parties and women professionals participated, many of these issues were discussed. Farida al-Naqqash, a secular activist from the Tajammu', argued that the question of why women do not participate in the political process has to be answered on different levels according to the different social classes women come from. A clearer definition of what is meant by political participation is needed. Al-Naqqash and others argue that the reformulation of 'political participation', so as to remove its negative and dangerous connotations, is necessary before the political discourse can change. This can only be done once it starts to appeal to and be understood by the different target groups.

Not to be forgotten, al-Naqqash maintains, is the oft-mentioned factor of illiteracy. In fact, studies carried out by the Tajammu' Party indicated that as many as 80 per cent of Egyptian women are illiterate, whilst only 15 per cent of the literate population is interested in the cause of women's liberation. This has clear repercussions when it comes to awareness of the implications of political participation, let alone interest in the process.

Further, it was stressed that general ignorance among the young educated female population (between 18 and 22 years of age) of the different rights and issues, was a major factor. One of the arguments raised was that if women are not introduced to political participation from an early age, it is highly doubtful that after reaching their forties or fifties and completing the tasks of rearing their children and providing for them, they will turn to politics, unless their interests in political activity had been nurtured from their youth.

The importance of unifying the efforts of the various activists and the groups, on the local and regional front, as well as providing some form of political training for girls in schools and elsewhere was stressed time and again. One of the rhetorical questions raised during the seminar was whether the impediments to unified action were a manifestation of the disease affecting many organizations of 'mixing the public [interests] with the private and considering the private to be more important than the public'.[16]

One of the interesting points in the debate concerns the reasons proposed by the secular women's groups for why large numbers of women *are* eagerly participating in Islamist groups. Many feel that the general cultural stagnation, which is congruent with resentments against the rich–poor division, leads men *and* women to seek refuge in the Islamist utopia of a just and egalitarian society, rich with authentic Islamic cultural norms and values. Most secular feminists maintain that this is a 'false consciousness' into which women are 'brainwashed', developed by Islamist groups which are strengthened and supported by 'money and weapons'.[17]

Interestingly, but not surprisingly, the Islamist women did not consider public participation a problem. As far as they were concerned, they *were* active and participating in the political process, albeit a different one. Their involvements in the various activities (traditional ones as well as the discussion groups and meetings) constituted active political participation. Further, since the whole Islamist movement itself is in the process of growth and consolidation, all its members are constantly mobilized. Just as there is no one reason why secular or Muslim women activists are attracted to political participation, the same goes for Islamist women. What is common to all women activists is a conviction that they can contribute to changing their society. The ideas they are attracted to naturally differ, and the determining difference in this case is the feelings towards 'the West'. In other words, a choice is being made depending on how 'authentic' to indigenous (Islamic) culture these women (and men) want to be.

Even though many of the women's committees within the diverse political parties, as well as the women's groups (NGOs), all stressed the importance of a dialogue to reach a common understanding with

Islamist women, few of them seemed to have taken any constructive initiative on that score. In fact, the general trend points increasingly towards an increased polarization in the respective positions.

Islamist women feel that the women's NGOs are all preaching a Western-style 'false' emancipation of women, and they contend that an Islamic society under the shari'a law (as interpreted by them) would give women all the dignity, respect and rights they need. Any other discourse is inauthentic and disruptive. For many of the Islamist women, there is an active involvement in a structural *jihad* to change society radically from the grassroots up.

Women's groups perceive Islamism as a threat to their very being and to all the achievements women have fought hard and long for. But they all agree that Islamism is not the only power they are fighting against. All the women's groups, with the exception of the NDP women's committees, openly state that their struggles are also directed against the government. The feelings among many women are that they are the first bargaining chips on the board of an undemocratic struggle for power. 'When you think about it', Ayida Saif Al-Dawla (NWRC) rhetorically asks, 'what is the worst that could happen to women if the Islamists actually were in power? There is no real democracy as it is and women's issues are already without political power'.[18]

A Tajammu' activist, Farida al-Naqqash, echoed the feelings of many women when she said that 'fighting on two fronts' has been a feature of secular women's groups since their inception. The fear now is that the state,

> instead of using feminism and women's groups as allies against the Islamists, is trying to weaken the feminists, thinking that this is the best way to avoid confrontation with the Islamists.

Al-Naqqash is referring to the inactivity on the part of government bodies to amend laws which have been critiqued, and to allow women's NGOs to set themselves up without harassment and control. As Hala Shukralla (NWRC) said, '[the] government should listen to feminist demands, instead of fighting to prove their superior Islamic-ness where women are concerned'.

Women's Right to Work and the Labour Laws

The Civil Servants System, promulgated by Law No. 47/1978, and the Public Sector Employees System, promulgated by Law No. 48/1978, were enacted in order to apply the principle of women's right to work. Both laws contain provisions to help women (and their spouses) working in the government and public sector to reconcile their duties to their families with their responsibilities to their place of employment in accordance with article 11 of the Constitution. These laws determined the following privileges:

1. The right of a husband or wife to unpaid leave to accompany his/her spouse working abroad for a period of not less than 6 months whether on secondment basis or not. Further, the law makes it compulsory that the administrative authority grant the request of the spouse in all cases.
2. The right of a female employee to take up to two years' unpaid leave to look after her child. This unpaid leave is granted three times during the employee's period of service. During the leave the state is responsible for paying both its quota and that of the female employee in the social insurance subscription or to pay her an indemnity equivalent to 25 per cent of her salary; the choice is hers.
3. The right of women to paid maternity leave for a period of three months. Such paid leave is granted three times during the employee's period of service, and is not deductible from the due annual leave.
4. The right of the competent administrative authority to permit female employees, on their request, to work on a part-time basis in consideration of half the salary and the annual or sick leave. In such a case, the female employee may exceptionally subscribe to social insurance under the Social Insurance Law.

Labour Law No. 137 of 1981 (Private Sector)

This law lays down the basic rules governing labour relations and the duties of both the employer and the employee. In one of its chapters, the Labour Law lays down the rules governing the employment of women. This law:

1. Requires the application of all provisions governing the employment of women without discrimination to men and women performing the same job, without prejudice to the rules governing the employment of women and granting them certain privileges or protecting them against abuse or mistreatment of employers.

2. Prohibits the employment of women between 8 p.m. and 7 a.m., except in certain types of work, the nature of which entails night-time work (e.g. hotels, restaurants, theatres, hospitals, etc.). This exception also applies to female executives filling senior posts. In such cases, employers are required to provide the necessary guarantees for the safety, protection and transport of female employees.

3. Prohibits the employment of women in work detrimental to their health or morals or in strenuous jobs (e.g. bakeries, underground work in mines, etc.).

4. Grants a female employee who has served the same employer for 6 months, the right to three fully paid maternity leaves of 50 days each during her period of service, without prejudice to the mandatory leave taken by a female employee during the 40 days following her confinement.

5. Grants a female employee two fully paid half-hour rest breaks daily to breast-feed her infant during the 18 months following her confinement.

6. Grants a female employee employed by an establishment having not less than 50 workers the right of up to one year's unpaid leave to look after her infant, three times during her service.

7. Requires an employer who employs more than 100 women in the same place to establish a nursery or to participate in one if the number of employees is fewer than 100.

Thus it is clear that essentially, the rights of women working in the public or private sector are not dissimilar. Where public sector employees are entitled to unpaid leave of up to two years three times during their period of service, their private sector counterparts are entitled to a maximum period of one year. Moreover, whereas the public sector female workers can obtain three months of maternity leave, the private sector counterparts are allowed 50 days.

The Labour Law in Practice

Although by law Egyptian women enjoy equal employment activities sometimes greater than those available in many 'developed' countries, the reality falls far short of the intentions. At best, as the Communication Group for the Enhancement of Women accurately describes it, a situation of 'incomplete equality' exists.

According to the *Statistical Yearbook* of June 1991 (Central Agency for Mobilization and Statistics), working women in Egypt are a minority, representing no more than 15 per cent of the total workforce in both the private and public sectors, whilst women make up about 33 per cent of the total number of university graduates. So in fact, whilst women constitute approximately half of the total population, their participation in production and development lags far behind their potential. Moreover, in certain areas the percentage of female workers is diminishing, in spite of the fact that these areas suffer from manpower shortages and a fall in the standards of services. Such areas include, among others, healthcare services, agriculture, communications and justice. To make matters worse, it is also clear from the statistics that more than 50 per cent of working women do not reach senior posts except after the age of 55. This illustrates all too well the fact that promotion opportunities to senior posts are not open to working women except towards the end of their working careers. Further, these statistics also indicate that working women spend a large part of their careers in public offices without the opportunity to perform a leading role.

Certain fields of work remain closed to women – such as the judiciary – whilst their representation in others remains only symbolic – e.g. defence. Furthermore, the dependency ratio in Egypt is 1:3. This means that 30–5 per cent of the population represent the productive force supporting the remaining 65–70 per cent.

In sum, there is a marked retreat from the principle of equality in the field of work, which is perceptible in certain unconstitutional practices. Notably, more and more advertisements are appearing in the newspapers for posts which specify that only men should apply. The main argument used to justify such prejudices are that the working women's productivity is low because she is preoccupied with domestic problems.

Feminists argue, however, that low productivity is a general social problem extending to both men and women, but the latter have to contend with the reality that despite provisions by the law to facilitate work for women, employers rarely take them into account. One such provision concerns the availability of affordable day care centres for the children of working mothers. Statistics indicate that the number of day care facilities available in 1989/90 was 4014, with a capacity for 369,473 children only.[19]

Feminists and lawyers working in this area also argue that the prevailing economic conditions do not allow women to afford time-saving modern household equipment, which can help to reduce their domestic workloads and channel their efforts into other productive activities. Further, it is also argued that embedded traditional norms and roles (such as household work being exclusively a woman's activity, without any help from the husband) simply lead to women assuming increased responsibility and so taking on more burdens.

Moreover, almost all feminists agree that the greatest threat undermining the principle of women's equality is the recent public call – by both religious and government figures – for women to return to their homes, thus relinquishing their right to work and their role in developing society and increasing production:

> Those who hold that women should content themselves with looking after their children conveniently overlook the fact that the number of women supporting their families is 25–30% of the total number of breadwinners.
>
> (The Communication Group 1992: 15)

The proponents of this view argue that taking women out of the job market is necessary to solve Egypt's economic and social crisis whether due to unemployment, low productivity, low standard of living, or transport and traffic problems, etc. The question remains, however, what should the families who are dependent on the working women's incomes do, were the latter to stay at home?

THE WOMEN AND WORK DEBATE

Another heated debate is, ironically, an old one that is resurfacing with a vengeance: namely, women's right to work, or more accurately, the *suitability* of women's work. The reasons why the old contentions recur are numerous, the most prominent of them being attributable to the deteriorating economy, which is in turn tied to and inseparable from the world economy. In Egypt, the problems are manifested in rising unemployment, declining productivity and increasing income disparities.

All too often government officials, as well as clergy and laymen, contend that one of the means of solving the unemployment problem is to 'persuade' working women to return to their homes (i.e. their husbands and families) and thus vacate their jobs for men. Some have gone so far as to suggest paying some of these women part of their salaries if they leave their jobs as an incentive to do so. In fact, a legal stipulation does exist which enables women to work half-time for half their wages.[20] Further attempts to keep women out of the job market centred on a proposal that women retire at the age of 50 (instead of the present retirement age of 60, or 55). As if that were not enough, many of the women's groups are protesting against the claims coming from certain sectors of society that by staying at home and retreating from their jobs, women would not only be solving the unemployment problem, but also problems of the declining standards of living, decreased productivity and even traffic congestion!

Statistics which indicate that women are the sole breadwinners in almost 30 per cent of all households seem to be ignored. They get lost in what appears to be a state campaign to remove women from the workforce, a project that goes hand in hand with a large-scale and highly controversial privatization programme. Tied to constraints raised by structural adjustment policies, the logic behind this laying off of women seems to be the desire on the part of the management of newly privatized enterprises to create more jobs with lower maternity and child care costs.

The pressures imposed by the International Monetary Fund (IMF) and the World Bank have had a number of repercussions on the whole situation of women and work and the ensuing debate. One of the stipulations was that the public sector become more competitive with the private sector. This seems to have been translated into the public sector copying the private sector's policies of employing women, which included short-term contracts and engaging under-age girls.[21] In so doing the public sector freed itself from the responsibility of providing economic and social rights to women, as well as gradually ridding itself – often through outright refusal of employment – of women employees. It is important to note that the public sector was one of the largest employers of women. As a result of the recent policies, women are forced increasingly into the informal sector where legal protection and rights are non-existent.

In this regard, it should be pointed out that none of the arguments that hold working women responsible for contributing to unemployment, takes into account the hundreds of poor women who work day and night in rural and urban areas. These women work for no wage or very minimal wages *outside* the formal sector. Therefore, they are neither competing with men for job opportunities in that field nor making demands on the social services (social security, maternity leave, and the like).

Further, secular and Muslim feminists contend that there is a concerted government effort to highlight the immorality and ensuing degradation of social mores, which result from the sexes mixing in the workplace. Both state and Islamists seem to be at once also deeply concerned with the fate of the working women's children. Congruent with this is the glorification of motherhood which is brought to the fore on every possible occasion. Religious spokesmen appear on television quoting the *Hadith* (Prophet's saying) that 'heaven lies at the feet of mothers' and extolling the virtues of this most sacred role of women. Meanwhile there is a simultaneous highlighting of 'results of various studies' that prove that children of working mothers (or mothers who are not able to devote their full time to motherhood) suffer psychologically and socially from this 'neglect'. It becomes a woman's national, patriotic and religious duty to devote herself to the rearing of her children to form a strong country for the future generation. The irony of this whole debate is that this is the same discourse that was used earlier in the century by proponents of the women's movement, who argued that it is precisely this glorified role of motherhood that necessitated and justified women's education first and then over time their involvement in the public sphere.

Women I spoke to from the various political parties and NGOs were particularly upset by a trend among employers, as manifested, among other things, in advertisements for employment. Many of these advertisements in the dailies stipulated that the applicants should be male. Protests against this were raised by some of the women activists, on the grounds that such claims infringed on women's constitutional rights, and that they were blatantly unfair since women applicants could be better qualified than men. However, the only noticeable change was a paraphrasing within certain ads, so that instead of asking for male applicants, the stipulation became 'completion of military service', which excludes women applicants. The continuation of this practice without any effective restraint is encouraging many commercial companies and banks in both the private and public sectors to give preference to males over females (The Communication Group: 16).

Muslim and secular feminists alike contend that Islamist influence on the women and work debate owes much to the same structural adjustment policies (SAP) and the IMF. This is succinctly expressed in a paper prepared by the Arab Women's Committee within the Arab Lawyers' Union. According to this research, Islamist regimes such as the Muslim Brotherhood were quick to seize the opportunity and step into the space left after the retreat of the government – in response to SAP stipulations – from the arena of social services. Islamist regimes hastened to invest in the now increasingly privatized sectors like education and health.

As well as existing as an ideological power, they [Islamists] also became a social and economic force. As owners of schools they play a big social role in a form of social conditioning based on the traditional sexual division of labour which ultimately leads to the retreat of women from participation in both the productive sphere and the general work sphere. And in the arena of health, these groups have set up clinics within mosques where they influence women's perceptions of themselves by encouraging them to refuse contraceptive methods and thereby fall into their traditional occupations as wife and mother only. Women doctors work in these clinics to encourage their women patients to attend the religious gatherings and the adoption of a backward position vis-à-vis women's roles in society and in the family.[22]

During late November 1994, Parliament discussed the proposals for a 'New Unified Labour Law' (NUL), which was eventually adopted in the same year. Some secular and Muslim women's groups campaigned against this new law, arguing that it was a blatant surrender to Islamist and conservative influence in society. This was in reference to clauses in the law which limited both the kinds (article 91) and the times (article 90) of work women were allowed to do. Article 90, for example, states that women should not be allowed to work from 8 p.m. to 7 a.m. without special permission from the Minister of Labour. Article 91 warns against employing women in areas which are 'harmful to either their health or their morals', nor should they be employed in 'hard labour'.[23]

The campaigns against the NUL did not present its enactment. But they did manage to raise some dust about the implications of the law on and for women, as well as mobilize women's and other concerned groups against it.

Campaigners also argued that the NUL deprived women of some of the benefits that earlier labour laws had guaranteed, such as limiting the number of paid maternity leaves to two instead of three. The rationale behind this was that state policies had to coincide with policies concerning tackling the 'population problem'. By limiting the number of maternity leaves, the government is intending to discourage women from having more than two children.

Islamist women spoken to on women's work stressed the aspect of women working for women (e.g. women doctors for female patients, women teachers for female students, and so on). As such, they are not only providing for particular needs of certain Muslim women, but constitute a necessity. If the situation and conditions demand that women work in mixed areas, then these women must protect themselves and signal their respectability by wearing the strictest kinds of veil necessary, which would at the same time not be a hindrance in the work. In thus keeping their dignity intact, the women were also avoiding unnecessarily testing situations with men and thereby abiding by their religious duty in the safest and best possible way. But these Islamist women also took care to teach themselves and their adherents the precise rights given to women to work, and rights and duties of Muslim men to maintain *their* dignity and act appropriately.

THE NATIONALITY LAW

An integral aspect of almost all the feminist debates, is that the Nationality or Citizenship Law is an obvious example of the second-rate status accorded to Egyptian women. There is a blatant legal discrimination between granting citizenship to children of an Egyptian father and a foreign mother, and children of an Egyptian mother and a foreign father. The children of an Egyptian father are automatically granted Egyptian citizenship, whilst those of an Egyptian mother are granted these rights only on certain conditions.

Law No. 26/1975 governs the terms and conditions for granting and withdrawing Egyptian nationality and has been subject to public debate during the past years. Article 2 of this law provides that any child born to an Egyptian father is automatically Egyptian. This is the basic requirement for acquiring Egyptian nationality, whether the child is born inside or outside Egypt.

On the other hand, the law clearly dictates that the children of an Egyptian mother married to a foreigner having a known nationality are not entitled to Egyptian nationality, irrespective of whether they have been born in Egypt or outside. Moreover, the children of an Egyptian mother and an unknown father or a father having an unknown or no nationality and born outside Egypt may not apply for Egyptian nationality until they reach the age of 21, subject to the following conditions:

1. that the decision to apply for Egyptian nationality should be made within one year from the date they reach their majority;

2. that they should have made Egypt their principal place of residence for at least five years prior to the submission of such an application;
3. that they should notify the Minister of Interior of their wish to become Egyptian and that the said Minister should not object within one year from the date he receives such notice.

When this law was passed in 1975 it obviously failed to anticipate situations where an Egyptian mother might be divorced or widowed and needed to live in Egypt with her 'foreign' children. Neither has the legislature foreseen the extent of the financial difficulties which an Egyptian mother would face in order to support her children who feel and live like Egyptians but are treated by the authorities as foreigners.

Effectively, the existing nationality law gives preferential treatment to the children of foreign mothers as compared to the children of an Egyptian mother. Meanwhile, there is a flagrant violation of the principle of equality between men and women when the children of the former are automatically and unconditionally granted nationality, whilst those of the latter do not enjoy the same rights.

This law causes a great deal of hardship to the mothers of children with foreign fathers born and raised in Egypt, and the children themselves. Children are subjected to official discrimination and suffer a consequent sense of alienation. Examples of what happens in such cases include having to pay tuition fees in foreign currency, difficulties in obtaining residency permits, work permits and admission to private schools. A further example of the difficulties faced is that basic schooling becomes highly problematic for these children. The reason is that high school fees – only a fraction of which is normally expected from Egyptian children – are demanded from these children, who are treated as 'foreign' children. The result is that many of these children cannot go to school. One story – of many – concerns three sisters who were unable to attend school until their non-Egyptian father died, at which point the school fees were waived.[24]

Apart from the ensuing hardships that the mothers of such children and the children themselves have to face, the discrepancy is an outright contravention of any claim to equality between the sexes. Women activists from a number of groups have formed pressure groups to lobby for change. As a result, the issue was discussed in Parliament and a special commission was set up in 1993 to study the issue and come up with amendments to this law. The proposals of the committee have been presented to the People's Assembly (the

Parliament) over the past few years and have in effect requested that Article (2) be amended to provide that children born to an Egyptian mother – irrespective of any other conditions – are automatically Egyptian. Results from the proposals of this Commission have yet to be seen. More likely, this was a tactic of the government to absorb some of the anger, appear to be delegating responsibility and taking women's demands seriously, whilst hoping that calm and amnesia will take over.

Islamist women's opinions on this issue vary. There are those who agree with most secular and Muslim feminists that the law is a blatant sign of inequality, notably the Labour Party women's committee. However, this is seen as a matter that can wait in terms of its importance and urgency.

Most interestingly, though not surprisingly, I found that the NDP's standpoint was one that endorses the law as it stands. Farkhanda Hasan, head of the women's committee said, 'we don't want any undesirable elements', explaining rhetorically, 'What if the fathers are from Arab countries which we have political problems with, for example? No, no. We must be very careful. We can't just leave it open.' Nevertheless, she continued, to my incredulity, 'Some amendments are needed which can allow for exceptions to be made'.

No alternatives – with the notable exception of the New Marriage Contract – are being envisaged to the existing laws as they stand. The emphasis of secular and Muslim activists in particular is on raising women's awareness of the existing laws as a means to countering ignorance – but not as a way towards creating a different legal structure. In other words, many women activists are currently concentrating on using the existing state, and its site of power, to set up their strategies, whilst the Islamists are arguing and actively setting up their alternative structures in the mosques or members' houses.

There are many other issues debated that take place in women's groups which are also aired in general debates within Egyptian civil society. Examples are debates on political orientation and identity – i.e. a secular identity versus an Islamic one – as well as an emotional and often heated debate on the issue of accepting foreign funding. Both these require a thesis in themselves. Suffice it here to say that the range of opinions is vast, and that the 'accusations' of being stooges of the West dog both men and women where secular orientations and the acceptance of foreign funding are concerned. Two debates cannot be lightly referred to in this context, owing to their significance as to government policy vis-à-vis feminist discursive practices. These are the debates on women and violence, and women and health.

WOMEN AND VIOLENCE

Rape and violence against women are issues that are taken up primarily if not solely by *some* women's NGOs. Because this issue is a relatively recent,[25] and still a sensitive one, elaborations on the ramifications and political implications of this issue by women's committees within political parties is still in the process of being born. More importantly, the distinction between rape and other forms of violence against women (e.g. domestic violence) has yet to be made clearly and explicitly. Until recently, 'rape' and 'violence against women' have been used interchangeably, since no other form of violence against women has been distinguished, or at least elaborated politically. The debates taking place in some parts of the Western world on punishment for rape *within* marriage is alien to Egyptian legal and cultural formulations.

Furthermore, the issue of rape remains an extremely sensitive, taboo and understudied issue. The information gathered here comes more from my own observations of the snippets dropped here and there about rape, and not from a comprehensive study on the issue. Basically, what little debate there is in the women's groups can be divided between those who contest certain, accepted, conventional reasons for rape, and those who advocate capital punishment for such a crime. As far as reasons go, conventional understanding, not uncommon elsewhere in the world, claims that women, in some way or other, are *themselves responsible* for their rape. This view is taken to the extreme in this context, to mean that *unveiled* women, or women who are 'improperly dressed', are a walking invitation to rapists.

Some feminists I spoke to argue that this perspective in itself constitutes 'a different form of rape – that which denies women their right to choose their dress, as well as their simple right *to be* in their own separate ways'.[26] Moreover, such groups argue that instead of putting the brunt of the blame on the women – something that is seen as unfair and unjustified at best – a more comprehensive attitude would be to study the roots of the problem.

Accordingly, the view held by most feminists is that the open-door, capitalist economy, which has led to economic hardship for an increasing percentage of the poor, not to mention the introduction of new and individualistic value systems, has important social repercussions. Fewer and fewer young people are able to afford to marry, which is perceived as the only permissible outlet for sexual relations. I am aware that this formulation indicates that rape is being confused with the fulfilment of sexual desire. Rape in a context of enforced repressed sexual desire *is* an extreme and hurtful (for the raped woman) form of fulfilment of that desire. Moreover, it is further claimed that fewer affordable activities are available for the average man as an energy outlet.[27] The more common explanation given for rape is that sexual repression, in extreme cases, finds an outlet in violent acts such as rape.

The solution then, as some secular and Muslim women activists see it, lies in tackling socio-economic problems. A study and reassessment of the educational curriculum is suggested, so that values of equality between men and women (instead of the prevailing polarity) can be taught. Provision of basic needs for people, like shelter, food, healthcare and education, are also seen as necessary means for dealing with the problem. Another suggestion is the organization of sports, camps and seminars where the energies of young men can be directed.

As far as punishment is concerned, the prevailing view among many feminists is that capital punishment is the best means to prevent such a crime. However, the women's groups are divided as to whether that is indeed the case. Some think that since this does not tackle the roots of the problem, rape will continue regardless of the punishment. They cite as an example the fact that although capital punishment is imposed for murder, this does not prevent murders from taking place.[28] Others feel that capital punishment should remain as a deterrent (if only because they feel the rapists deserve death), but that this should not be mutually exclusive of the imperative to deal with the problem from its social-economic angle as well. (The latter refers to the problems faced by youth who wish to marry.)

Whatever the debates on causes and punishments, most feminists admitted that the rape issue needs more attention and interest on their part. The Al-Nadim Centre, set up in the early 1990s to deal with women victims of violence, is in itself both a novel idea and a sign of the increased awareness. Because of the uniqueness of this enterprise, the Centre is currently working on studies on violence against women in Egypt, whilst simultaneously looking for cooperation from other similar centres in different parts of the world. Moreover, the conference on 'Women's Health and CEDAW' had as one of its recommendations that the issue of women's safety was to be prioritized in the coming years in the form of study groups and seminars on the means of combating violence, not just in Egypt, but in coordination with the rest of the Arab world.

Islamist women I spoke to saw rape as a symptom of the lack of religious values in the society. It was argued that rape was imported into the traditional value systems along with Western cultural hegemony – i.e. it is alien to the Islamic culture.

> When you look at when the phenomenon started, you will find it happened at the same time the invasion that took place in our society – schools, universities and other cultural institutions – by Western values as indicated by American soaps such 'Dallas', 'Falcon Crest' and the like.[29]

According to some Islamist women, the only way to eradicate rape was to re-educate men, women and children about Islam and thus reinstate Islamic values and morality. Any other means, especially the existing penal code, are superficial and ineffective. They do, however, agree that economic conditions play a part, since financial complications make it very difficult for young man to get married, but they argue that these are secondary to the issue of morality and Islamic values. To them, rape is synonymous with the loss of the collective community of Islam, with its values of cleanliness and purity. It is implied quite strongly that if there were to be an 'Islamic society' as envisaged by Islamists, such social ills would be reduced or eradicated altogether. The fact is that to expect Islamists to have a solution to this issue is rather premature. After all, which political movement had clear solutions to all of society's social ills before they came to power? Moreover, as long as Islamist activists themselves, and their followers, believe in the utopia of a quasi-perfect society, how can it be discredited as long as it remains untried?

WOMEN AND HEALTH

Only during the preparations for and during the ICPD did the issue of women's reproductive rights begin to be actively discussed amongst most feminists. In my previous fieldwork in Egypt, I noticed that very few feminists (and then usually secular ones) would raise the issue spontaneously. This situation changed slightly, though not radically, as the preparations for the ICPD were underway. My explanations for the relative silence on this issue are two-fold. On the one hand, the

Egyptian government is in favour of family planning to reduce the so-called 'population explosion'. Contraception, in the form of the pill and the coil, are encouraged, and the pill in fact is supplied at heavily subsidized prices and is almost free. Family planning clinics are readily available, and advertisements about the necessity to reduce the size of the family have become a part-and-parcel of local popular discourse. The latter can be seen in the fact that jokes are made about these advertisements, which appear on television almost daily.

On the other hand, what is openly problematic for some women's groups, in relation to reproductive rights, is the issue of abortion, which is a very tricky one. Government policy is supposedly based on religious interpretations, and indicates that pregnant women are allowed a legal abortion only if their health is threatened. Abortion in this event can take place within the first three months of pregnancy. However, arguing for women's entitlement to legal abortion in general, or even in particular cases of rape or incest, is highly controversial. In a campaign, strengthened prior to and during the ICPD, in which the New Woman Research Centre (NWRC), supported by other ostensibly 'liberal' groups, played an important role, the call for legal abortion in the case of rape or incest was made. The furore surrounding this issue fed into already existing antagonisms and suspicions that the ICPD as a whole was a Western conspiracy to rid the Muslim world of its Islamic values by legalizing abortion, calling for women's equality and destroying family values. No matter what the logic or content of the argumentation of these feminists, they were not only being unheeded, but they were being attacked personally, whilst former 'liberal' allies hastened to distance themselves from them. In short, the issue of women's own opinions, practices and warnings about this government-sponsored family planning process remains relatively little discussed at the level of NGOs. Silence is more telling than any commotion in this regard.

Ironically, this is an issue in which Islamist women agree wholeheartedly with the government. As Heba Ra'uf a young Islamist said to me scornfully during the ICPD, 'I am here with a child at home and another inside me, so that should indicate what I feel about abortion'. As far as Islamist activists are concerned, the whole argument for the legalization of abortion is nothing but a blatant call for immorality. Legal abortion is seen as a ticket for women to 'lose their head', 'scorn motherhood to the extreme' and 'become wanton'. Besides, as another Islamist, Abiyya Badr, argues, why should women suddenly decide they do not want to have their baby on their own? After all a decision [to have one] has already been made before, and this is human life which took both mother and father to produce. If women were allowed to abort, it means that the responsibilities towards husband and family can be taken lightly then!

Almost all the Islamist women I spoke to considered that rape and incest were too insignificant to warrant legalizing abortion. And anyway, they maintained that the raped woman should not hold the unborn child responsible for her rape. Unsafe abortions were not seen as a reason to legalize abortion but, on the contrary, an affirmation of the necessity of the opposite. In short, Islamist women consistently refused to acknowledge or accept any arguments in favour of legalizing abortion. On the contrary, the very discussion of the need for this was seen as highly immoral and a sign of social decay.

Another issue discussed under women's health is that of female circumcision. Again the issue was heavily debated and became highly charged during the ICPD. This, however, is an issue on which *all* feminists in Egypt agree. The practice of female circumcision in all its forms is entirely rejected and disapproved of by secular, Muslim and Islamists alike. During the ICPD it was noticeable that all these tendencies vehemently called for the abolition of this practice by law. And yet I found two aspects of this debate highly significant. First, none of these feminists, despite agreeing on this important issue, were prepared to form a joint action or front. On the contrary, the norm was to remain concerned with the numerous issues which divide these women, rather than that which would unite them. Secondly, the government stance becomes all the more interesting, since it refused to abide by its earlier promises to ban the practice, and instead came up with a far milder law to restrict the practice to doctors. The question is why, despite Islamist women activists' stance against circumcision, did the government feel obliged to maintain the practice? The answer, I believe, lies in the following. Islamist males (i.e. the heard voices) did not condemn the practice. On the contrary, they were either conveniently silent, or they criticized the government stance on everything from hosting the conference, to allowing all sorts of issues to be discussed there.[30]

Moreover, the strongest voice of official Islam – i.e. Sheikh al-Azhar – refrained from condemning the practice. Instead, he almost sanctified it as an Islamic custom, the interference with which is considered unacceptable from a cultural and religious point of view. There was open disagreement in opinions on this issue between Sheikh al-Azhar and the Grand Mufti (another voice of official Islam).[31] The latter openly and clearly denounced the practice as un-Islamic. Yet his was a cry in the wilderness as far as male voices were concerned. Hence, the discourses of Islamist *women* activists, even if resonating with those of other feminists, are not the determining factor as far as government decisions are concerned. The debate on circumcision and its repercussions have proved more definitively than any other debate to be indicative of government policy and feminist discourses. It is the male voices, whether Islamist or simply conservative, which carry weight in government policy-making. This is a very important fact which seems to have been ignored so far by most feminists, who are too busy homogenizing the government stance whilst emphasizing their internal differences. Whilst the former may be accurate, the persistence of the latter is, in my opinion, not only blinding but counterproductive.

CONCLUSION

Whether Islamist, Muslim or secular, feminists are fighting for a better society. Yet each holds on to the belief that their better society is threatened by 'the Others' who suffer from a collective false consciousness. Islamists believe that secular feminists are 'followers of the West' at worst, and 'deluded women' at best. Secular feminists believe that Islamists are influenced by, if not propagating, 'terrorist and anti-women rhetoric'. Both see the other as the enemy. Meanwhile, in this circus, the government plays on the fears of all: appointing a strong and secular woman as the head of the ruling party's women's committee, whose main idea is that feminism is unnecessary and is a thing of the past; whilst Islamizing their media programmes and yet rounding up 'Islamist terrorists' indiscriminately.

Ignorance of the law is seen as the biggest problem by secular and Muslim feminists. The latter argue that the law itself needs to be amended, whereas Islamist feminists call for it to be scrapped altogether in favour of another set of male-interpreted laws (the shari'a). Effectively, all groups are moving around and remaining mired in the same androcentric argument. It is this androcentrism that has emerged most clearly from reviewing the various laws. The implicit and explicit gender bias underlines a masculine discursive character which permeates the laws, and seems to be based on a dualism of men as rational credible beings and women as emotional (and incredible) beings. Illustrations of this can be found in, among others, the following cases: in the PSL wives (irrational and incredible) seeking a divorce must do so on conditions which a male judge (rational and credible) must approve; in the Criminal Code women prostitutes (irrational and incredible) are testified against by the same men (rational and credible) who bedded them; and yet again in the case of abduction where the kidnapper (rational, credible) is asked to marry the woman (irrational) or be hanged!

Feminists who wish to challenge the law, therefore, have to pursue their struggles outside the courtroom. Assumptions that rationality and justice are male attributes must be consistently and fundamentally challenged. Such assumptions are manifested by the exclusion of women from the judiciary. Hence, campaigning for women to be appointed as judges, which is already taking place in Egypt, indicates a growing awareness in that direction.

The power implications of this struggle are highly significant. This is an arena where feminists may realize that the shifting balance of power is seldom theirs except on particular occasions: international events such as the Nairobi Conference, the ICPD and Beijing, where the credibility of the state and its international 'image' leave it vulnerable to agreeing to certain secular and Muslim feminist demands. On the other hand, Islamist feminists work with the realization that they are part of a movement of opposition. As such, theirs are issues which form part of a larger pressure group, capable of at least influencing state decisions – even if only for the sake of temporary compromise. The latter is best illustrated perhaps by the events surrounding 'Jihan's Law', when the government was forced to amend the law after it was declared unconstitutional. The ability to influence decision-making is very much integral to feminist power. The law is an important arena where such a power is seen to be time-, issue- and context-bound, and thus fluid in diverse ways. Debates surrounding the different legal issues indicate that secular, Muslim and Islamist feminists have a long struggle ahead of them to realize their different sources of power and relative strengths vis-à-vis the Egyptian state, and thus be able positively to influence the course of the legal trends.

In the next chapters, Islamist gender ideology is looked at in more detail, to highlight further the nuances in relationship between Islamist ideology and feminist consciousness.

7 Islamism and Gender: Male Perspectives

In this chapter, I highlight the different male Islamists' ideas and claims with respect to the position of women in society and the roles they are 'allowed' (according to certain interpretations). Having realized by this stage that men's voices in general receive a great deal more coverage and are more powerful than women's voices, I took a conscious decision to limit male Islamists' voices. The male Islamists whose works I examine are *Sheikh Muhammad Al-Ghazali, Sheikh Muhammad Mitwalli Al-Sha'rawi, Sayyid Qutb, Sheikh Yusuf al-Qaradawi* and *Adil Husayn*. My choice of these male Islamist voices is controversial – and deliberately so. The controversy lies in the fact that some of them are arguably voices of official or state Islam, i.e. Al-Sha'rawi and Al-Ghazali. Indeed, these two men have appeared and continue to appear frequently on state-controlled television. I have shown, through the voices of the various feminists, that the state does not object to certain aspects of Islamist ideas – especially those that concern women. I have relied on the many Islamists I spoke to, to recommend whom they considered the influential male Islamists in their lives. The men who are presented in this chapter, therefore, and who have not been interviewed, are the ones that were mentioned in answer to my questions, and in the course of many talks held with Islamist activists. These men are also known for remaining relatively silent on some of the activities carried out by the more radical Islamist groups (e.g. the murder of Faraj Fuda and the assassination attempt on Najib Mahfuz).[1]

I do not present everything the chosen male Islamists have to say about the position and role of women within Islam, but instead I highlight their perspectives on specific issues of contention today, some of which were also discussed in preceding chapters – i.e. the veil, women's work and male–female equality, women's right to divorce, female circumcision and feminism. Polygamy and male control (*qawâma*) *per se* are not, in the works I analyse, always written about as independent issues, but are often implicit in the men's opinions on divorce and equality of the sexes. This is also valid as far as feminists are concerned, since polygamy is not discussed as an issue in itself, but more as an aspect of the PSL.[2] This fact is part-and-parcel of the discursive realities of feminist groups, wherein scholarly, serious and popular challenges to Quranic interpretations (of both polygamy and *qawâma*) remain few and far between.

Moreover, I do not consider everything these male Islamists have written or said about these topics, but I analyse their latest books which are written *specifically on women*. In this way I could present their voices, and give space to what they themselves feel relevant to list in a book written on women. The only exception to this criterion is Sayyid Qutb who, to my knowledge, never has devoted a book to women. However, since Islamist activists interviewed mentioned him frequently, I have looked at his book *Signposts*.

What I found striking in the different Islamist approaches is that it seems almost impossible to describe an Islamist viewpoint on women that does not take into account, and in fact compares itself to some understanding of, women's issues in 'the West'. Thus, the position of Muslim women is always juxtaposed against that of their Western counterparts. Another reference point frequently used to compare women's rights and roles in Islam with 'other', less fortunate situations is that of the era of the *jahiliyya* (ignorance) or pre-Islamic times. The arguments on women's rights in Islam are often, if not always, portrayed in direct opposition or comparison either to their sisters in the West, or to the first generation of Islamic women. The implication is that the history of Muslim women is never accurately portrayed if not done in comparison to what came before and what came after.

SAYYID QUTB

Qutb's contributions and extrapolations on women's issues all come within the framework of the family:

> The family is the basis of the society, and the basis of the family is the division of labour between husband and wife, and the upbringing of children is the most important function of the family. Such a society [in which this happens] is indeed civilized. In the Islamic system of life, this kind of a family provides the environment under which human values and morals develop and grow in the new generation. These values and morals cannot exist apart from the family unit.
>
> (Qutb 1991: 182–3)

The family is thus conceived as the most important political, social and cultural unit in any society. Its importance is inseparable from the coherent functioning and allocation of responsibilities between men and women. The family system and the relationship between the sexes determines the whole character of society and the extent to which it is either civilized or backward – i.e. Islamic or *jahili* respectively.

Qutb was explicit in separating good Muslims from immoral Westerners. This dichotomy persists in all his references and examples to underline his meanings. So where the family is concerned, Qutb argued that havoc would ensue if Muslim societies were to copy Western ones. In the latter, according to him, free sexual relationships and illegitimate children form the basis of society, the relationship between man and woman is based on lust, passion and impulse, and the division of work is not based on family responsibility or 'natural gifts'.

Qutb posits that in Western societies, a woman's role is merely to be attractive, sexy and flirtatious, and she is freed from her fundamental responsibility of bringing up children. This situation, seen as unnatural, is made worse if the woman chooses a career over family responsibilities. By preferring to use her ability for material production rather than for training the next generation, she is exposing the underlying norm of that corrupt society which values material production more than 'the development of human character'. These societies, Qutb argues, have a backward civilization from the human point of view, and are consequently seen as *jahili* in Islamic terms (ibid.: 183).

> These societies which give ascendance to physical desires and animalistic morals cannot be considered civilized, no matter how much progress they may make in industry or science.
>
> (ibid.: 184)

Qutb's tirade is levelled against 'all modern *jahili* societies' (ibid.), in which, he claims, 'the meaning of "morality" is limited to such an extent that all those aspects which distinguish man from animal are considered beyond its sphere'. According to Qutb,

> A progressive society lays down the foundation of a family system in which human desires find satisfaction, as well as providing for the future generation to be brought up in such a manner that it will continue the human civilization.
>
> (ibid.: 185–6)

Such a society and progressive family system must be based on Islamic norms, which must, above all, forbid free sexual activity. Those norms are the only guarantor of civilization, as far as Qutb is concerned. The family thus becomes not merely the most important unit in society, but is the cradle of Islamic civilization. Qutb's stratification of gender roles within the family is not elaborated to any great length. But his reference to natural gifts indicates the priority of motherhood and domesticity for women, whilst simultaneously *not* ruling out that women may be involved in other capacities. The emphasis on the family unit is therefore not exclusive of a public role for women, as long as it falls within the framework of furthering Islamic civilization.

Based on his perceptions of Western societies, it seems safe to deduce that Qutb did not think much – if anything at all – of feminism. As part-and-parcel of that Western immoral, *jahili* society, feminism would probably have been perceived as one of the instigators of the moral degeneration and lack of ethics that characterize them.

It is difficult to find any references to Qutb's position on female circumcision. But one can assume that it is only recently (especially during and after the ICPD) that the whole issue of female circumcision has become controversial. Before the recent furore, the practice was rarely publicly questioned.

Qutb's political legacy was picked up, elaborated and developed in many ways by others. That it has had a profound impact is unquestionable. However, Qutb's ideology is to be distinguished from others precisely because of its flagrantly political agenda. People such as Al-Sha'rawi, Al-Ghazali and Al-Qaradawi have toned down the political potential and present their views as primarily socially relevant. Qutb minced no words in clearly identifying the rulers of his times as morally corrupt, and laying down a basis for their overthrow and alternatives. Yet Al-Qaradawi and others talk and publish on all aspects of social relations – whilst carefully avoiding any direct reference to the regime or its rulers. Partly for that reason, they have been afforded officially sanctioned podiums, and have managed to reach larger and not consistently politicized audiences.

SHEIKH MUHAMMAD MITWALLI AL-SHA'RAWI

Sheikh Al-Sha'rawi is best known by almost all Egyptians for his elaborate and simplified interpretations of the Quran, which have been broadcast on prime-time national television and radio channels, for the past ten years or so. A graduate of Al-Azhar, Al-Sha'rawi has many years' experience in teaching the Quran in religious institutions in Egypt, Saudi Arabia and Algeria. Immensely popular mostly for his manner of explaining the intricacies of Quranic and general Islamic stipulations in a simple and interactive manner, Al-Sha'rawi is a formidable religious figure who appeals to Egyptians across the board. Why am I referring to him as an Islamist? The reason is that both implicit and explicit in Al-Sha'rawi's proselytization is a persistent and often veiled call for the Islamization of the state and society. This will become clearer in the following exposé of his ideas on women, which are from his book *Al-Mar'a al-Muslima* (The Muslim Woman).[3]

On Equality between the Sexes and Women's Non-Domestic Work

Al-Sha'rawi begins by stating that women and men are equal in their attempt to increase in piety and gain God's grace. His main point of departure however, is the near cliché that:

> man is characterized by decisiveness. And the meaning of decisiveness: that the capacity of reason is what controls his actions, and the capacity of emotion is almost non-existent. Woman will be exposed to situations which require emotion before reason, and man will be exposed to situations which require reason before emotion.
>
> (Al-Sha'rawi 1992: 73)

He elaborates on this point by giving an example – something which he is quite well known for as most of these examples tend to be somewhat crude but nevertheless realistic. In my opinion, this example is indicative not only of his views and attitudes, but also of the class he addresses and influences most. Al-Sha'rawi gives the example of a husband:

> The toiling man when he comes to rest at night, what would his position be if he hears his small child crying? He will then only see that his child is spoiling his sleep, and disturbing his rest. So he may let forth some curses on the child, and curse the mother of the child, and tell her: 'Shut this child up, because I want to rest'. *This is the logic of reason*, because he wants to wake up full of energy in order to carry out his job for the child and its mother. So the man wants to shut him up, but the woman takes the baby further away and

tries to calm it down, *this is the logic of emotion.*

(ibid.: 74; emphasis added)

Al-Sha'rawi shows here how he views the realm of rationality to be masculine and realm of emotion to be feminine. He also uses biological reductionism to state that God clearly outlined the differing functions of man and woman by the chemical differences that are supposed to exist in their cells. Woman's cells, allegedly, contain certain chemicals which 'give her softness, and give her tenderness', whereas in man, these cells contain chemicals which

> give him roughness, and give him perseverance for his mission, because this creature [man] is there for struggle and labour and defense and she is created to bear, to bear in her womb so she must be meticulous, giving, soft and supple and able to endure carrying for nine months, and then be tender to her newborn, all this requires the mission of emotion, tenderness more so than in man, so it should not be said that: women are better than men. It should also not be said that: man is better than her.

(ibid.: 24)

He then goes on to say that woman's occupation is tenderness. If she wants to work, he asserts, she can do so 'within the kingdom of her house: minister of health, minister of education, minister of finance, and a judge among her children' (ibid.: 76).

Some proponents of woman's work outside the home argue that women are 'forced' to do so in order to share the burden of expenses, and improve the family's standard of living. Al-Sha'rawi answers this by arguing that this is 'an alteration of one of Islam's issues', meaning that (in his interpretation) Islam declares that women are the responsibility of the men of the family. That is to say, a woman should be looked after by her father, her husband or her brother(s). In his opinion, only women who do not have a man to look after them, or if they do, but that man happens to be incapable/disabled, can consider working outside the home.

Moreover, he argues, it is the corrupt social mores of modern times that have made people reverse the normal equation, which is that incomes should dictate the standards of living, and not vice versa. This reversal, he claims, is responsible for many of the problems facing society today as increased expectations have led to people putting the cart before the horse. This in turn has led to many mistaken attitudes and increasing frustrations and reversals in the natural order of things. He furthers this critique of society (and implicitly of the state) by arguing that society should be responsible for alleviating the plight of such women instead of letting them be forced to leave their homes and go out to work. 'It is the responsibility of the society that if they see a woman who has been forced out into an arena [of work] to perform that job for her so she can return to her natural place' (ibid.: 78). Al-Sha'rawi goes on to say that a woman's venturing outside to work should therefore: (a) only be in cases of absolute need; and (b) even then, be temporary – she should go back to the home at the first opportunity; (c) close or distant society must take over the responsibility of providing for her; and (d) she should not forget that she is female, so that as she goes to work out of necessity, she must be suitably attired – so as not to arouse the 'natural desires' of men (ibid.: 81).

Al-Sha'rawi states that if people are unhappy with their situation and want a better standard of living, then the man should 'move in his life and pay the price' and go out himself to do more than one job, and thereby earn the extra income. 'Pickiness' or 'choosiness' as to the type of work they can do, according to Al-Sha'rawi, is irrelevant in this case. 'Why do you want her to do your work?', he asks of men,

> when there are things she cannot do in your line of work ... and if you want her to do your work, then I want you to do her work ... I want you to bear children ... and I want you to breastfeed instead of her ... So why do you want her in your field? ... So let us leave the woman to her kind, and let us leave the matter of her work to necessity.
>
> (ibid.: 84)

Moreover, a woman outside the home is a constant threat, Al-Sha'-rawi implies, to all other housewives. This is an argument to which he returns and which he also uses to justify the wearing of the veil, as we shall see. His argument goes along the following lines: a working woman is also one who will be seen on the street by men. These men have wives at home who have grown 'old and wrinkled from age and childbearing'. Seeing these young attractive women in their full bloom on the streets, he argues, makes them lust after them and become aware of their own wife's failings. This, in turn, will lead to the man unfairly picking on his wife and creating domestic dishar-mony and chaos. Not only husbands however, but young men of impressionable age and those who are frustrated because of the eco-nomic difficulties in the way of marriage will also 'find himself assailed by these fires in the street, so what can he do? So the woman [out on the street] will entice disruption' (ibid.: 82).

On the Veil (*Hijab*)

Al-Sha'rawi is adamant about the need for *all* Muslim women to wear the veil. He advocates that *if* women are to leave the confines of their home, they are to do so only with a veil. His arguments for it are couched in terms of the veil as a means of ensuring security for a woman, as well as a source of respect for her:

> Suppose a man is married to a woman, has lived with her for a long time, until her beauty has withered, till she has become undesirable, neither beautiful nor attractive ... If her husband only sees *her* every day, she would not change in his eyes, so that the change was stolen from the husband because it [change] does not come suddenly but it comes creeping. As you would see your son when he is born, and then seeing him continuously, so he never grows in your eyes ... So if [the husband] goes out to the street and sees a beautiful unveiled girl in the prime of her youth, at her best, uncovered, made up, what would his position be? He will begin comparing, and when he compares he will find a woman in her youth, and the other [the wife] in her worst years. His equilibrium will be shaken, and thus occurs all the disruption within homes.
>
> (ibid.: 87–8)

To illustrate his point further about men noticing (or not) the ageing of their wives, Al-Sha'rawi gives an example of an apartment, by likening the experience of living in an apartment for a long time (and thereby not noticing that it looks the worse for wear) to living with the wife. That is, only if the man leaves the apartment and sees a newer one, will he notice that his own is in a poor state of repair. By such a comparison, Al-Sha'rawi makes sure that his point is understood by everyone. But his point has several important implications: men own their apartments – they also own their wives. Moreover, apartments can and are changed; is he implying the legitimacy of changing wives? An apartment is lived in, one does not respect an apartment for it is not seen as a subject, but more as an object. In short, the metaphor of the apartment is loaded with connotations.

   The justification, then, as Al-Sha'rawi claims, is that by veiling themselves (in their youth) women are supposedly protecting themselves (and by implication other women) from broken marriages, and (hopefully) hiding from their husbands the ravages of time. Hence, women are the means of future security and continuing respect. No mention is made, however, of the remotest possibility that these same women may find their own old husbands repulsive. After all, since the criteria are looks, then men are not meant to be beautiful or attractive. One cannot help but wonder exactly which of the sexes Al-Sha'rawi is denigrating.

After justifying the veil in that manner, Al-Sha'rawi elaborates on the religious symbolism of it. The veil is not only (according to his interpretation) commanded by God and therefore an imperative for all Muslim women, but it also denotes the 'true' and 'original' sign of faith. As an example he mentions the wives of the Prophet in support of his argument.

Al-Sha'rawi delineates what he perceives as the requirements of a veil. By citing passages from the Quran and a variety of *Hadiths* (Prophet's sayings), he concludes that women are to show their faces and hands only; they are not to dress in an elegant or attractive manner; their dress must not show the contours of their body; they must not wear any perfume; they must not resemble men in their dress; and theirs must not resemble the dress of the non-believers.

On Women's Right to Divorce

Not surprisingly, Al-Sha'rawi does not actually allude to women's right to ask for a divorce, but rather to the fact that men's right to divorce is actually a blessing in disguise for women. His is an attempt to justify and explain the benefits of that right being firmly in the hands of men:

> When it comes to divorce for men, there is the fear that we will tell him to explain the reasons for the divorce and so he does, then these might form a constraint if the wife wants to find another husband, or if the husband wants to find another wife.

(ibid.: 60)

In other words, men can be counted upon to be discreet and therefore not spoil the chances for either to resume life with another partner. This is therefore supposed to justify why men have the right to divorce and can do so simply by pronouncing a phrase – presumably in the presence of witnesses.

Al-Sha'rawi goes on to say that the 'enemies of Islam' take up this divorce issue out of their own frustrations with broken families and disloyal husbands who are stuck with and unable to divorce the wives they dislike because of religious decrees (ibid.: 58). The stated implication is that in comparison with other societies and religions the Islamic divorce proceedings (if rightly followed) are merciful and less painful to both partners. Further, Al-Sha'rawi argues that the high number of divorce cases[4] which are stuck in the courts for years is not so much a condemnation of the divorce process *per se*, but of the marriage process. The latter is due to a lack of implementing the proper Islamic standards of (the couple's) meeting. If the whole procedure of marriage, Al-Sha'rawi maintains, were to be done in the proper Islamic way, divorce would not be a problem for the courts in the first place, especially since Islam contains advice in cases of trouble between married couples.[5] Nowhere in his explanation does Al-Sha'rawi allude to the fact that, in practice, much of the spirit of this policy of mercy is completely thwarted and misused by men. Consequently, no mention is made of the options that should be open to women. But then Al-Sha'rawi is unlikely to consider that women should have an independent say in any matter.

On Female Circumcision

Because of his immense popularity and influence, Al-Sha'rawi was one of those whose opinion was sought to clarify and settle the heated controversy that followed the debates in the ICPD.

Al-Sha'rawi was, and is, not surprisingly, unwilling to condemn the custom in any way. His contribution revolved around refuting the terminology and again declaring that the practice is essentially meant to give respect to women. According to Al-Sha'rawi, the term 'circumcision' should only be used in reference to males. What should take place for females is an operation which he refers to as *khafd* or reduction. The condition for carrying out this operation is that the clitoris is

> longer than the edges so only the excess is cut off because its extension makes it susceptible to rubbing on the clothes, so the female remains susceptible to excitement and throws herself on males, which eliminates [their] respect for her.[6]

Al-Sha'rawi does speak out against the more extreme forms of circumcision claiming that these tend to affect couple's sexual lives.

According to Al-Sha'rawi, extreme forms of circumcision were for-
bidden by the prophet

> because it reduces [the woman's] sexual appetite compared to that
> of her husband so he develops a complex, and it may be that this
> would be a reason for her to hate her life with that man except that
> out of shame she would not say so, so then she has to ask for a
> divorce for another reason!! [sic]
>
> (ibid.)

In short, Al-Sha'rawi seems to be saying, more extreme forms of
circumcision lead only to more headache and suffering for the *men*,
whereas what he calls *khafd* is a source of respect and guarantor of
pride for *women*.

On Feminism

Feminism is not recognized by Al-Sha'rawi (and for that matter all the
other Islamists and conservative Muslim scholars) as a theory or a
school of thought. In fact, there was no Arabic word for 'feminism'
until relatively recently. The word currently being used is *niswi* or
nisa'i – both of which mean 'related to woman'. Feminism is viewed
as part-and-parcel of a Western, and therefore inherently antagonistic,
ideology and set of norms and values, which are intent on destroying
everything good and Islamic. Thus, feminism and any of its calls on
the equality of the sexes, women's rights, and so on are in fact part of
the discourse of 'the enemies of Islam'. The latter are referred to quite
frequently in any countering Islamist discourse. It is always 'the
enemies of Islam' who are not only discrediting Islam in
general, but, as another male Islamist puts it, using women's issues
as the avenue through which they attack Islamic heritage and
culture.[7]

The 'enemies of Islam' are, according to Al-Sha'rawi and others,
'the Orientalists and the non-believers', who bring in harmful ideas
which are non-Islamic and, in fact, Christian (ibid.: 16). But worse, we
are warned – and here is where the relevance to local secular feminist
initiatives comes in – are the 'Occidentalists'[8] who are Muslims themselves, but have been brainwashed into transferring poisonous ideas
into their own societies under the guise of modernizing them (ibid.). In
sum, feminists are to be considered those brainwashed Occidentalist
enemies of Islam.

SHEIKH MUHAMMAD AL-GHAZALI

Al-Ghazali, one of the ambiguous mouthpieces of establishment Islam, was previously known and respected as a 'moderate', if not progressive, religious scholar, whose views were in no way radically opposed to the existing regime, and who proposed no overhaul of societal values, but general, overall Islamic guidance. This image, however, was rather crudely shattered when he testified, in the capacity of an Islamic scholar and expert, in favour of legitimizing the killing of apostates (*murtadd*) *especially when the state fails to deal appropriately with this renegade itself.*[9] This occurred after a spate of attacks on certain state figures (among whom were the Prime Minister, Speaker of Parliament, and the Minister of Interior), and especially in the case of Cairo University's Nasr Abu Zaid,[10] who was declared an apostate because of his writings. Al-Ghazali's position in this matter, apart from coming as a shock to many Egyptian intellectuals, also set him apart from other conservative Muslim scholars and highlighted his opposition to existing aspects of state and society.

Al-Ghazali's ideas on women were expressed in his book *Qadaya al-Mar'a Bayn al-Taqalid al-Rakida wa al-Wafida* (The Woman's Issues: Between Stagnating and Imported Traditions). As far as Al-Ghazali is concerned, the women's issue is a marginal one which is being (mis)-used by two camps – both of which are threatening Islam and Islamic society. These two camps are the Westerners/Orientalists *and* the extremists within Islam itself. As to the latter, Al-Ghazali says,

> A pessimistic evil is attacking Islam due to the seclusion of some of its followers within certain jurisprudential ideas (*Ara' Fiqhiyya*) ... and attempting to present them as the core of the belief [Islam] and its great values. The man who loses the whole market because he prefers one shop to another or one agent to another is not called a trader.
>
> (Al-Ghazali 1990: 29)

On Veiling, Equality and Women in the Labour Market

It is a woman's right to have a beautiful appearance, after she is perfect of mind and decent of character. Does the Indian Sari which exposes a part of the belly and back afford this beauty? Does the European dress that shows the lower thighs, and lifts – upon sitting down – to the upper thighs, afford this beauty? The truth must be said that those who make such clothes do not bestow on the woman her pride, nor do they wish her dignity, but they inflame evil instincts against her.

(Al-Ghazali 1990: 193)

Al-Ghazali's main point does not differ much from Al-Sha'rawi in that he believes in the necessity of wearing the veil. Though sharing Al-Sha'rawi's reasoning that the veil provides women with dignity and maintains their pride, Al-Ghazali differs significantly in his approach to justifying veiling. Whereas Al-Sha'rawi was advocating that women should not go out of their homes at all (and if they do the veil serves to protect the men on the streets), Al-Ghazali urges that women should impress society – men and women alike – with their cultural talents and 'beneficial' qualities instead. This is an interesting point since the issue of women's (veiled) appearance in public is significant not only because of the symbolism implied therewith, but also because of its implicit acceptance of women's presence in the public sphere in general.

Al-Ghazali objects to modern European clothes and 'non-Islamic clothes' in general, because they are supposedly focusing men's and society's attention on women's bodies, and thereby detracting from women's dignity. He emphasizes his point by saying that 'women have a right to make themselves beautiful (*tatajammal*), but not to display their charms (*tatabarraj*)' (ibid.: 193). Moreover, he claims that modern culture is responsible for this 'demeaning', as well as being accountable for the religiously unacceptable situation where women dress in 'men's clothes'. The latter case, in his opinion, renders it difficult to distinguish between the two sexes. He further claims that 'great women are innocent from these sick happenings' and cites Margaret Thatcher, former Prime Minister of the United Kingdom, as one such highly regarded, decently dressed woman.

Apart from the doubtful wisdom – as far as political tendencies go – of his choice of Margaret Thatcher, it remains very telling that he cites her at all. Not only a very public figure, but a *leader* of a nation, Al-Ghazali is openly yet conditionally emphasizing the legitimacy of such public roles for women. He stresses his qualification by stating that

The attempts to eliminate natural differences between the sexes is a form of absurdity, and the difference that is impossible to erase is the intellectual capacity and what the human personality can claim in terms of values and abilities, and in these fields women may excel and men may excel...and cloth has no bearing on this excellence.

(ibid.: 194)

This eloquent treatise on equality of the sexes is placed within the context of the Quran, and it is repeatedly emphasized that women and men are equal in the eyes of God in so far as their faith goes. Also within the Quran lies the claim that men have a certain 'supervisory' role over women. This supervision, Al-Ghazali immediately expounds, is not a negation of the equality, but merely corresponds to the greater responsibilities that men have. Significantly, Al-Ghazali likens the sort of custodianship men have over women to that of government over society/people. Neither signifies a denial of some status of equality between ruler and ruled, and therefore should not be taken as an excuse for oppression and humiliation (ibid.: 36). This is highly suggestive because apart from inadvertently indicating that the relationship between men and women implies a hierarchy of sorts, his intentional reference to the state not so subtly conveys a broader and more political message: that the subjecthood of citizens to the state should not justify the latter's oppression of its people.

This supervisory role highlights men's responsibility and sacrifice. In Al-Ghazali's opinion, the problem in Islamic societies is that ignorance has dominated men *and* women, and that the relationship between the two sexes has been looked at only from the point of view of desire. This at the expense of realizing that the relationship between men and women (in a marriage) is meant to be one of partnership and sharing. He then laments that '[this] great message of the *umma* [nation] in the world is unknown to either fathers or mothers' (ibid.: 37). In fact, he argues that women's issues

are surrounded by mental, moral, social and economic crisis, so that the situation calls for the intelligent revision of certain verses, and of inherited religious opinions (*fatawi*), and bad traditions which leave their imprint on people's actions.

(ibid.: 177)

The former is a progressive argument in itself, though the specific forms of 'bad traditions' are not elaborated upon. Al-Ghazali does show his true colours by arguing that certain jobs are better for women than others, for where occupations are concerned, he rejects equality of the sexes. In his opinion, 'it is not fitting for women that they work in areas which do not complement their nature' (ibid.: 39). He then elaborates on what he means. He argues, for example, that policewomen may check other women, but to work as traffic wardens is unacceptable, because that is too strenuous; men are more capable as pilots, whilst the job of air hostess for women should be scrapped – at least for flights that entail overnight stays in hotels and staying away from the family; whilst peasant women may sow seed, but should not be exposed to more vigorous labour.

Moreover, women's job options – not to mention their mobility – are further limited by Al-Ghazali when he states that women should not travel unaccompanied.[11] Referring to the loose morals of European culture, Al-Ghazali emphasized that as long as these existed and Islamic society was weak against it, no security would prevail. It follows, according to his logic, that women travelling alone will always risk falling prey to all sorts of evil.

As far as military professions for women are concerned, Al-Ghazali cites the (by now) expected specializations:

> It is possible for women believers to have an honourable presence in the field of Islamic *jihad* the essence of which is the treatment of the sick, preparation of medicines, transport of the injured, preparation of food and drink, writing letters, and carrying out some managerial duties.
>
> (ibid.: 170)

After citing some textual backing for these kinds of occupations, Al-Ghazali then criticizes those who 'go crazy' when they hear that women have any role at all to play in war times. Al-Ghazali stresses his belief that war is being waged against Islam on its own terrain, and from all quarters. This state of war then, not only justifies, but in fact renders necessary women's participation. Ironically, Al-Ghazali elsewhere mourns the fact that 'the feminine characteristics of softness and delicacy are almost disappearing due to the harshness of the jobs assigned to female labourers' (ibid.: 38).

It is difficult to see how he can reconcile these two points, unless women's participation in the state of war is meant to enhance their 'delicate' qualities.

On Divorce Rights

Al-Ghazali goes to great length to explain the religious procedures of divorce and the rationale behind them. His aim is to clarify that divorce, if properly understood and placed in the right context – neither of which currently occurs according to him – is not meant to be an injustice. Al-Ghazali again criticizes 'narrowminded' and 'unjustified' interpretations which lead to broken homes and shattered families. He emphasizes that mercy and goodwill towards their wives should dominate men's decisions and actions when divorcing them. He implicitly advocates that women should not be mistreated in any way by their husbands, but then hastens to say that this 'kindness' should not, in turn, be misused by women themselves. All in all, the emphasis is on trying to make men more tolerant towards women. No mention is made of the God-given licence for women to share in the right to divorce (i.e. *'isma*), so that, despite devoting over 15 pages to the issue of divorce, women's right to divorce is at best taboo and at worst non-existent.

On Female Circumcision

Al-Ghazali's opinion on this subject remains unknown since he maintains an ambiguous position. Neither outrightly condemning, nor openly condoning, Al-Ghazali seems to share Al-Sha'rawi's view. In other words, tacitly admitting the existence of the practice before the advent of Islam, whilst at the same time claiming that the prophet's *Sunna* indicates a toning down of the process with the gradual intention of eliminating it. Al-Ghazali gives the example of slavery which was also gradually abolished from Islamic societies. Yet nowhere is female circumcision as heavily criticized as other practices, which are harmful to females and which Islam supposedly clearly abolished.[12] The ambiguity is such that one is left wondering whether Al-Ghazali, were he to have daughters, would have them circumcised.

On Feminism

Feminism is assumed to be part of European and American society in which licentiousness and corrupt morals are rampant. When an Egyptian man is about to more there, he is advised by Al-Ghazali to marry an Egyptian woman before he leaves. This, Al-Ghazali argues, is to prevent the man from being dominated by the stronger yet immoral Western woman, who will bring his children up as atheists. Western woman's influence is such that Egyptian men are warned that instead of him prevailing (which would be the 'normal' course of events if he were to marry a good Muslim woman), *she* will guide *him* away from God's true ways. The latter, of course, is the sure path to calamity, as that is how the man ends up losing everything.

The dominance of Western women is possible since, as Muslims, men are already mistakenly suffering from a sense of 'inferiority' vis-à-vis the West. This point is made lest the reader erroneously assume that even in the evil West women could be unconditionally powerful. But it has to be said that Al-Ghazali is as critical of the West and Western ideas (and by implication feminism) as he is of the 'fools' who have undermined Islam by their narrow and baseless interpretations. Both are tarnishing the image of Islam, misunderstanding it and ultimately waging war against it. But when it comes to Western ideas and feminists, the approach Al-Ghazali seems to advocate is to beware and ignore them, whereas in the case of radical and limiting interpretations from within (so to speak), some form of discussion is preferred.

Al-Ghazali's rather contradictory approach to women's issues belies the familiar tone of patriarchy and patrony that many women followers nevertheless do not question. Couched in apparently elevating and 'progressive' language, Al-Ghazali's message on these issues is essentially no different from Al-Sha'rawi's. In fact, similar textual references are quoted in both men's work, and to the same end. Al-Sha'rawi, however, is more crude and blunt in his ideas, whereas Al-Ghazali is subtle and succeeds in sounding more condescending.

YUSUF AL-QARADAWI

Not unlike the others, Dr Yusuf Al-Qaradawi (1991) also starts his book *Fatawi Mu'asira lil Mar'a wal 'Usra al-Muslima* (Recent Fatwas for the Muslim Woman and Family) from the premiss that Islam has been misrepresented and little understood. In his book dealing with women's issues, Al-Qaradawi is basically answering questions from and about women all over the Arab Muslim world. It is noticeable, however, that in comparison with the others, his manner of dealing with the issues involves more Quranic and *Hadith* quotations and justifications. Al-Qaradawi's answers to the diverse questions reflect a conservative approach rather than a dynamic one. His manner is altogether less innovative.

In his first chapter, in answer to a question on whether women are all evil, Al-Qaradawi seems to refute this by referring to Quranic verses and *Hadiths*. However, he does point out that women are considered (like children and wealth) to be a source of *'fitna'* (temptation which leads to turmoil), since they are more wily than men. This age we live in, Al-Qaradawi argues, epitomizes the height of women's *fitna*. The 'destroyers', he warns, use women to undermine inherited values and customs in the name of development and modernization. What is interesting here is not so much the message itself – which is old news by now – but that Al-Qaradawi, unlike the previous sheikhs, directs his warnings (and call to arms) to Muslim *women*:

> It is a Muslim woman's duty to be aware of these conspiracies, and to prevent herself from being used as a tool for destruction in the hands of the inimical powers to Islam, and to return to what the women of the *umma* were doing during its (the *umma*'s) best centuries: the well-behaved girl, the decent wife, the good mother, and the generous person who works for the betterment of her religion and *Umma*.
>
> (Al-Qaradawi 1991: 11)

On Equality of the Sexes and Women's Non-Domestic Work

> Woman's servicing of her husband is kindness as God ordained it . . . As for the entertainment of women by the man carrying out household duties – sweeping, mixing, cooking, washing . . . etc. – this is not kindness. Especially since the man works and toils outside the house. It is therefore just that the woman works inside it.
>
> (ibid.: 63)

Unlike Al-Sha'rawi and Al-Ghazali, Al-Qaradawi has no explicit opinion on women working outside the house. It is likely that no one would ask his opinion on that matter anyway, since it is understood from his other advice that women should work in the home only. This implication is to be seen not only from the above quote, but also from most of what Al-Qaradawi has to say about women's rights vis-à-vis men or their husbands.

As Al-Qaradawi puts it, 'every right [of women] is met with duties' (ibid.). Women's rights, according to Al-Qaradawi, are summarized in expenses, clothing, accommodation, as well as her dowry money (which she gets before marriage). That is not to say that Al-Qaradawi does not respond to the woman's plea for some purely emotional sustenance from her husband. In fact, Al-Qaradawi argues strongly in favour of men being emotionally considerate, gentle and compassionate with their 'dutiful' wives. In return for these rights come women's duties and responsibilities towards their husbands.

In that respect, Al-Qaradawi goes one step further than his colleagues, by addressing the issue of sexual relations between husband and wife, fully and explicitly. He assumes that men's passions and sexual urges are greater than those of women; hence the need for women to comply with men's demands as part of their duties. However, he does stress and variously justify the importance of women also being sexually gratified.

In his justification of women's domestic work, Al-Qaradawi cites examples of famous women who lived during the time of the Prophet. These women were allegedly engaged in a variety of domestic tasks, including grooming and cleaning their husbands' horses, carrying heavy containers of water on their heads over long distances, and so on. Al-Qaradawi argues that though this very difficult work was done before the eyes of the Prophet, he never spoke against it. Hence the implication, Al-Qaradawi asserts, that this is natural and expected of women. Al-Qaradawi's arguments on women's rights and duties vis-à-vis men can be summarized in the following quote:

> This issue actually resolves itself, since the real Muslim woman serves her husband and her home out of natural disposition or instinct, and as part of the traditions that the Muslim society has inherited generation after generation. And the renegade and violent woman does not look to the opinion of religion, and does not care for the sayings of the teachers to her or about her.
>
> (ibid.: 64)

Al-Qaradawi's extrapolations make it clear that women have certain roles inside the home, while men's spheres are outside. This is not because of circumstances, but is as a matter of the rights and responsibilities of each sex towards the other. Nowhere does he explicitly refer to women who work – either out of choice or necessity – outside the domestic sphere. It is to be inferred that this situation would be abnormal, or at least, occur only under extenuating circumstances.

Like the others though, Al-Qaradawi postulates that in times of war women do have a public role to play. This roles is, in effect, an extension of the domestic tasks of cleaning, tending the sick, and the like. At any rate, if Al-Qaradawi could justify hard domestic duties carried out centuries ago, one would not like to think what he would sanction for women today with all the 'pampering' domestic appliances now available. On the other hand, perhaps precisely because domesticity is relatively easier today, and in the name of hard work, one might suggest – with obvious sarcasm, but nevertheless based on his logic – that he would urge women to enter the world and toil away.

On Veiling

> It is not permissible for women to show their beauty to strangers, except that which is apparent, and what is apparent are the face and hands. This is the most reasonable, simple, and suitable saying for the nature of our times. As for women going out in the manner we see in some capitals and some countries, that is something which cannot be sanctified by religion, or manners, or logic.
>
> (ibid.: 23–4)

Al-Qaradawi does not dispute or in any way question the necessity of donning a veil for any Muslim woman. On the contrary he documents all the traditional references which allegedly justify it. The only issue of contention however, according to him, is whether the veil should cover the face (thus be referred to as a *niqab*) and hands or not. He is in favour of a veil that does *not* cover the face and hands. In his opinion, people who veil women – as in keeping them behind closed doors – have understandable justifications, but it remains a non-Islamic custom.

Al-Qaradawi expresses surprise that people should even question whether short dresses for women are Islamic. The answer is self-evident in his opinion. In fact, he expresses disappointment and heavy sarcasm by claiming that cats, and other animals, do not question their instincts, whereas Muslims seem to have lost touch with [these] basics.

Al-Qaradawi's criteria for 'the Islamic dress' are identical to those of Al-Sha'rawi. Al-Qaradawi believes that alterations in dress such as one sees in fashion nowadays, are not only almost heretical, but catastrophic. This catastrophe, as he sees it, is that fashion indicates loose morals, which in turn point to the inability of men to control their women. This weakness of men is a sign of the weakness of religion itself, a terrible situation which Al-Qaradawi valiantly decries. He issues an impassioned appeal for men to regain their masculinity and impose their will over women – if not for the sake of religion, then for the sake of their manhood (ibid.: 26).

It is clear from Al-Qaradawi's appeal, then, that manhood and religion are one and the same. Anything that indicates women's choice would also indicate loss of manhood. It would seem in this discourse that faith and masculinity are both threatened by women's rights to independence, and that liberation or freedom for women is permissible only so long as it enhances the religion–manhood pairing. This dichotomy of thought has been implicit in much of what was said earlier, but Al-Qaradawi must be given the credit for decrying it so openly and without any attempt at disguising it.

On Women's Right to Divorce

Al-Qaradawi does not disagree with Al-Sha'rawi and Al-Ghazali. The right to divorce is *par excellence* man's. Women are made to be the sponge for men's anger. In all the references to divorce that Al-Qaradawi mentions, he is dealing with various situations in which it is the men who have divorced their wives. In most of the cases cited in the book, husbands are writing to ask his opinion on the implications of uttering the divorce statement in anger (i.e. 'I divorce thee thrice').[13] Al-Qaradawi obligingly cites religious sources which would nullify a divorce uttered in anger. Nowhere is any consideration given to the fact that the divorced wives have themselves any right to resent this treatment and the whole seemingly simple divorce process. Even less consideration is given to the rights of an angry wife to be divorced. The implication is that anger is forgivable in men, but simply a matter of emotional disposition in women, which can be overlooked. If Al-Qaradawi regards women's choice of dress to be effacing to masculinity, it follows that the right to divorce need not even be considered. For divorce must be more serious than dress, and women are presumed to have no choice in either.

On Female Circumcision

Al-Qaradawi does not 'waste time' dwelling on this issue. His opinion is brief (half a page) and to the point: he recommends what is now commonly referred to as 'light circumcision' for girls. Though acknowledging that there is much disagreement on the issue on the part of both doctors and Islamic scholars and countries alike, Al-Qaradawi says:

> For those of you who find it safer for your daughters go ahead [and do it], I support that, especially during our modern times, and those

who leave it have no obligation, because it is not more than nobility
for women.

(ibid.: 29)

One does not know whether to be insulted or relieved by Al-Qaradawi's by now not surprising attitude. Though he openly recommends
it, his justification for not having to do it is equally insulting: it is
'*only*' a matter of enhancing women's nobleness – i.e. no great loss if
missed.

Having surveyed Al-Qaradawi's opinions on these different issues,
one can imagine that his opinions on feminism, which he does not
refer to explicitly, would not differ from those of his contemporaries.
Though Al-Qaradawi himself does not explicitly say anything about
feminism and Westernism *per se*, his publisher could not resist the
opportunity to do so himself. Consequently he (who is nameless, but
signs as 'the publisher' to the introduction to the book) refers to those
who call for women's liberation as *shayatin al-ins* (human devils) who

> push for vice and present it to women as though it were advance-
> ment and liberation, cloaking [woman's] rebellion against her
> instincts as if this was equality which will liberate her from man's
> control and oppression!

(ibid.: 6)

But what should be voiced is that despite these and his own opinions,
Al-Qaradawi is highly respected and much cited by many Islamist
women activists. Whether this influence comes with his other political
ideas and standpoints, or because of an ignorance of his comprehensive views on women's issues, is debatable. What is certain is that many
of the women interviewed who cited him were very active in the public
arena, as we shall see in the next chapter.

'ADIL HUSAYN

As a writer and member of the Islamist-oriented Labour Party
Husayn is an interesting example of a leftist-turned-Islamist intellectual. Moreover, he is to be distinguished from the above-mentioned
Islamists by his open espousal and defence of political Islam and his
appeal to the younger generation of intellectual Islamist leaders. As
such, his choice as a representative of Islamist thought here is
arguably the least controversial. Not a graduate of Al-Azhar,

Husayn's initial academic training was in the relatively secular Cairo University. His political participation began during his university years. Husayn's shift from politics of the left to those of the right is not unique, but one of many such political switches. Evidence of his earlier political tendencies (or declarations) are still traceable in his argumentation. Though Husayn, in an elaborate article on '*Al-Mar'a al-'Arabiya: Nadhra Mustaqbaliyya*' (The Arab Woman: A Futuristic Outlook)[14] does not mention female circumcision or women's divorce rights, he does present an intriguing exegesis about the other topics of equality, women's work and dress (Husayn 1993: 5–28). His writings are interesting because they are one of the most lucid and sophisticated elaborations of a particular Islamist stance on women.

Husayn sets out three main principles which, according to him, govern the general Islamic view on women. The first is an admission of the biological and emotional differences between the sexes. This in turn has important social consequences, exemplified by a division of labour between men and women. The second principle is, as he puts it, 'the admission of the total *humanity* of woman and her right to independent action to seek fortune with man in this life and the hereafter' (ibid.: 9; emphasis added). The third principle – and the most crucial to his ideas on equality – is that of *qawâma* (or men's leadership of women). He hastens to qualify what he means by this (referring all the time to the various relevant verses of the Quran). Husayn argues that

> *qawâma* definitely does not mean that women should be excluded from participation in all matters, and at different levels. Nor is there a meaning to an understanding that the difference between [the] two roles gives man twice as much as woman in society as based on the rules of inheritance or testimony.[15] The rules of inheritance do not reflect the basis of appreciation and respect (*fadl*), just as those of testimony do not reflect an evaluation of woman's actual capacities... But the issues are determined according to constructed and interrelated social-economic considerations, and I believe that [these rules] are not understood correctly... outside that context... the role of a particular woman in society is to be determined... by the fact that she is a woman from a particular class etc.... and from a certain section within that class.
>
> (ibid.: 10–11)

On Equality between the Sexes

Husayn argues that, historically speaking, change has been occurring in almost every section of the globe. Yet he maintains the one thing that does not change is the specific division of labour between the sexes. 'The world of civilization deduces from this that the consistent division is a norm, which must have a rationale for its repetition' (ibid.: 14), Husayn asserts. In fact, he critiques feminists indirectly here, by saying that those who explain the repetition as merely a fatal curse or ideological idiocy are people who refuse to acknowledge the practical mechanisms of civilization. He further argues that

> modern historical experience has proved once again that the distinction between humans is based on pragmatic reasons, and hence its regulation is possible but its abolition is impossible... The calls for equality between male and female are considered a grave mistake. We notice it in the animal kingdom as a whole, and it is a natural issue and has no relation to culture or ideological upbringing.
>
> (ibid.: 14–15)

Not only that, but Husayn argues that by accepting the distinctions, the necessary division of roles is also accepted. To argue for equality, he contends, is actually 'the essence of injustice', and can only be sustained for short periods with all forms of oppression (ibid.). Instead he argues that

> In an ideal social organization the equality would not mean equivalence in individual roles, or equality in their [man and woman's] material and emotional share, but it means that every individual enjoys equal opportunities to develop the God-created assets, without obstructions or biases imposed by society's conditions to strangle the assets of the weak. Justice means that the role of the individual is determined according to the owned capacities and not because these limits are the maximum others determine.
>
> (ibid.: 15)

This is a reference to how Husayn perceives that (Western) feminism imposes roles on women which are unsuitable. Though he does not mention feminism by name, his reference is to 'the Other', which in Islamist discourse *is* the essentialized West. And ideals of equality between the sexes, which he is openly attacking, have not exactly been proposed by colonial powers *per se*, but by what is regarded as

Western feminist discourse. Further, his outright condemnation of equality – because it is (a) forced and (b) unjust – is reminiscent of binary Islamist discourse on imposed and inauthentic ideas.

Husayn argues for using a 'middle paradigm, or a paradigm of conjunctions' based on his proclamations that Islam neither calls for total equality nor total difference between man and woman, 'but its [Islam's] vision is intermediate or connected containing an admission of the facets of complementarity and facets of difference' (ibid.: 8). Husayn also refers to a middle paradigm, in order to distinguish between main issues and auxiliary or secondary ones in Islam. Interestingly, he cites dress as one of these secondary issues. Here, he differs markedly from his colleagues, who insist that veiling, and women's dress in general, is central to any discourse on women and Islam, and take veiling as an undisputable given.

On Veiling

> In my opinion the suitable dress for a woman [need be] in accordance with the main principles mentioned ... (especially the first and second), so it must be that which reflects the difference between man and woman and guarantees the persistence of a [decent] relationship between them (*al-ihtisham*), and it must also facilitate the movement necessary for the social duties which Islam put forth, in addition to consideration of the climate (degree of heat and humidity – the nature of the work ... etc.)
>
> (ibid.: 12)

Husayn's formulations are either deliberately ambiguous or simply confusing. For what reflects the difference between men and women? The traditional Islamic dress for men – which many young and old men occasionally don – is a *jallabiyya*, or long tunic. Can it be argued then, that women should not wear dresses or *jallabiyyas* themselves? Moreover, what should a dress 'in accordance with woman's basic humanity' and 'psychological and biological difference to man' look like? Instead of clarifying what he means, Husayn goes on to criticize the big fuss made about dress:

> It is amazing that the fanatics of the issue of dress and its description, end up by negating all that Islam in its origin has given women, so that her style of life will complement her dress description as if this were to be the basis of the basics! ... even though the correct logic contradicts what they arrived at, that is to develop the

dress in the manner which suits woman's performance of her social functions.

(ibid.: 12)

On the face of it, it could be argued that Husayn is contradicting himself. For on the one hand, he argues for *ihtisham* (modesty), whilst on the other hand, he criticizes those who are arguing for the same thing though more elaborately. Yet it is precisely his ambiguity that renders it difficult to determine whether he has said anything he can contradict.

In order to determine the 'social functions' that Husayn talks of, let us review his ideas on women's work.

On Women and Work

Husayn places his arguments on women and work within an elaborate ideal of alternative development. He argues that the kinds of socio-economic development imposed on the Muslim world have created relations of dependency. This form of development, Husayn contends, erroneously called for all available human power to participate in the public sphere, in order to cope with the fast-changing and uncontrolled socio-economic dynamics. An example of this is the distressing emergence of the nuclear family and the emotional and social instability that this apparently leads to. These dynamics also entailed the call for all men and women to enter the public arena in order to participate in the expanding government structures. 'As if', Husayn remarks,

> creating the illusion that women were not already working when they were inside their homes... as though women's traditional roles represented hidden unemployment... so if for the sake of argument this untrue assumption is accepted, then the women were being asked to enter public structures when there was a lack of productive work opportunities, which meant congesting the management and service sectors, without real need for their efforts. Hence the hidden unemployment in the homes (assuming it is such) has been transformed into hidden unemployment outside the home.

(ibid.: 20)

What he calls for and deems necessary is 'independent Arab Islamic development which is reconciled to its history' (ibid.). What this means, basically, is a development that responds to the two most important problems facing the Muslim world: enlarging the capacities of available human resources and creating the opportunities for these resources to thrive, and facing the external enemies. This would entail, according to Husayn, *increasing* the birthrate to populate the under-populated areas. Presumably, this would simultaneously increase the area of potential growth, whilst securing the 'endangered lands on the borders of enemies' (i.e. Israel):

> In this case ... such a plan would ... view the situation of woman's work outside the home from that perspective. We can claim that the aim of the quick increase in the population in turn enforces the value of family stability, and the thematic importance of women's work inside the home.
>
> (ibid.: 24)

Husayn justifies this by arguing that day-care centres (which he stresses are rare – a reference to a government shortcoming) and schools are no compensation for a mother's care, especially during the first years of life. In an attempt to glorify the domestic role, Husayn declares:

> What I wish to ascertain is that what we are advocating for women here, is an invitation to a grand central developmental role, a factor of removing the thick clouds that surround the understanding of development.
>
> (ibid.: 26)

Husayn then adopts some aspects of feminist discourse (i.e. the oppression of women) to reach the main thrust of his argument to justify women's domestic roles. He contends that

> woman has suffered from long oppression, missed out culturally and has been tied to her home, so that practically all that Islam has ordained in terms of rights and principles has been taken from her.

Husayn points out (quite rightly) that women's going out to work in the name of equality, whilst at the same tune performing their child-bearing duties, has obviously not eliminated their oppression. He admits, however, that women have gained in self-confidence and independence. But the price for these was, he maintains, both person-ally and socially more 'dangerous'. Thus he advocates that

> woman maintains her present characteristics of self-confidence, and the benefits of social, cultural and political participation, without being forced to be sliced out of her house to work to obtain these

benefits. Because the work she performs in the home is equivalent to (if not more than) the work performed by any male or female labourer outside the home in terms of economic and social value. And in a society based on cash economies I do not see what prevents the local community or the state from *providing a regular exchange in cash to this woman in return for the roles she performs for her family and society, it being the case that hers is a situation like that of any other worker in other spheres.*

(ibid.: 27; emphasis added)

This is, in my opinion, a superb example of the problematic I referred to earlier, namely twisted logic. In this case, Husayn has used and twisted opposing logic – the patriarchal and the revolutionary – encased in a velvet cushion of Islam, to come up with a re-evaluated traditional role. In a sense, Husayn has retrieved (or recycled) his Marxist dialectics of positing a thesis (women's Islamic liberating work as part of development) to an antithesis (current development as oppressive to women) to form the synthesis (Islamic development which will liberate women by returning them to the home). But this synthesis has a postmodern twist. That is, there is a novelty to the traditional, there are multiple meanings to domesticity, motherhood and the home – not only the one interpretation. Put differently, women inside the home are not oppressed, but in fact, they are actively *countering* this oppression. The value of their social, economic and political roles is not less, but more and of deeper significance, than their public work.

CONCLUSION

Male Islamists employ a dichotomy in their argumentation. Rational/ emotional, wise/foolish, good/evil, strong/weak and natural/imposed where the former is associated with the male and the latter with the female. In itself this dichotomization is not new, as binary thought is an integral aspect of Islamist thought, itself based on us/them and good/bad distinctions. The Islamist regime of truth and disciplinary power is reflected here in the precise allocation of roles for men and women which all Islamists agree with, albeit formulated differently. There is almost no difference in these men's opinions on the roles that women are meant to occupy and the subservient nature that the emotional (woman) must cede to the rational (man). The discipline being referred to here is formulated precisely in the manner in which they impose their ideas – different men dictate the same ideas all the time. Though they attempt to phrase their ideas in a way that would seem as if women were being given positive status and recognition (with the exception of Al-Sha'rawi, who is cruder) the main gist of what they have to say is that women should not assume too much power – if any. The final word is the man's, and the 'public' domain remains male-dominated.

What is important to note is that the Islamist male standpoints herein portrayed differ little from those of other conservative male Muslim thinkers. Hence, my insistence on referring to the two men whose ideas fall within this grey area: Al-Sha'rawi and Al-Ghazali, both of whom are also adopted by state-run media as official Islam spokesmen. The reason this is significant has to do with the rationale I gave at the beginning of this chapter: there are certain similarities in the state's perception of gender and those of Islamists. I refer to this as the grey area, where Islamist male gender ideology meets with conservative male gender tenets. This is the arena where, in my opinion, feminists need to direct their resources, since it is also the area where struggles for ideological hegemony between Islamists and the state are least fierce, and hence most dangerous for feminists. For where the two regimes agree most, feminists lose most, since this actually means that feminists have to fight both regimes. This is a reality expressed by Muslim and secular feminists earlier on.

The two men most cited by men *and* women Islamists, Qutb and Al-Qaradawi, are those who also have the most conservative and narrow-minded attitudes when it comes to women's issues. It must be said though that they were cited not so much for their gender ideas, as for their vehement demands for an Islamic society and veiled demands for a just Islamic system. All the men cited are eloquent speakers who are convincing in argumentation and discussion. Together, they appeal to almost all strata of Egyptian society, from illiterates to intellectuals.

Nevertheless, this has been the most difficult chapter to write. Being a Muslim feminist, I found that the men Islamists have a logic that is difficult to agree with. There were many times when I felt a compelling urge to close their books and stop reading them – 'Adil Husayn being the notable exception thanks to the influence of his earlier political convictions. Reading the way they described women and hearing some of their sermons on television, I found what they had to say degrading, condescending and patriarchal. The only validity I claim in this text in particular is that of their own words as presented in their quotes, and that of my situatedness as a woman – presumably one of those they refer to. Doubtful validities they may be, but let me juxtapose them against the validities in the lives and words of the Islamist feminists, in the following pages.

8 Gender and Islamism: Three Generations of Women's Perspectives

Having surveyed the male perspectives, I shall focus here on those of the Islamist women activists. I first elaborate why I chose these specific women and then I present and analyse the works of the selected Islamist women activists starting with the eldest. The women chosen are *Zaynab Al-Ghazali, Safinaz Qazim* and *Heba Ra'uf*. This chapter does not attempt to map out all the intricacies and details of Islamist women's lives and work methods comprehensively. In fact, as in the previous chapters, it is the voices of some of these Islamist feminists that are chosen to highlight their viewpoints on certain issues, such as feminism or *Qadiyyat al-Mar'a* ('the woman's issue'), Islamisms and the state. As such, the chapter sketches continuities and changes in their ideas and actions, and highlights the characteristics and particularities of Islamist feminisms.

A notable difference between these women and their male counterparts (with the exception of Sayyid Qutb) is that the women surveyed here are activists in the real sense of the word. Whether it is Zaynab Al-Ghazali (born in 1917), Safinaz Qazim (born *c.*1939) or Heba Ra'uf (born *c.*1965), all three are politically active and have been so since their teens: joining demonstrations, giving talks, organizing protests and, above all, writing. These women are active in the field of women's issues – writing, advising, campaigning, ostensibly in the name of all Muslims, but also on specific issues related to women. Each of them has admitted to realizing that women are oppressed in today's world, and each of them, in her own way, combats this oppression in the name of a proper Islamic society and state. They are thus presented as Islamist feminists.[1]

I chose these three because each has a following among many of the women Islamists I interviewed. In the case of Zaynab Al-Ghazali,[2] her reputation as 'a soldier of God' is almost legendary not only among women, but also among men Islamists. These women each represents a different generation of Islamist women leaders. Qualities of assertiveness, eloquence and the ability to attract a following are attributed to them (sometimes in less kind terms) by both their Islamist followers as well as their feminist colleagues – both Muslims and secular.

Another reason I chose these women has to do with my personal interactions with many Islamist women, and with these especially. With the exception of Al-Ghazali whom I did not interview, because she was unavailable, the other two women, Qazim and Ra'uf, impressed me. I approached them warily, and mostly only in my capacity as a researcher. Unlike the secular and Muslim feminists, I did not feel comfortable to stress my identity as an activist at the start of our meetings. By our second meeting, however, I felt able to share that aspect of my person, whilst emphasizing that I was there to seek their knowledge and opinion on women's issues for my research.

Both Qazim and Ra'uf were generous with their time – Ra'uf somewhat less so as she was always on the move from one place to another. Tracking her down was often difficult, and she constantly obliged me by inviting me to come to her house. In fact, I met them both in their homes and felt at ease in middle-class surroundings which were very similar to those of my family home. Ra'uf made a point of being available to anyone who wished to speak to her, whereas Qazim, with many more years' experience and care behind her, was comparatively less so. Qazim first insisted on knowing where and why I was doing my research, and initially was very cautious about presenting me with her articles and works. This, she later explained to me, had to do with a few bitter experiences with plagiarism of her work. Later on, however, and after searching in vain for some of her out-of-print works and telling her this, she produced her copies and gave them to me.

Compared to other Islamist women I met, Qazim and Ra'uf were most eloquent as to their beliefs and the reasons behind their activism. I am not able to give voice to all those I met, so I chose the ones that I felt were most concerned with the socio-political consequences of their gender identity, and could elaborate their ideas on who they were and why they were doing their work. I was given many a story that echoed the argumentation in some of the books I surveyed in the previous chapter. But I was seeking then, and am attempting now, to present the voices of the *feminists* among these women. I sought those who (a) were aware and consistently tackling specific issues relating to women; (b) could elaborate on their innovative reasons for joining Islamist movements and believing in Islamism; and (c) whose insights were novel and yet could be seen on a continuum.

Zaynab Al-Ghazali set up her own Muslim Women's Association at the age of 18, in 1936. The MWA had to contend with continuous harassment and eventually banning by the Nasser regime. Al-Ghazali herself was imprisoned and tortured. Representing the next generation of Islamist women's activism, Safinaz Qazim was highly impressed with Malcolm X when she met him during her years as a Literature student in the United States. Since her return to Cairo, she has campaigned vigorously for an Islamic society. She was also imprisoned by Sadat during the latter's 'purge' of all oppositionists in September 1981. Refusing to join any one group, Qazim levels her criticism and proposals for alternatives principally through her pen. Heba Ra'uf, the youngest and of the contemporary generation, uses different platforms to air her ideas and declare her Islamist solidarity, including Cairo University (where she is lecturer and is completing her PhD), and the Muslim Brotherhood–Labour Party Alliance. Ra'uf also edits the 'woman's page' in the Labour party newspaper *Al-Sha'b*.

ZAYNAB AL-GHAZALI

It is true that I am over seventy [years of age] but my call has not been defeated. My voice will continue to ring till the last day of my life. I am still able to practise the *Da'wa* through giving lessons to some of the Muslim sisters and attending Islamic conferences, and I pray to Allah to grant me success and help me to accomplish my desires to elevate Islam and Muslims.

(Al-Hashimi 1990: 53)

Al-Ghazali's career continues to revolve around actively establishing the groundwork and basis for an Islamist movement in Egypt. Though starting her political life as a member in Huda Sha'rawi's[3] feminist group, Al-Ghazali was soon drawn to Islamic lectures at Al-Azhar. From there she moved decisively and quickly in the direction of a politicized Islamic consciousness.

She resigned from the Egyptian Feminist Union and founded her own group, the Muslim Woman's Association, in 1936. One of her major publications is her memoirs of her prison years under Nasser, which she wrote as an explicit documentation of the atrocities. She has written innumerable articles published in Islamic newspapers and magazines throughout the Muslim world. She has also lectured extensively in Egypt, Pakistan, the USA and Saudi Arabia. Many books have been written about her, since she maintains a formidable influence among men and women Islamists in many parts of the Muslim world.

Al-Ghazali's basic tenets regarding the role that Muslim women should occupy is a secular feminists' nightmare. She begins by arguing that there is no such thing as a separate 'women's issue' within Islam. In fact she maintains that

> If we study the secret behind the backwardness of Muslims, we will find that one of its first causes is the imagining of issues invented by the enemies of Islam in order to attract the Muslim people's attention away from the large issue of returning Islam to its former pride and glory, to steal [Islam's] world from the circle of retardation or what they call 'developing', or Third World.
>
> (Al-Ghazali 1986: 44)

She maintains that Islam's perception of men and women is unified. It is as a nature that has divided into two, and neither is complete without the other. Having said that however, Al-Ghazali then proceeds to outline in detail what is expected of women in any Islamic society. Of the Muslim girl, Al-Ghazali says,

> It is the duty of the Muslim girl to diligently attend to performing her prayers at the right time. To make sure she respects and obeys her parents and treats them well because obedience to them is obedience to God almighty. Also to wear the proper and [religiously] ordained dress... In school or university to be the good example for her colleagues so she makes sure she achieves the highest of grades in her lessons and thus becomes an example in positive achievements and practical achievements.
>
> (Al-Ghazali 1988a: 48)

Thus, a good Muslim girl's responsibility is to God and parents. It is principally a matter of obedience. The status of parents is holy and sacred as is that of God. What emerges is a girl who accepts, obeys and is passive until it comes to acting as a religious beacon, or example, for the rest of the community – then, activism of a sort is expected. These values sound somewhat contradictory, especially since nowhere does Al-Ghazali urge that the activism should be turned against parents who may not be particularly religious. So that, on the one hand, the girl has a duty to be religiously active, but on the other hand, she must also be obedient. Yet it can also be seen as an inculcation of the values of listening to and obeying one's elders. What is most interesting is that while Al-Ghazali stresses time and again that there is no separate issue for men and women, she nevertheless addresses the above specifically for girls. I have yet to find a similar message dedicated to boys.

In a paper entitled *Dawr al-Mar'a fi bina' al-Mujtama'* (The Role of Women in the Building of Society), which she presented at the conference of Muslim Women in Lahore (November 1985), Al-Ghazali stated:

> Woman's role in society is to be a mother, to be a wife... What has happened since we have left the circle of natural disposition to the circle of invention... Generations whose brain cells have been poisoned by drugs so they have become skeletons and human distortions, an ugly picture for a human drawing ... For a few limited pennies we have sold our motherhood and then we ask about the role of women in society? What kind of a society is this where the home that forms the seed of the society has been ruined by tearing women between home and the workplace.
>
> (Al-Ghazali 1985: 4)

Like her male colleagues, Al-Ghazali sees that this terrible state of affairs is a result of a 'Western conspiracy'. She warns that

> The West, which has lied and fraudulently claimed that they have liberated women, will be faced with the natural end of the circle of time when things return to their natural order. Then they will know that they have destroyed both home and work the day they betrayed the world and called for the necessity of women being rented in order to obtain her food and drink from the fruits of her own labour, so she became a human distortion and an available commodity for the lust of the wolves. So do not be fooled by her being a Prime Minister. Women's skill in the rearing of her sons and preparing them for their leading and productive roles in society is far more valuable and useful.
>
> (ibid.)

No distinction is made between all these different Western influences she talks about. This lack of specification and constant homogenization of the 'forces of evil' is typical of Islamist perceptions of an 'external threat' to Islam. Al-Ghazali argues that Zionism is this external force which is declaring the Muslim world's doom. It is Zionists, she argues, who have 'ordered the Muslims to become "hippies", and order Muslim women to bare their bodies and they order Muslims to export from their countries singers and dancers' (Al-Ghazali 1983: 24).

It is notable that by 'Muslims', Al-Ghazali is actually referring to 'Arabs', the seeming implication being that non-Arabs are non-Muslims. Also noteworthy is the fact that whether they are hippies, bare-bodied, singers and dancers, they are all supposedly terrible cases. Here too, we are faced with a homogenization of a wide category of people and occupations who are the result of the equally homogenized category of Zionists. This elusive category of 'they' are also the ones calling for secularism. In other words, the 'enemies of Islam', in Al-Ghazali's opinion, call for further heretical things such as the separation of religion and politics. This separation is viewed by Al-Ghazali as a 'crime', which all Islamic countries are perpetuating, since 'Islam cannot live as long as it is separated from its laws' (ibid.: 23). Moreover, she argues that 'a society's worth can be measured by its leaders'. This reference alludes to Arab leaders (most of whom are still active today), none of whom is, in Al-Ghazali's opinion, worthy of leadership over a Muslim society. Herein lie Al-Ghazali's opinions on the current state.

As Al-Ghazali continuously and repeatedly emphasizes, women's main and indeed only role – in her words, 'firstly and secondly and thirdly' – is to be a good wife and mother. The role of the mother is to bring up the next generations of Muslim children to be heavily indoctrinated in Islam.

When referring to the role Afghan women should play during their struggles against the Russian occupation, Al-Ghazali stresses the aspect of encouragement. In her opinion, Afghani women could contribute to the *jihad* against the Russians by

> injecting the *mujahidin* (fighters) with enthusiasm with her tender and enthusiastic words to the child, the youth and the elderly men. An enthusiasm with which she can renew the souls of *jihad* for *jihad*.
> (Al-Ghazali 1988b: 27)

Women's role during conflicts is, therefore, a continuation of their role as mothers and wives. Theirs is primarily a vocal endeavour to inspire male fighters – all this, even though she refers in the same interview to the Muslim woman *combatants* during the early years of Islam. But it seems that as far as contemporary Muslim women go, 'giving hope with tender words' and 'honest motherhood' is about as active as they need be (ibid.).

Nowhere does she address the situation of women who are either
unmarried or unable to bear children. What kinds of roles are envisaged
by Al-Ghazali for these women? Herself childless, Al-Ghazali has
poured her heart into Islamist activism. Judging by her example then,
motherless women can become full-time soldiers of God. Not only that
however, but Al-Ghazali literally holds women responsible for the sorry
state of Islamic culture and all Islamic societies. Addressing herself to
women in an article entitled 'My Lady!', Al-Ghazali pontificates:

Yes my lady you are responsible for our dependency on those non-
Muslims who are the callers for disbelief, immorality and chaos...
With you women have gone to adorning themselves and rebelling
against our religion and all our inheritances... Yes my lady you are
responsible for all this decline of Islamic culture and its supremacy,
its advancement and giving to life, that giving which has been
assigned by God for the Islamic community in order to be the
best community ever revealed to people.

(quoted in Al-Hashimi 1990: 115)

Al-Ghazali states that because women are unable and/or unwilling to
put all their energies and efforts into being good wives and good
mothers, the family and home has suffered, and with it the whole
Islamic society. So women, according to her line of reasoning, are the
reason why everything is going wrong in the Muslim world. Women
are, at this rate, quite formidable and powerful figures. Women's
duties as wives and mothers, she reiterates, are far more important
than working in a company, factory or laboratory:

God in His infinite wisdom has created with His creativity and
power the woman's natural disposition in such a way that she
specializes in making a man happy and comfortable, so he [the
man] can improve his productivity and do his duty wisely and
observantly by her, and she will not find this man unless we find
him the protective family which is clever with its capabilities.

(ibid.)

Al-Ghazali argues this point by saying that a man cannot bear to do
more than God has assigned him. So why, then, she questions rhetorically, does woman want to carry the double burden (of family and
work) simultaneously?

My daughter, what have you got from the calls for equality, and
what have you got for deviating from your disposition?... The

disposition of women that ordains her to live in order to build ... To build men ... to build great women who build men to become a great *umma* [nation].

(ibid.)

Hence women's roles as indirect builders (but builders nevertheless) of the Muslim nation.

Not that there is an inequality being called for, Al-Ghazali hastens to point out. Quite the contrary, using a verse from the Quran to stress her point, Al-Ghazali says that women are equal to men when it comes to faith and belief. God does not distinguish the efforts of the two sexes. So what more in terms of equality does the Muslim woman want? asks Al-Ghazali. The irony lies not so much in what Al-Ghazali preaches, but in her own lifestyle. She herself declares about her work: 'For I pledged to Allah on the day I established the Group [Muslim Women] that I would never submit my life to anybody beside Him' (Al-Ghazali 1995: 14). Moreover, she describes her marriage to her husband as 'only a contingent worldly event, but brotherhood in Allah is everlasting: it does not elapse nor can it be measured in the world and all that is therein' (ibid.: 169). Here she clearly implies that there are more important things than marriage, namely, spreading the Islamic *Da'wa* or faith. Is one to understand that hers is a very special case then? Is she the only Muslim woman allowed actively to proselytize in the name of her faith?

Al-Ghazali divorced her first husband because she felt he was preventing her from her mission of being an Islamist activist (Ahmed 1992: 200). But what about her primary mission as a Muslim woman, to be a good wife? In another article she writes that

A woman asking her husband for divorce is a crime that deserves punishment,[4] for is there anything more terrible than a woman threatening the nest of her marriage and her motherhood?

(Al-Ghazali 1989: 48)

Yet she openly admits she was the one who asked her first husband for divorce, and she stipulated to her second husband that he was not to interfere in her Islamist activism. In view of this, it becomes increasingly obvious that Al-Ghazali seems to apply double standards: one for herself and the other for other Muslim women. Her own essentially public role and her private life contradict what she preaches.

Another interesting point about Al-Ghazali's activism is its seemingly total lack of sympathy for the less fortunate women in her society. After writing in excruciating detail about the torture she was subjected to in Nasser's prison, she outlines a scene where she was made to wait in a queue in prison whilst all the prisoners were being counted.[5] This queue contained women who were imprisoned for theft, prostitution and murder. This is what Al-Ghazali has to say about these women:

> Our fellow inmates' souls were clearly saturated with depravity and the wards locked in the evil they contained. Humanity here had sunk to the lowest of the low... What had happened to us whilst in the military prison in terms of humiliation, flogging, beatings, executions and starvation was nothing compared to what we were witnessing on our first night in this prison. Here we were in front of a straying herd lost in the dungeons of *jahiliyya*. Women who claimed to be liberated, were rather slaves of whims and desires. Their crimes had submerged them entirely and they had forgotten their humanity, purity, honour and dignity. Nothing but animals with no meaning to their lives except eating and intercourse. Blind animals led by blind men on a road which zigzagged endlessly in front of them. Those who want corruption on this earth, the people of atheism and falsehood, of evil and crime, had helped these women to sink into this abyss of profanity.
>
> (Al-Ghazali 1995: 175–6)

Al-Ghazali then proceeds to move her Islamist protégée (who was also in prison with her) away from the queue saying to the warden:

> *Al-Ghazali*: We'll stand separately, we don't belong to this [group].
> *Warden*: What are you saying?
> *Al-Ghazali*: We'll stand alone.
> *Warden*: Are these not Allah's creatures like you?
>
> (ibid.: 177)

Al-Ghazali does not respond and moves away. Then she continues with her story.

However, Al-Ghazali's position was to shift with the passage of time. When asked, in the 1980s, direct and specific questions about the roles that Muslim women should play in modern societies, Al-Ghazali began to talk of 'choice'. Thus, in comparison with her above-quoted discourse, a change takes place in which she acknowledges that women should themselves determine in what way they wish to participate in society. The following illustrates this shift in her discourse:

There is an attempt to curtail Muslim women's roles in life and this is a baseless attempt. In my opinion a Muslim woman can work on two levels: the first is that she brings up her children in the spirit of Islam, and in our circumstances she must explain to them that their land in Palestine and Afghanistan is unjustly taken and God's orders are delayed, and that their inescapable duty is to change these corrupt circumstances in the Islamic world. The second level is that she herself joins in this *jihad* [struggle], and in the absence of Islamic law I see it as a duty of every Muslim. It is up to the Muslim [woman] to balance it out and arrive at the most positive outcome to this situation.

(Al-Ghazali 1985: 38)

In other words, Al-Ghazali argues along similar lines to Qutb, Al-Ghazali and Al-Qaradawi, that as long as Islamic law is absent, Muslims are in some state of war. In such a situation, women have an important and active role to play, which they must determine for themselves. Yet, the role visualized by Al-Ghazali is one in which she hastens to deny any inequality between men and women, and in which women's work in the name of Islam is a duty.

The subtle alteration in her discourse may well coincide with an increasing sense of urgency felt by the Islamists to reach their political goals quicker. On the other hand, Al-Ghazali herself may have realized that after 30 years of activism, the younger generation was going to have to be involved on its own terms. This generation is relatively less influenced by her, saturated with certain Western influences and on the lookout for newer discourses.

SAFINAZ QAZIM

I wish we had no feminism here [in Egypt] at all.[6]

Though by no means sharing the same social impact and consequent 'grandeur' of Al-Ghazali, Qazim remains a figure to be reckoned with. In her early fifties, she is of the generation that learned and was guided by Al-Ghazali, and forms a link between her and the Islamists of the 1990s who are in their twenties and early thirties.

In our first meeting, I was struck by the fact that her bookshelf boasted a picture of Khalid Al-Islambuli, Sadat's assassin. Qazim sat under that picture, and held forth about Islamism and feminism. She was one of those imprisoned by Sadat during his last days[7] and consequently views Al-Islambuli as a 'liberator, who freed me from [state] oppression and tyranny'.

The reasons why Qazim's standing differs from that of Al-Ghazali are varied. Al-Ghazali's linkages with Hasan Al-Banna, the founder of the Muslim Brotherhood, has lent her some of the latter's allure and legitimacy. Qazim can claim no such historic and deep link to the Muslim Brotherhood in its entirety. Moreover, as the first publicly active woman Islamist, Al-Ghazali's reputation remains unrivalled.

Preferring to work alone and not be part of any group or movement, Qazim thus affirms her lack of confidence in institutions and contemporary organizations – whether governmental or not. Moreover, whilst Al-Ghazali has travelled extensively to preach her gospel, Qazim, since returning from a study trip to the United States in the late 1970s, has refrained from extensive travel. Al-Ghazali's Islamic education was more extensive and long-standing than that of Qazim. The latter's initial education and training was in journalism and the arts, and her Islamic knowledge is derived from her extensive readings and study of Islam. Many a book has been written about Al-Ghazali, but Qazim has yet to have a biography written about her.

Nevertheless, Qazim's viewpoints are interesting precisely because of the characteristics that differentiate her from Al-Ghazali. Qazim speaks from the standpoint of a Muslim woman who was Westernized in both outlook and demeanour, lived in the West for a few years in the 'heady sixties', and 'came to Islam' as a result of these contacts with the Western world. She comes into Islam with first-hand experience of being a Muslim, Arab, middle-class, woman intellectual who was faced with negative Western reactions to all these different aspects of her identity. Much of Qazim's writings tends to be illustrative and allegorical.

Her heaviest criticisms are levelled against all aspects of Muslim society which she perceives as being 'ape imitations of the West' (Qazim 1986: 21). In her criticisms she sketches the dichotomy which she believes 'the West' tries to impose, to discredit and eliminate cultural authenticity and religion:

In the face of Europe stands the cancelled world with its cultures and beliefs, wherein all its achievements have been reduced to completing the tools necessary to imitate Europe – most important of which are 'Westernization' and 'Secularization'... This so that the cancelled world can come forward with its accreditation papers to be accepted within 'modernity': And in this cancelled world, wars take place which end up in secular dictatorships which force their masses to take religion lightly and eliminate it from their worlds, if not forcing them in some instances to atheism. All this while whipping these countries into obedience so that they become dutiful apes obliged to imitate this statue of worship: 'Europe'.

(ibid.).

She refers to this age as that of *'euro-ameri-zionism'*. She also predicts the fall of 'euro-ameri-zionism' in much the same way as the Roman and Persian empires. In her perception,

the euro-ameri-zionist age and the age of Islam are two opposite ages: antagonists: every right in the euro-ameri-zionist age is a wrong in the Islamic one and all that is good in the Islamic age is hated and waged war against in the euro-ameri-zionist age. It is impossible to combine the ages, impossible to be neutral among them, and it is impossible to continue and link between them.

(ibid.: 23)

Nor is there any possibility of a smooth transition between them anyway, Qazim asserts. In fact, she maintains that the move from one age to the other has to be free, radical and thorough. This transformation is to be as though 'the magic has broken away from the swans, monkeys, and pigs and returned them to their humanity and humaneness' (ibid.).

Unlike Al-Ghazali, Qazim does not allude to her prison torment *per se*, but always uses the context of comparisons with life in general. She sees prison itself as a testing of her faith, as well as a metaphor which describes the state of political and moral corruption the country is in. She maintains that 'prison for me is the emergency laws, and the exceptional laws that allow the minister of interior to arrest and imprison a citizen without declaring any reason!' (ibid.: 27). Qazim decries state power which does not treat people as citizens, but rather as 'hostages or captives' with which it can do as it pleases.

At the same time, however, she sees other civil institutions in society (such as human rights and civil liberties associations) as being no better. Qazim contends that these institutions include among their members people of 'intense backwardness and ugliness [of character], and have a residue of suspicious and primitive behaviour which abuses freedom and human rights' (ibid.: 28). In fact, she maintains that 'we might well prefer the police of injustice and criminal statehood to these' (ibid.).

In effect, Qazim is describing the feelings reiterated by many Islamists, that both state and non-Islamic or secular institutions are a failure. This argument has a logical conclusion which is encased in their calls for an 'Islamic solution' to all problems. The Islamic solution is attractive precisely because it is 'new' – in the sense that it has not been tried yet. This is supposedly in contrast to other avenues offered by the state and by secular organizations, which, they argue, have proved their inefficacy, as well as their sharing of similar diseases: corruption and hypocrisy of their members.

Qazim, unlike Al-Ghazali, openly admits that women have been and continue to be oppressed. This oppression is manifested in their ignorance of religion and of their rights and obligations within it. Were they to be knowledgeable, she argues, unhappiness caused by fighting with family, with society, with culture would not feature so much. Instead, women would be valued, respected and stronger. She maintains, however, that this oppression has little to do with their sex and more with general tyranny. Thus she refuses to acknowledge it as simply a matter of women's oppression:

> There has been oppression against women, but that is a result of ignorance (*jahiliyya*) and barbarism (*hamajiyya*). These are pre-Islamic legacies. It is very important to make a distinction between our heritage (*irth*) and what actually takes place. It is not the oppression of man to woman, but the oppression of someone who does not fear God to a fellow human being.[8]

She insists that 'there are issues which are far more serious than women's oppression or inability to obtain her rights, like the forbiddance of believing in the one God'.[9] Here she is referring again to the impact of Western hegemony which she perceives as being idolatry.

With this in mind, Qazim's opinions on feminism, or any so-called 'Western-inspired' movement to secure women's rights, is predictable. She sees feminism as an aspect of Western societies which arose out of the excess repression and liberalization that they underwent. Qazim says of feminism:

> I am one of its most ardent enemies, be it here or in the rest of the world. There is a general principle within Islam that there must be justice. It follows that as a Muslim I can play and take a role in my society. I have no case that is 'woman's', rather I have a case of a

victim of injustice. It could be described that as a Muslim who *happens* to be a woman, I deal with a victim of injustice who also *happens* to be a woman. This is a fundamental difference with a feminist. A feminist works from the conviction and basis that she is aiding those of her sex.[10]

Qazim's emphasis on justice is closely tied to her ideas on respect – that is, respect between members of the family and society at large, as well as the respect between state and citizens. She perceives that today's society and politics are based on tyranny in all relations, hence her perceptions of injustice.

Moreover, feminism is perceived by Qazim to be the embodiment of much misrepresentation and harm to women. She sees feminism, not unlike the aforementioned women activists, as divisive because of its sexism: 'feminism ultimately leads to a fight between two camps: men and women'. She also contends that feminism is as bad as, if not worse than, Zionism. In fact, she describes and equates feminism and Zionism with 'women's nationalism'. Both, she claims, attempt to be separatist and claim a certain space as exclusively their own at the expense of another integral segment of society (Qazim 1994a: 45). In an interview with Qazim published in *Al-Ahram Weekly*, she asserts that

I am all for women's liberation ... In my view, a woman's commitment to shari'a is the highest degree of liberation a woman can achieve. It is true that many of the rights which shari'a grants to women are violated, but it is also true that women should strive to gain those rights. In doing so, women should seek those rights as human beings, avoiding the sexist perspective.[11]

To Qazim, feminism is a movement which 'is not for women's liberation, it is a movement which chains women [to a certain erroneous idea] and alienates women from their humanity'.[12] In sum, it is unnecessary. But as far as contentions around women's equality go, Qazim maintains that 'Allah gave certain different blessings to men and women, but these are partial differences that do not mean inequalities – there is a unity of kind'.[13]

Qazim's argument revolves around the by now familiar theme, that women are in fact preferred (by God) to men because of their childbearing functions, whereas men are preferred over women because of their physical strengths and their concomitant capacity to be financial providers. Hence, in this functional preference lies the equality between the sexes:

The basis in Islam is the equality between man and woman despite the admission of the difference between them. Difference does not mean inequality... One should not desire the attributes of the other. For Allah is just. And ultimately there is balance.

(Qazim 1994b: 103)

As for the issue of female circumcision, Qazim responded by saying it was too horrible for her even to begin to imagine it. She underlined her opinion that such practices are a hangover from pre-Islamic times, and should therefore be gradually eradicated.[14] Herself a mother of a daughter, she has not even considered subjecting her daughter to this practice. However, Qazim does comment that 'it is ironical that the continuous attempts to associate female genital mutilation with Islam are made by Western countries where women have had to suffer from the chastity belt for hundreds of years'.[15]

Another important aspect of Qazim's ideas is her belief that *some commandments in the Quran are simply to be obeyed, without question.* One of these commandments relates to the *hijab*, or the veil, and the other to husbands' rights to beat their errant wives. With respect to the latter she says,

A Muslim woman should not object to the Quranic text. If God, in His holy book, says that it is the man who can beat a woman for disobeying His orders, then a woman has to accept God's will.[16]

As far as the veil goes, Qazim argues that it too is an unquestionable Islamic injunction and thus 'primarily a matter of obedience' (ibid.). The next main argument for wearing of the *hijab* is, according to Qazim, that it forces men to deal with a veiled woman on an equal footing, because they will be attracted by her mental rather than her physical attributes.

When describing a scene on an Egyptian beach, where women were bathing whilst fully clothed, Qazim comments,

despite everything the Islamic conscience is victor, slowly the awareness opens to the belief: Islamic ideology and the Egyptians decide that their beaches will reflect the precepts of their religion! 'Thank God': I said it with my heart jumping in joy with the waves.

(Qazim 1982: 49)

Qazim maintains that the veil is what enables women to have a pronounced and as open a public appearance as they wish. With the veil, Muslim women can achieve all the rights accorded them by Islam. According to her, Islam,

> which is the religion of freedom and liberation and the honouring of human beings, [has given women the right] to education, choice of husband, inheritance, work, consultation, and the effective participation in building their emerging societies.
>
> (Qazim 1994b: 117)

Qazim's message, then, reads that women can enjoy many rights so long as they pay the necessary price of obedience to God. This price is essential because it delineates a fundamental point that Muslims are stating: that we are proud and superior to Western influences. Obedience to Allah's laws – as opposed to man-made ones – is a reaffirmation of cultural authenticity and unique identities as Muslims in a heathen world.

Qazim's argument, and one that is not foreign to Islamism, is that by labelling their opponents' arguments as Western, contentious issues are dismissed. This is one of the delegitimizing tactics employed by Islamists, by which they effectively disregard and circumvent attempts to deal with potential and actual matters leading to dissent, e.g. blind obedience and non-questioning of authority.

Interestingly, Qazim, like Al-Ghazali, is divorced. Neither of these women seems to be oppressed, weak or ignorant of her rights. More to the point, both these women were able to *exercise* their rights and obtain the desired results. And therein lie the most crucial aspects of these two Islamist women's activism: strength of character, self-confidence, knowledge of religion, explicit views and goals for the future, and above all, determination.

HEBA RA'UF

Heba Ra'uf is in her early thirties, a wife and mother of two, and is a teaching assistant in the Political Science Department at Cairo University. Having received a relatively exclusive Western (German and English) education up to university, Ra'uf is an interesting and telling example, not only of the motivations behind recourse to Islamism, but also of the *empowering* potential it can represent for many Muslim women. These points are clarified in Ra'uf's own words about her experience in a German secondary school:

Nobody has to explain to me what it means to be preached to, what missionarism is, or what it is like to have one's own culture ridiculed and demeaned by another! At school they [the foreign teachers] were adept at making us feel inferior. Though there was a chapel for Christian students to pray there once a week, they refused to give us a room to pray for our five prayers a day! Although other students were allowed to wear whatever they liked, I was not allowed to put on the proper *tarha* (head scarf), instead I was restricted in the way I covered my hair ... If you did not have a boyfriend you were very strange, in fact, something must be wrong with you and your customs that forbid this. They tried to impress upon us that they were the civilized Westerners, and that those of us who tried to be good Muslims were very strange.[17]

Islam for Ra'uf was a means to reinstate her identity in the face of perceived contempt and/or disregard. It was thus an empowering tool to work through her anger and resentment. In fact, there is an immense amount of anger springing from misunderstandings and misconceptions of Western society. Western eccentricities, often termed immoral behaviour – which is threatening to our authentic Islamic culture – are seen in the open and 'shameless' quest for homosexuality[18] to be normalized and viewed 'positively'. This issue of what is happening around homosexuality is seen to be an indicator of the levels of moral degradation that the West has come to, and of what will happen to us if we embrace the same cultural and social beliefs.

Misperceptions about the Western 'Other' abound in Heba's Islamist ideas: 'The top school curriculum-setters in France are homosexuals!'[19] Apparently, there is a fear that the openness involved in declaring homosexuality will lead to its spreading to others, whereas containment (i.e. if occurring discreetly) and public disdain will reduce the rate of dissemination: 'I don't want this openness, I am against homosexuality, let them practise it inside their homes!'[20]

Another perception of the Western 'Other' has to do with ideas that 'the West' purportedly has on motherhood. 'The West' supposedly discredits and sees motherhood as unnecessary:

20 years from now, motherhood in the West will be a matter of adoption, and adoption under the guise of a do-gooder charitable goal [said sarcastically]. Why else is there a negative birth rate in France? – because motherhood is becoming unnecessary![21]

Armed with her negative experiences and misconceptions, which in themselves were a culmination of similarly infuriating encounters with other Western influences, Ra'uf explains that she felt she had to make a choice. On the point of going to university, Ra'uf realized she had to choose how she would act for the rest of her life. Either she would 'give in' and become Western-oriented, or she would seek an alternative authenticity from her own cultural background – Islam. She chose the latter. In effect, Ra'uf was seeking a means to assert both her independence vis-à-vis unwelcome patterns of self-definition and her simultaneous willingness to be part of a collectivity with a legitimate self-affirmative mission. Full of her memories of oppressive 'Westernism', she opted for what she felt satisfied her need for some form of affirmation against 'Westernism' in all its forms. This provided her with a sanctified sense of value and purpose.

Ra'uf was tutored by the two giants of Islamist activism: Zaynab Al-Ghazali and Safinaz Qazim. Ra'uf in effect represents the younger generation of Islamist women activist-leaders in Egypt. However, the continuity she represents should not be taken to mean identical points of departure, or even conclusions. Ra'uf's discourse represents an important difference from that of her male and female colleagues.

It is not uncommon to hear an outright denial, from many Islamist men and women activists, of 'the woman's issue' since, it is argued, Islam refers to the issues of *bani Adam*, or the human race. Ra'uf, while supporting the importance of the larger struggle, has nevertheless diligently shifted her focus in such a manner, so as clearly and yet subtly, to give women's issues some centrality. She has achieved this in a number of ways.

First, Ra'uf's Master's degree was devoted to an elaborate and carefully thought out dissertation which respected traditional authoritative Islamic texts, but came out with refreshing and novel interpretations on women's roles. Ra'uf then confidently argued and subsequently *proved*, that according to highly valued Islamic scholarship, women were allowed to occupy the highest public functions *as long as they were qualified*. Distinctions therefore should not be based on gender, but on qualifications. Arguing thus, Ra'uf effectively backed up the claim that qualified women should be entitled to occupy such positions as heads of state or judges. This is an extremely contentious point however, especially among the ranks of the Muslim Brotherhood itself. Adopting this stance and simultaneously endearing herself to many of the younger Islamist women,[22] Ra'uf combines courage with political acumen.

Secondly, Ra'uf's public stance whether with younger female Islamist 'conscripts', or via her work as an editor of the woman's page in
Al-Sha'b,[23] also highlight her relatively 'liberal' stance. According to
her,

> women become more influential in traditional societies in transition
> characterized by a lack of a stable base. The weighing scale should
> be God, for if affairs are left to men only they will be despots, and if
> left only to women, they will be malignant.[24]

Ra'uf also explicitly states that she laughs 'at mosque preachers who
address women, because they do not enter into politics but try to
concentrate on women-related things only'.[25] She is referring here
to traditional preachers, and some of those who are busy signing up
new conscripts, who only talk about women's duties and obligations.
According to Ra'uf, this kind of proselytizing is unproductive since it
separates women's issues from broader political participation. Judging
from her Islamist colleagues' critique of feminism, this sounds like
'feminism in reverse'.

Thirdly, Ra'uf's standpoint on women, a cornerstone of her overall
Islamist advocation, is relatively innovative. In an interview with
Middle East Report, she argues that women's liberation in Muslim
societies 'necessitates a revival of Islamic thought and a renewal
within Islamic jurisprudence'. Moreover, in the same article she claims
that her aim is not to reconstruct Islamic law (as opposed to deconstructing it), but 'actually defending Islam from stagnation and bias'
(Ra'uf Ezzat 1994: 26).

Despite her approach to women's rights, Ra'uf adamantly refuses
to recognize the legitimacy of feminism or feminist advocacy on
women's rights, claiming it to be divisive and individualistic. Feminism is, according to her, 'not necessary', since Islam is not only a way
of life but a 'very political existence'. Moreover, feminism is but a
vestige of the West, which does not apply to Islamic cultures. Ra'uf
argues,

> Feminism aims only at women, has one ever heard of 'masculin-
> ism'? In order to address the whole issue of women's oppression,
> one must address the whole society. It is both men and women who
> have to be targeted, especially since we must aim to change the
> traditional way of thinking of the whole fabric of society.[26]

Effectively, Ra'uf maintains that an Islamic liberation movement
targets both men and women together, with the aim of changing the

existing mentalities which result in gender oppression. Like many other women activists, she believes that feminism in its current form is divisive and would thus not benefit liberation.

On Family/On State

According to Ra'uf, relativism – a theoretical ill resulting from Western influence – means that calamities like homosexuality are seen as normal and acceptable to the rest of society:

> That is my problem with postmodernism – there is no room for religion at all because there is this denial of absolutes. There have to be certain absolutes in our society, otherwise everything becomes relative, and anything permissible and, even worse, you become the idiot who is being pig-headed, and the person in the wrong. Islam is a combination of the absolute with the relative.[27]

Relativism, according to her, is tied in with the loss of such basic values as the extended family and the growth of individualism – another negative heritage of Westernism.

Ra'uf criticizes the lack of political significance accredited to the family both in certain traditional Islamic interpretations and in Western studies. She claims that both streams of thought traditionally emphasize the family as a purely social unit, performing functions such as affection, fulfilment of sexual desires, and so on. Both ignore the vital political role that the family functions have. 'Instead of elevating the role of the family to regard it to be as important as any public activism, the family was denigrated as a "private" matter.'[28] This occurs, she asserts, despite the famous feminist dictum of 'the personal is political', thereby proving that feminism has failed in its own message.

Ra'uf argues that, alternatively, Islamic political theory considers the family as an essential political unit. In her schema, the proper Muslim family becomes the means to women's liberation. The family (in the extended sense) is perceived as the essential political unit in a Muslim society. In this analysis she extends the teachings of an Islamist scholar who deeply influenced her Islamist tendencies – Sayyid Qutb, who viewed the family as 'the basis of society' (Qutb 1991: 182).[29]

Ra'uf takes this argument further along two main themes. The first is that political authority should be vested in the family as opposed to the state. The state, especially in its present form, is ill equipped to handle all the responsibilities which are wrongly expected of it. As a religiously corrupt regime, the legitimacy of the state becomes highly questionable. Further, Westernization has defiled the government's policies, resulting in the spread of destructive Western values of individualism, which in turn have contributed to the breakdown of Islamic family values. She maintains that it was precisely these values of solidarity at all times, and mutual respect, protection and status for family members, with their consequent dependable structures, which offered women protection. Their absence is the principal cause behind women's oppression.

Ra'uf's central argument, and what she builds up to, is that the family as a unit is a micro-process of the state, wherein the same procedures for management and articulation take place. The importance of the family, according to her, is that in undemocratic societies, it becomes the one public/private institution that the state *cannot* ban: 'No state can ever forbid people to have families.'[30] Thus, the family effectively becomes the main bulwark of freedom for all its members – men and women – against state oppression. In the same manner, the family also becomes the guarantor of freedoms among its members.

Ra'uf's second theme follows from this. She argues that the dichotomy between public and private (a vestige of some Western feminist and anthropological theories) is a falsehood, since the private (i.e. the family) is a microcosm of the larger public arena where power is exercised.[31] Ra'uf thus effectively appropriates the feminist dictum of 'the personal is the political' herself, and adds the dimension of the family to it. In her theorization, the personal (woman) is the public (family) is the political (state). Further, she contends that just as *shura* (consultation) should be realized in the running of the state, so it should also take place in the running of the family. As Ra'uf states, 'Islam considers the family as the starting point for any real Islamic society. The same values [operating in the macro public arena] should dominate.'[32]

Ra'uf argues that women should be actively involved in the running, management and defence of their Islamic nation (*umma*). 'Military service should become obligatory for women as well as for men', she states, since the Muslim nation is effectively in a state of war. Her argument here resonates somewhat with the claims made by other Islamists (e.g. Muhammad Al-Ghazali) who nevertheless go on to restrict women's military duties to nursing the injured, preparing meals, and so on.

Ra'uf maintains that 'raising children is a very important political function', and thus the

> Family is not an obstacle, it can be turned into an obstacle. Women who stay at home for some time bringing up children, are participating in protecting that unit [the family] in society; practising social socialization, giving their children certain probably positive values. Then these women can go and perform other public and equally important roles. No one has 24 hours to devote to only one sphere.[33]

Ra'uf's last sentence is in direct contradiction to Al-Ghazali's earlier affirmations. Nevertheless, there is an obvious idealization of the family in much of Ra'uf's argumentation, notably with regard to its liberating potential for women. She ignores the fact that much of the oppression and violence women suffer is a result of the internalization of certain harmful social norms and their practice *within* families. Practices such as female circumcision, for example, are carried out at the behest of mothers on their own daughters. Though the state plays a role in institutionalizing oppressive patriarchal structures, to idealize the family in opposition to the state is to perpetrate the same dichotomy of thought that Ra'uf herself tends to criticize – 'we must stop thinking and seeing things in dichotomies'.[34]

But one must keep in mind that Ra'uf's is primarily a political message against the existing state structure, as well as an attempted formulation of some form of 'Islamic' women's liberation. In the context of the former, taking the family as the central unit of analysis and action, Ra'uf is actually appealing to traditional and generally acceptable values, while simultaneously cloaking a woman-centred appeal. The latter is not feasible for her to be forthright about, since it risks bringing her in direct confrontation not only with her male colleagues, but with current Islamist treatises. Hers is the innovative but veiled language of a minority within the Islamist current. Nevertheless, it remains significant that she attempts to develop this minority discourse from the platform of a majority force. The latter is in reference to the wide popular social base that the Muslim Brotherhood occupies in present-day Egypt.

Ra'uf describes her goal as that of changing the dominant paradigm 'from within'. By using the traditional sources she pays her respect to them, while simultaneously seeking their reinterpretation and innovation. Similarly, she strategically places herself within the dominant Islamist trend, but actively works to promote her version of what it is that women should be doing. Ra'uf presents a personal political example, which is legitimized by a tactically placed religious discourse.

Though Ra'uf continues to amass support – especially from women student circles – for her opinions, long-term consistency and effectiveness of her views remain questionable. For one thing, Ra'uf's self-definition as an 'Islamist' seems to fluctuate depending on her audience. Within the space of a few weeks she described herself as an 'Islamist' once in a personal interview, then retracted and negated the term, then again appeared describing herself as such. Her retraction of the term occurred during another personal interview in which she said:

> 'Islamist' is an exclusive terminology. As if an Islamist is different from the average Muslim and can be more violent, militant, politically conscious and active. I describe myself as what I understand an average Muslim should be. I do not pretend to be idealistic. If others are not average Muslims that is another story – my duty is then to try and improve them.[35]

Although in this interview she presents herself as an 'average Muslim', she clearly states that 'I declare myself an Islamist' (Ra'uf Ezzat 1994: 26). The question that comes to mind is, if she seems to be prepared to compromise on her self-definition, will she do the same with her opinions on the necessity to reinterpret and innovate on issues relating to women? Her current standpoint is motivated by political ambition. When faced with the exigencies of *realpolitik*, her advocacy of 'an Islamic women's liberation movement' may risk ending up as nothing more than what Egyptians would call *ahlam al-siba* – 'dreams of youth'.

What is significant about Ra'uf is her gradual but definite shift away from the patriarchal emphasis of Al-Ghazali and Qazim's main arguments. Though much of her discourse carries within it the vestiges of anti-Westernism and anti-feminism, she nevertheless elaborates and emphasizes women's roles. Whereas she maintains, along with her mentors, that there is no such thing as a separate women's issue, she develops an elaborate structure which serves to protect and enhance women's socio-political roles and rights – the family. By intentionally breaking down the barrier between public and private, Ra'uf has quite cleverly created a way out of the glorification of motherhood as women's only role. She thus implies that *motherhood and the family are political roles*. By stating it in such a way she is deconstructing and reconstructing Muslim women's roles. Indeed, male Islamists such as Qutb and Husayn have stressed the importance of women's domestic role within an Islamic society. But theirs was a quest to reconstruct the social glorification of motherhood which in itself is not new. What *is* new however, is precisely that which Ra'uf herself has formulated and in many ways defined: the *political mother*. It can be argued, however, that Ra'uf's call for political mothers is merely what Al-Ghazali has typified for a long time, in her role as political activist and mentor for younger men and women Islamists. Yet Al-Ghazali acted out political motherhood whilst preaching domesticity and an indirect political role as the primary role for other women. Ra'uf, on the other hand, has theorized the role, is living it and sees it as part-and-parcel of any woman's involvement within Islamism. It is important to note that Ra'uf's formulation of political motherhood seemingly excludes barren women. However, Al-Ghazali's living out the role indicates that infertility need not be a deterrent – after all, a barren woman can still fulfil the role of the 'political mother'. Moreover, if the family is the political arena and the constituent of a state, then sisters are also capable of playing an important guiding political role as members of this family-state.[36]

Ra'uf has sought a liberating discourse of empowerment from within an Islamist hegemonic paradigm, effectively creating a sub-narrative to the grander narratives of Islam. In sticking to and arguing within the dominant paradigms, Ra'uf has maintained a continuity with Al-Ghazali and Qazim and other male Islamists. Yet in calling for *women's liberation* from within that hegemonic paradigm, she has attempted to make a break – which is in apparent contradiction to her argument that women do not need a separate issue. By emphasizing the family, Ra'uf is seeking to bridge 'the gap' between men and women and arguing for a collective (Muslim) enterprise, which is contrasted to Western individualistic and divisive feminism. Yet, as I shall argue shortly, she effectively participates in creating consent for, and thus perpetuating the hegemony of, male Islamist ideology.

What is consistent in the arguments made by both men and women Islamists is the dichotomy in analysis and presentation: good/bad, Muslim/Western (or non-Muslim), legitimate/non-legitimate, public/private, man/woman. By constantly maintaining these binarisms, Islamists are using certain forms of reflexivity which are part of their discursive strategies and disciplinary power. To be with them is to be good, Muslim and legitimate, whereas to be against them is to be bad, Western and illegitimate.

By employing such divisive binarisms as a means (intentional or otherwise) of disciplinary power, Islamists are accomplishing two things. First, they are continuously strengthening their power base by delineating who/what they are against. And secondly, they are co-opting all the 'womanpower' they need to carry out what is effectively an Islamic revolution. This latter aspect of co-opting womanpower, however, is done quite cleverly with a built-in safety mechanism, so to speak: the justification *to exclude them legitimately later on.* For not only has the domestic sphere become glorified, but motherhood itself is now the ultimate political occupation which only women can excel at. By elaborating her thesis of women's liberation via the family, Ra'uf is thus sanctioning the bases that once in power, Islamists can tell their women members to continue their *jihad* and *da'wa within* the politicized family. So women are not necessarily being told to 'go back to the home', for in a sense, even at the peak of their activism, they have never left the home. The implications of such an elaboration remain to be seen.

BY WAY OF CONCLUSION

In the first chapter I said that one cannot be an Islamist woman activist without wearing the veil, for it is taken as a sign of acceptance of and devotion to Islamism. But Islamist feminists do not all wear the same form of *hijab*. On the contrary, in the case of Al-Ghazali, Qazim and Ra'uf, it seems that the more they advocate women's rights, the more stringent the form of veil. Al-Ghazali for example, often satisfies herself with a simpler *hijab*, while Ra'uf wears the *khimar*.[37]

Similarly, Islamist feminists do not all 'wear their ideas' in the same fashion. Al-Ghazali's views, though championing some ideal of womanhood, nevertheless remain a traditional visualization of women as obedient wives, wonderful mothers and great soldiers of God. Yet the latter appellation refers more adequately to her than to her advocacy of other Muslim women's roles. The contradictory stances she takes between, on the one hand, her public and assertive role and on the other, the private obedient role she advocates for Muslim girls and women, negates much of what she says. Nevertheless, Al-Ghazali remains an Islamist pioneer and one who has tutored and mothered generations of Islamist men and women. Also important to keep in mind is that Al-Ghazali's ideas on women did not remain static throughout her career. In fact, her conceptualization of women's roles witnessed a gradual shift in the 1980s owing to the exigencies of the political enterprise, and the demand for a broader power base, which necessitated a more active participation of women in Islamist movements.

The Islamist discourse of the 1970s was capable of reaching and mobilizing Qazim, who, though sympathetic to the Muslim Brotherhood's ideology, remained detached from any party or group. Qazim wholeheartedly shares Al-Ghazali's belief that Islamism is the only way forward for all Muslim societies. Moreover, both women share the view, albeit formulated differently, that the current Egyptian state is a miserable failure and totally under the thumb of corrupt Western ideologies. Both decry the savagery of the state in their own way, as well as emphasize its illegetimacy as a structure of authority.

As far as feminism is concerned, Qazim's ideas are far more elaborate and critically targeted than Al-Ghazali's. The reasons for this lie in the fact that feminism – and especially a secularized and Westernized version of it – became more problematic at around the same time that Islamism itself became a dominant feature of Egyptian political life, i.e. during the mid–1970s and 1980s. Furthermore, with both a literary background and a spell in the United States, Qazim was far more exposed to radical Western feminist theory, which she took to be the meaning of all feminisms. The latter meant that whilst she was more prepared than Al-Ghazali to recognize and admit the oppression of women, she was more vehement and clear in her opposition to the manner in which 'feminism' is propagated. Also, being of the generation of Farkhanda Hasan (the NDP Women's Committee) and Asmahan Shukri (Labour Party Women's Committee),[38] it is not novel that Qazim perceives feminism as 'unnecessary'. Where she goes further than any other Egyptian feminist is in her depiction of feminism as a sister to Zionist ideology, and part of a grander 'euro-ameri-zionist' scheme.

Ra'uf constitutes a continuity with Al-Ghazali and Qazim in so far as she herself is a disciple of Muslim Brotherhood thought, is a believer in their 'Islam is the solution' slogan, and sees the power of the state as repressive and illegitimate. Ra'uf, Al-Ghazali and Qazim are all in the same continuum in so far as they share and perpetrate the dichotomous visualization of Islamist thinking, with all its resulting exclusion of the ideas of 'the Other'. All three women are popular leaders with their own set of 'disciples', thereby furthering Islamism through using and developing their disciplinary power, and remaining firmly under – and benefiting from – Islamist hegemony in Egyptian society. Moreover, all three Islamist feminists would not be seen dead with 'feminism' as a self-definition. So strong is their antagonism to the term, that they are not interested in *hearing* of its different reconstructions and multiple conceptualizations.

Where Ra'uf breaks with her former mentors – men and women activists – is to use the same dichotomizing strategies and hegemonic framework to argue for a more openly feminist stance. And here feminism is used in the sense in which I defined it earlier: as an awareness of women's oppression because of their gender, and the willingness to undermine this oppression directly, and create an egalitarian society. Ra'uf seemingly argues for an authoritative family to replace the state and a political mother within that family – state structure as a source of authority. By so advocating, Ra'uf is simultaneously calling for a mechanism that would protect women, whilst paving the road for women to become leaders within it.

Effectively, when looking at Islamist feminism, we began with 'natural dispositions', moved to the dictatorship of society and state by euro-ameri-zionism, and ended up with family states and political mothers. In the following and final chapter, I look at where the journey to understand and analyse the dynamics of feminisms, Islamisms and the state has brought us.

9 Conclusion: Feminism, Islamisms and the State. Or: The Power of Feminisms

The journey I started, to explore the interaction between feminisms, Islamisms and the state in Egypt, has taken me among Islamist men and women activists, secular and Muslim women activists, a variety of laws and debates, and different struggles for power and hegemony. I highlighted and analysed the power struggles between the state, with its personalized nature, and Islamists in their diversity, through the perceptions of diverse Egyptian feminists. Above all, this has been a journey that has given prevalence to and emphasized diverse Egyptian feminisms.

I have found the most frustrating aspect in the writing of this research to be the inability to bring out all the feminist voices. Ultimately, the women I bring out here are only a fraction of the many, many feminists for whom the struggles for women's rights are a defining aspect of their lives. And whose endeavours, both daily and long-term, have shaped, and continue to shape, much of the dynamics of hegemonic power plays.

The most enriching aspect of this project has been meeting these women again and again in the text and renewing my knowledge of them and their discourses throughout. Above all, I am fortified by being able to identify the diversity of women's struggles, and to understand that feminisms are all the better for their differences. Both the researcher and activist aspects of me have gained in knowledge, insight and understanding. The journey of fieldwork and writing has also meant contrasting the different textual validities of representation and discourse respectively. What the different feminists have to say about Islamism, state and feminism was presented by situating and comparing their words.

In the following pages, I summarize the salient aspects of the power dynamics between Islamisms, feminisms and the state. It must be said that as a conclusion, it is quite a difficult chapter to write. For how can one *conclude* on issues that are still to this very moment relevant

233

and *ongoing* dynamics? How does one sum up over 20 years of currently highly pertinent and very crucial activism? Yet I have attempted to capture a moment in the midst of these power dynamics which are constantly shifting. The first section, therefore, maps out the different dynamics of feminisms, Islamisms and the state, primarily in terms of their relevance to and effects on the power of Egyptian feminisms. I identify the main aspects of the different Egyptian feminisms surveyed herein; briefly examine the Islamist–state dynamics; recapitulate the different Islamist viewpoints on gender relations and the ensuing feminist reactions and/or interventions. In the second section I argue for an Egyptian feminist politics of difference. And in the third and final section of this chapter I briefly present other possible avenues of research.

FEMINISMS – TOGETHER YET APART

By working with a postmodern definition of feminism which is based on cultural and historical specificities, as well as localization and pluri-vocality, this research has identified three main feminist streams in Egypt: secular, Islamist and Muslim. These different feminisms remain very much within the upper and middle classes, though the Islamist streams have a potentially larger audience, owing to Islamist use of a hegemonic language of Islam, coupled with different forms of activisms that Islamism itself advocates among all social and economic classes. The term feminism has functioned as an identification technique to map out all the women who acknowledge that women are oppressed by different means and in many ways, and who actively seek to rectify this injustice by diverse methods. Though they generally rarely referred to themselves as feminists – and some strongly opposed the term – it is important to highlight the feminist consciousness these different women represented. Within each stream diversity and contextual specificity are represented by the different articulations of opinions. Nevertheless, I also tried to generalize some of their aspects in order to analyse the larger power dynamics between Islamist thought, feminist activisms and state laws.

At one end of the political spectrum is secular feminism represented by the Tajammu' Party and the New Woman Research Centre (NWRC). Both call for total equality between the sexes, attempt to ground their ideas on women's rights outside religious frameworks and unanimously perceive Islamism as enemy No. 1, and the state as already Islamist to all intents and purposes. As far as most secular feminists are concerned, their antagonism towards any discourse which involves 'Islam' is paralleled only by their intense dislike and suspicion of what they perceive as a hegemonic political Islam. They see the solution, more or less, in terms of insisting that the state adopt secularist ideas which specifically avoid mixing politics with religion and where the latter ought to remain exclusively a private affair of individuals, which should not be mixed with politics at any state or other level. In their manner of rejecting any discourses of emancipation within religious frameworks, secular feminists are effectively risking both estrangement from, as well as the exclusion of, many contemporary Egyptian women activists. In that respect, secular feminists maintain a politics of Othering – where 'the Other' is the one who thinks differently vis-à-vis religion.

At the other end of the political spectrum are the Islamist feminists who are publicly represented to some extent by the Labour Party and independent activists such as Heba Ra'uf. Islamist feminists, like their male Islamist counterparts, frame their whole political and social agendas firmly within a framework of political Islam. Both Islamist men and women are cautious of losing each other's support in their common political struggle, this has certain implications on the feminists' ideas, i.e. emphasizing equity and compatibility, as opposed to calling for equality which would be potentially divisive. The disciplinary power of Islamists corresponds to Islamist feminists' own strategies of exclusion of 'Others' and the demarcation of society between 'us' (Islamists) and 'them' (non-Islamists). Their perceptions of the state are directly opposed to those of the secularists and identical to those of their male colleagues. As far as they are concerned, the state oppresses all in society – men as well as women – precisely because of the lack of true Islamic laws, as a result of succumbing to dominant Western ideology. Women, according to Islamist feminists, are especially oppressed in this regard, because Islamism's hegemonic power is being opposed by repressive state power. The latter has implications for the life-style being imposed on women (and men) which contravenes their natural dispositions and oppresses them through Western – and thus inauthentic – political, social and economic demands. In their manner of adopting the disciplinary techniques (of their male Islamist colleagues) of excluding those who argue for diversity of Islamic political and social practices, Islamist feminists risk alienating many potential recruits. Perceived as such, both Islamist and secular feminists adopt the politics of Othering, or the exclusion of 'the Other' from their discourses.

In between these two feminist streams are Muslim feminists. Their ideas are illustrated by the Nasserist political party and to some extent the Bint-al-Ard group. These feminists perceive the state as a guilty bystander and sometimes knowing accomplice of general Islamist (*not* Islamist feminist) perceptions and allocations of gender roles. Muslim feminists, whilst sometimes advocating that religion is for God and politics is for people, effectively argue along lines which acknowledge the importance of Islam culturally and politically. They generally maintain that no argument for women's issues, placed outside Islam, will gain popular support in a country in which the master narrative of Islam structures and influences the lives of people. Muslim feminists see the development of an Islamic (feminist) counter-discourse as essential, if the false power of Islamist hegemonic knowledge is to be challenged and alternative explanations of reality formulated. In that sense, Muslim feminist thought and agendas fall within the advocated Foucauldian–Gramscian paradigm against hegemonic truth and related power dynamics. Hence, I maintain that their role is the most crucial within the dynamic of state–Islamisms–feminisms. Technically, Muslim feminists can bridge the ideological divide between feminists since by their very nature they combine various religious convictions coupled with an intent to shun extremism from either side. Muslim feminists can be either the outcasts or the trendsetters – depending on the politics they choose and the climate within which they function.

Moreover, even when certain women *claimed* secularism[1] as the basis of their activism (e.g. Nasserist women), this merely indicated a selective appropriation of religious material. In other words, though secularism was touted, efforts were simultaneously being made to 'present the correct understanding of Islamic values'. Put differently, though they claim that their agendas are free of religious argumentation and rationalization, these women cannot avoid the dominant political situation around them. This political situation is characterized by the fact that political discourse is itself geared towards and firmly placed within a larger framework of 'who is the better Muslim?' or 'what is the *real* Islam?' Thus, it becomes rather unrealistic to assume that secularism indeed indicates that religious discourses do not feature. More likely, what differs is the extent and the emphasis in which religion is appropriated in different argumentations.

The strategies adopted by feminists therefore differ among the groups themselves, but also among individuals within the group. Those involved in political parties have tended to be less flexible in their ability to feature their discourse outside some form of Islamic framework – as the case of the Tajammu' indicates. The New Woman Research Centre (NWRC), on the other hand, is comparatively less bothered to legitimize its arguments within an Islamic or religious framework. The reason for this discrepancy is directly related to the distance from actual state repressive power and its incumbent dominant discourse. Political parties – apart from the ruling NDP – are nevertheless in a predicament since they are 'permitted' by the government to be in the opposition. Such groups have comparatively less manoeuvrability in distancing themselves sufficiently from the hegemonic discourses and thus in creating their own.

The situation is equally valid for other (women's) NGOs registered under Law No. 32/1964 with the Ministry of Social Affairs. This is a significant aspect of state disciplinary power, which highlights the capacity of the state not only to control opposition, but to make sure that the same discourse it perpetuates, will dominate. I see a built-in destructive device in such disciplinary power techniques. For as long as the state discourse on Islam remains reactive to Islamism, this characteristic will eventually dominate and typify the discourses of the state-allowed 'opposition' NGOs. Eventually, the only credible and significant discourse of opposition will be that of the Islamists – who have themselves historically introduced, developed and refined the discourse of political Islam. The state is fighting a losing battle on a terrain not its own, and through its repressive power forcing other women's groups – which are potential sites of alternative opposition discourse – to risk losing the battle along with it.

The phrase 'women have no political power' was often repeated during my various interviews and in lectures and seminars which dealt with the gender issue. Apart from finding this statement to be inaccurate, I see it as nevertheless significant. Through their very existence as feminists and in their diversity of resistances to state power, feminists already do have power. Yet the recurrence of this phrase indicates both a dissatisfaction with their present power and/or a certain blindness to it. These diverse feminists want the ability to change the existing social relations in society, in whatever way the different streams see fit. For them, power lies in the ability to amend the laws that affect them: either by replacing them with other man-made laws, or by supposedly God-ordained shari'a. In short, though perceived from different standpoints, power is associated with the state and male Islamists. Secular and Muslim feminists see both as coercive forms of power. Islamists perceive the state power as the coercive one, and Islamist power as potentially libratory by virtue of its claim to authentic Islam.

Whether in NGOs or political parties or both, feminists of all streams are actively involved in debates and actions, but are nevertheless somewhat sceptical. This scepticism is not only of the current Islamist–state dynamics, but also of their own abilities to change the society. The most hopeful of the feminists were to be found in the ruling National Democratic Party (NDP), and within Islamist movements. The former, I believe, are buttressed by the forces of the state's power. And the latter doggedly motivated by the hegemonic ideology of resistance that Islamism is to Islamist activists.

Whether hopeful or sceptical or alternately both, Egyptian feminists of all persuasions are actively involved in discussions on state laws affecting women. Most feminists agree that the current laws are oppressive and need some form of change. The Family, Nationality and Labour Laws and the Criminal Code are perceived as being biased against women. In many cases secular and Muslim feminists distinguished between the letter of the law and its application, arguing for the necessity of more effective implementation. Islamist feminists see no need for civil laws in the first place and advocate the implementation of the shari'a. As state weapons, it can be argued that the laws affecting women have so far succeeded in acting as a form of disciplinary technique which depends on dichotomies of rational/emotional and credible/incredible. This latter form of institutionalized state power thus effectively excludes feminist counter-discourses as the 'unusual', incredible and irrational discourse of 'the Other'. Thus constituted, law has an affinity with power while at the same time being congruent with the disqualification of women's accounts and experiences. Feminists who wish to challenge the law, therefore, have to deconstruct the assumptions that rationality and justice are male attributes. By so doing they are perforce challenging the nature and edifices of male power in the society as a whole.

This endeavour has yet to be attempted. Secular and Muslim feminists perceive the greatest problem to be women's ignorance of the laws themselves, and argue that these laws need amending. Islamist feminists call for them to be scrapped altogether in favour of another set of male-interpreted laws – the shari'a. By merely increasing awareness – and implicitly some form of acceptance – of existing laws,

secular and Muslim feminists are remaining mired in the same androcentric argumentation. Secular feminists have managed to touch the
tip of the iceberg as it were, by challenging the gender bias of the laws.
On the whole however, the tendency among secular and Muslim
feminists is to demand *amendments* to the laws, as opposed to
attempting to formulate alternatives to the masculine discursive character of state laws. Islamist feminists' proposed alternative of shari'a
will fare no better.

Moreover, I believe that challenging the nature of naturalistic
assumptions to male superiority must go in tandem with the refine-
ment of feminism *as a theoretical tool of analysis*. The latter is a fact
which Egyptian feminisms, involved in the struggle to survive within
the different sites of power, cannot yet boast of. The need for a
theoretical tool of analysis is justified further when analysing some
of the debates that take place among feminists. In this case, the
particular debate around female circumcision is most relevant in so
far as it portrays inter- and intra-feminist power dynamics. Although
Islamist feminists for once agree with other feminists on the need to
ban the practice, the determining factor as far as influencing state laws
was the standpoint of males, whether Islamists (e.g. Al-Sha'rawi) or
simply conservative (e.g. Sheikh Al-Azhar). This is a very important
fact which seems to have been ignored so far by most feminists, who
are often too preoccupied with homogenizing state positions whilst
emphasizing their internal differences. This counterproductive non-
analysis of the situation could be substantially enriched by feminist
studies which could expound and formulate common feminist objectives and argumentations. These could highlight situated points of
weakness in state positions, and provide alternative analyses of
debates and consequent dynamics, which may in turn broaden avenues and forms of feminist activism and strategies.

Whether secular, Muslim or Islamist, feminists as groups and as
individuals are involved in constant struggles for hegemony. These
contentions in many ways mirror the ones being waged by Islamists
and the state, in so far as they involve hegemonizing ideas on how to
live and how to view 'the Other'. These disputes in themselves are
ample matter for further research, but suffice it to re-emphasize the
diversity within the groups of feminists. It is clear from their opinions
that both secular and Islamist feminists see no middle ground – either
one is religious or one is not. There does not seem to be an awareness
that there are shades of both secular political inclinations and religious observance. The polarization between the two streams is such

that it reinforces the exclusivity each group intentionally or inadvertently maintains vis-à-vis the other and outsiders – the latter may well include potential recruits.

STATE AND ISLAMISTS – DIVIDED YET UNITED IN POWER AND ON WOMEN?

I have put forth the contention that Islamists are not only to be seen as politico-religious organizations, but also as *regimes*. By identifying them as such – in the same manner that states are also regimes – the (non-)similarity in the methods of commanding power, establishing their ideological hegemony and acting out their disciplinary techniques can be comparably analysed. This in turn has enabled me to point out that religious regimes need not stand in opposition to a secular one, as originally maintained by Bax (1991) when developing the concept. I further contend that religious regimes contest with one another from different power positions. The Egyptian state has always argued along the lines of a 'holier than thou' discourse vis-à-vis Islamists in general. The religious discourse has thus featured in, developed and constituted the main site of the ongoing power struggles. I reinforce Bax's contention that one of the important differences between religious regimes (such as the Muslim Brotherhood) and the state lies in their sources of power. In Egypt the legitimacy of both regimes, and thus to some extent their power base, is based on a similar discourse. The state has the backup of its sources of repressive power (army, police and law), as well as international recognition as the 'legitimate' state. Yet I argue against Bax's idea that the interdependencies between the regimes are *continuously* antagonistic, since this supposes that there can be no points of potential – if rather tacit – consensus. I find Gramsci's elaboration of power as a dialectical interaction between unequal parties in which one (the state) is dominant and the other (Islamists) is subordinate more to the point here. This dialectical interaction better illustrates the interplay of coercion and consent that forms the dynamic of this power relationship. In the process of negotiation of power relations a certain consent to the status quo takes place whereby the state selectively appropriates some of the discourse on women and maintains a silence on others. Not only is the state appropriating some Islamist discourses on women, but certain tactics of delegitimization and violence as well. This is illustrated by the fact that as Islamists dismiss secular feminist discourse as Western and illegitimat and denounce the 1979 PSL (Personal Status Laws) as 'Jihan's Law', the state has also manipulated some women – in this case, wives of suspected Islamist militants. The latter are reported to be illegally arrested and tortured in prison as a way of taunting their husbands or forcing them to confess 'their crimes'. Regardless of the total accuracy of these reports, their likelihood further adds to the dimensions and dynamics of power discussed here. The ruling regime's disciplinary mechanisms and repressive power are acted out on women, i.e. women's bodies are once again the site of power contestations, not unlike what some Islamists maintain vis-à-vis the necessity of the veil – though the degree of violence perpetrated can be contested.

When arguments are based on the same discourse, the potential for consent is warranted and expected. As long as the discourse revolves around 'who is the better Muslim' of the two powers, then within that discourse itself both points of tacit accord *and* of glaring differences can be found, depending on the reader and interpreter of the discourse. The fact is that the closer and 'holier' the grounds of legitimation of power, the more the emphasis seems to be on delegitimizing the opponents' discourses – as opposed to creating an alternative discourse to offer different explanations of reality. The tactic of delegitimization in this case is two-fold. On the one hand, the discourse of Islam itself is selectively appropriated by the state. And on the other hand, the apparatuses of repressive power are kept firmly under state control. In this manner, the state not only manages to maintain its unproductive power, believing that it holds the reins of the popular discourse of Islam, and manipulating it.

And yet by moving from the polarities of good/bad, right/wrong, powerful/powerless, the analysis of the power relations between Islamists and the state can be perceived differently. In this regard, the conceptualization of postmodernism as a decentring from the centre to the periphery is relevant. If the centre is the state and the periphery is Islamist regimes (in their diversity), then the negotiation of power relations and the fluidity of power indicates that at some point 'the periphery' and 'centre' may well change places. Effectively, discourses elaborated by Islamist regimes are becoming centres, or focal power points, while still reacting to state forms of power. This is not to argue for a continuation in the polarity between centre and periphery, but rather to illustrate the shifting centrality of the discourses and their power at given points on time. The awareness of this shifting centrality is an important focus of attention for feminists, since it may well stress 'which way the wind is blowing', and thus enable effective and timely mobilization.

The state's attempts at manipulation of Islamic discourse ('we are the better Muslims') and the repressive power its structures maintain (seen in crackdowns on 'Islamist terrorists'), illuminate the crisis of legitimacy the discourses of the Egyptian government face. Here again the state's self-defeating devices are underscored. For in the power struggles, Islamist regimes are merely, as mentioned above, furthering the discourses they are themselves inventing and hence masters of. The latter are *discourses of resistance to state power* which as in the Foucauldian definition is *productive power*. The state's attempts to manipulate these discourses itself using its official Islamic establishment triggers a self-defeating mechanism, for the discourse of the state is centred on maintaining repressive and thus *unproductive power*. The implications of thus characterizing the different forms of power highlight possible future configurations, wherein unproductive forms of power may cede hegemonic credibility to other forms of productive power. The result is, as we see each day, a cycle in which unproductive power delegitimizes itself, and discourses of 'Islam' *per se* dominate almost all political interactions.

ISLAMISMS AND FEMINISMS – DEVELOPING APART YET TOGETHER

When discussing men and women Islamists, patterns in relations of power are traced between Islamist activists and their joint calls for an Islamic state and society. This pattern is the continuous assertion by both men and women Islamists that 'there is no woman's issue, but there is a social issue', without clearly specifying which existing aspects of tradition or practices are harmful to women. The mere establishment of shari'a and the creation of an Islamic state will not automatically guarantee women their rights. Nevertheless, Islamist regimes lack a clear outline or specification as to how women are going to enjoy these rights accorded to them by shari'a. Not only that, but Islamist feminists' tendency to insist on ignoring a specific 'women's issue' in this debate can prove unhelpful if and when Islamists come to power. This is a real risk since studies of earlier liberation and/or nationalist movements indicated that promises of more egalitarian lives and laws for involved women activists repeatedly fail to materialize once the male revolutionaries achieve power.

The review of male Islamist views on gender roles indicated that the majority agree on the importance of women's traditional role of motherhood. The difference in their perceptions lies in the manner in which motherhood is being politicized as a major and integral societal role, without which the Islamist revolution cannot be accomplished. Put differently, women within the home are not oppressed, but, they are actively *countering* this oppression. The value of their social, economic and political roles is not less, but more and different in significance, than their public work.

The Islamist regime of truth and disciplinary power is reflected here in the precise allocation of roles for men and women which all Islamists agree with, albeit formulated differently. The discipline being referred to here is precisely in the manner in which male Islamists impose their ideas – different men dictate the same ideas all the time. Though they attempt to phrase their ideas in a way that would seem as if women were being given positive status and recognition – with some exceptions – the main message remains the same.

What is important to note is that Islamist male standpoints differ little from those of other conservative male Muslim thinkers. Hence the state appropriation of some of the Islamist/conservative male thinkers as their own spokesmen on women's issues. The reason this is significant has to do with the grey area where Islamist male gender ideology meets conservative male gender tenets. This is precisely the same area in which state gender beliefs are grounded. Although the struggle for power and hegemony between state and Islamist regimes continues, consent on women's issues is manufactured within these grey areas.

Islamist feminists, whilst agreeing that women's primary role is mainly as wives and mothers, demonstrate through their own lives and activism that their Islamism can be an emancipatory discourse. The mother of Islamist women activists, Al-Ghazali, divorced her first husband (since she had the *'isma*[2]) and stipulated to her second that her work for God came first. Indeed, her public activism is part of the much boasted heritage of the Egyptian Islamist movement. Qazim also divorced her first husband, also suffered imprisonment and also furiously employed her pen and her words for the public activism she maintained in the name of fighting for Islamic justice. Ra'uf emphasizes her *choice* of the 'Islamic path', wrote a thesis defending women's Islamic rights to become political leaders and judges, and is one of the spokespeople and proselytizers for the Islamist movement. None of these women argued – like their Islamist male colleagues openly and often ingeniously do – that women's work outside the home is unnecessary. On the contrary, through their varying discourse and their public activism, they are continuously demonstrating the necessity of public activism for all soldiers of Allah – regardless of gender. Moreover, Islamist feminists have devoted their lives and their work to finding means through which women can understand and gain their Islamic rights. The generational progression of Islamist feminism indicates not a tacit acceptance of secondary roles, but a complex elaboration of their status as Muslims who are equal with men, before Allah and in the perceived struggle for an Islamic *umma*.

What is consistent in the arguments proposed by both men and women Islamists is the dichotomy in analysis and presentation which is part of their own discursive strategies and disciplinary power. By constantly maintaining binarisms, Islamists are validating their own form of hegemonic discourse. For to be with them is to be good, Muslim and legitimate, whereas to be against them is bad, Western and illegitimate. By employing such divisive binarisms as a means (intentional or otherwise) of disciplinary power, male Islamists are following a two-pronged strategy. First, they are continuously strengthening their power base by delineating who or what they are against. And secondly, they are co-opting all the 'womanpower' they need whilst ensuring that when they are no longer needed, they can be legitimately discarded. For not only has the domestic sphere become glorified, but motherhood itself is now the ultimate political occupation which only women can excel at.

Islamist feminists like Ra'uf argue that women's liberation is via the family. What this potentially justifies is that once in power, Islamists can tell their women members to continue their *jihad* and *da'wa within* the politicized family. In other words, women will not be urged to 'go back to their home'. For their greatest acts of political participation have been in the broader spheres of the home. Yet, one of the most significant contributions of Islamist feminisms, championed by Ra'uf especially, is precisely the transgressing of divisive binarism when it comes to women's activism. For what Ra'uf effectively argues for is the blurring – if not total discarding – of the public/private distinction. By formulating the family as a political site of power and resistance (to the state), Ra'uf is arguing for the public role in what is taken to be a principally private domain. Ra'uf's ideas are gaining much acceptance and support, especially among the younger generation of Islamist women. What remains to be seen, however, is the extent to which Ra'uf's arguments will be popular among male Islamists once the implications of her discourse are realized.

In the long run, such a discourse as developed by Ra'uf will challenge the male Islamists' views on rationality and goodness being exclusively male characteristics. By arguing against the fine line between public and private, Ra'uf is paving the way for two things. First, the logical extension of her argument is that the public space for women's activism is interchangeable with the extended family. So, rhetorically speaking, where does the family end and the state/public space begin? Secondly, Ra'uf's argument legitimizes women's occupation of such public roles as are currently refuted by the most moderate of Islamists: leadership of the whole Islamic community and the judiciary – both 'rational', male roles.

Nevertheless, Ra'uf perpetuates the assertion made by both men and women Islamists that 'there is no woman's issue, but there is a social issue'. She refrains from clearly specifying which existing aspects of lifestyles or customs are harmful to women, not to mention un-Islamic (e.g. circumcision, domestic violence and rape). This is occurring simultaneously with a rising religious conservatism in the society as a whole, whereby certain religious practices that are harmful to women become more deep-seated and incorporated into 'Islam'. These supposedly 'Islamic' customs, compounded by the lack of a comprehensive specification of women's rights on the part of Islamist women in the Islamist movement, indicate that existing harmful practices (a) continue to be (mis)perceived as Islamic, and (b) are institutionalized as such (in the event of Islamists seizing state power and institutionalizing their values).

ISLAMISMS, FEMINISMS AND THE STATE: THE POWERS OF RESISTANCE AND THE RESISTANCES OF POWER

Contemporary feminisms have, by their very existence on the political and social scene today, accomplished a great deal. I would venture to say that Islamisms have, in fact, enriched the contemporary feminist movement, in so far as they have galvanized, mobilized and given added and new significance and multiple forms of women's activisms. This is not to argue that Islamisms are 'the best thing that ever happened' to feminisms. But it is in their resistances to both Islamist gender ideologies – whether propagated by the state or Islamist groups, as well as in their resistances to competing secular ideologies

– that feminisms take on and develop new and diverse forms of power relationships. This is in line with Foucault's assertion that by resisting power they already have power. This enhances their present discourses and empowers them to further and create spaces for future alternatives.

Discourses are central to the diverse power-games taking place. What is undoubtedly true is that whether secular, Muslim or Islamist, the claim to some form of power defines and redefines the discourses and their resulting relationships. Islamists' power resides in their resistances to the state. Whether it is the Muslim Brotherhood or the *Jihad*, both are movements that aim for state power using similar disciplinary mechanisms – those of exclusion. One is either 'with them' or 'against them'; there is no middle way. Foucault concentrated on institutions and the individualizations and disciplinary practices which created divisions in society. What I have highlighted is that disciplinary practices of division also take place at group level and the exclusion is thus of entire groups and not just of individuals. Moreover, the exclusion is not random but tactical, and occurs simultaneously with different strategies of inclusion. Groups like the Muslim Brotherhood, for example, are simultaneously excluding those who disagree with their strategies for achieving power, whilst including certain voices (e.g. women's) which they can use to further their political ambitions. For Islamist regimes the quest for ideological hegemony and productive power constitutes a priority, especially vis-à-vis the state's repressive power.

Islamist discourses, however, are not the only ones that carry out exclusionary policies of 'the Other'. In fact, feminisms are also exclusionary. By believing that 'the Other' suffers from a false consciousness, whether they are Islamist, Muslim or secular feminists, they are effectively delegitimizing the discourse of 'the Other' and excluding each other. By rejecting the term that defines their activism and attempting to fit into broader political agendas, such as those in political parties, feminists are simultaneously seeking a wider public at the expense of prioritizing women's issues. This strategy, though popular with many women's groups, risks in the long run repeating what took place in earlier nationalist liberation movements. Indeed, the problems faced by society are common to both men and women and both need to strive alongside each other for a better future. Nevertheless, in a situation where hegemonic power is shifting and is not localized in one arena, to decide against prioritizing a particular issue is to lose the primacy of that issue in a moment of the struggle.

For in the next round of interactions, the alliances between the different powers will shift, and the positionality of the discourses will also change. Feminists may gain the upper hand at a particular moment in time – e.g. when the Egyptian state, in an attempt to improve its international image, approved the Personal Status Laws in 1985 just before the Nairobi Women's Conference. Ten years later, the ruling party adopted the New Marriage Contract drafted by secular and Muslim feminists, just before the official delegation left for the Beijing Women's Conference. *These are moments of productive power for secular and Muslim feminists.* It is in the run-up to and preparations for these international events that the state is prepared to use its leverage to adopt proposals advocated by some feminists – even though these proposals themselves are compromises. Once these feminists return to Egypt after such an event, the power balance has necessarily shifted – now the moment is for the Islamists, and the tensions shift between the regime and Islamist groups. In these moments Islamist feminists and Islamists decry all forms of secularism and critique the evil and false consciousness of secular feminists. In November 1995, parliamentary elections meant that the government had to call on all its repressive power to clamp down on all Islamists. Though repressive, the moment of power belonged to the state.

Perhaps the most inclusive strategy of all has been and continues to be that of the state. The latter occasionally strategically appropriates the most woman-unfriendly aspects of Islamist discourse, whilst electing an obvious secular feminist to head its women committee, whose duty it is 'to prove' women's achievements in all areas of work and activism. These apparent contradictions are indications of strategic alliances undertaken by the state to attempt to maintain its dominance. Depending on where the state is and what role(s) it occupies, its allegiances and interests will shift. In such manipulations of discourse, the state effectively nurtures the schisms among feminists which ensure its continued dominance.

One is thus reminded of Sawicki's (1991: 26) assertion that 'there are no privileged or fundamental coalitions in history, but rather a series of unstable and shifting ones'. Being the wielder of repressive power, the state is in a position to shift its alliances relatively easily. Nevertheless, Islamist regimes are themselves shifting alliances to increase their popular and institutional power and hegemonic bases. The alliance formed between the Muslim Brotherhood and the Wafd Party in the 1984 parliamentary elections and the following alliance with the Labour Party for the 1987 parliamentary elections are ample evidence.

FEMINIST ALLIANCES AND A POLITICS OF DIFFERENCE?

Political alliances with other feminists are necessary for feminists if they are to shift their power bases and empower themselves to counterbalance the diverse hegemonic influences. Many of the feminists interviewed echoed the need for such an alliance. In fact, feminism can mobilize individuals from diverse sites in the social field and thereby use difference as a resource. Here I would reinforce Audre Lorde's call for a 'politics of difference' (Lorde 1984: 115). Lorde claims that it is not women's differences that separate them but rather their 'refusal to recognize those differences, and to reexamine the distortions which result from our misnaming them and their effects upon human behaviour and expectation'. Lorde suggests that feminists should devise ways of discovering and utilizing their differences as a source for creative change. Learning to live and struggle with many of the differences may be one of the keys to disarming the power of male norms which have all been internalized to varying degrees (ibid.).

Sawicki (1991: 32) takes this further by arguing that although a politics of difference does not offer feminists a morality derived from a universal theory of oppression, it need not lapse into a form of pluralism in which anything goes. What Egyptian feminists can and need to do, I reiterate, is to develop theoretical analyses on the basis of which generalizations can be made. These would help to identify patterns in relations of power and thereby recognize the relative effectiveness or ineffectiveness, safety or danger of particular practices. The relative importance of male voices in the formulation of state laws and decisions is a practice that feminist analysis can trace and counter. Egyptian feminists could realize that whether secular or Islamist, looking at their different activisms exclusively in light of victimization and/or false consciousness will not provide the necessary shifts in their strategies for power. On the contrary, by identifying the state as the prime mover in the power game, feminists may be able to find more common ground in their struggles than is currently the case.

A politics of difference is necessarily no blueprint. For in a feminist politics of difference, theory and moral judgements are geared to specific contexts, but it does require that categories (notably 'Islamism' and 'feminism') be clear and provisional. This is in order to shed light on possible strategies and enable shifting coalitions between different feminisms. This would enable the fluidity of power bases and alliances. What is certain is that differences are ambiguous; they may be used either to divide or to enrich feminist politics. Sawicki elaborates that

> If we [feminists] are not the ones to give voice to them [differences], then history suggests that they will continue to be either misnamed and distorted, or simply reduced to silence.
>
> (1991: 32)

So far, differences have been used to divide Egyptian feminists, and thus to hold back the elaboration of feminist politics, an elaboration of which could extend feminisms beyond resistance and towards hegemony. The Islamist feminist from the women's committee in the Islamist Labour Party herself suggested areas where women from diverse political orientations can agree. Women's literacy and the encouragement of women to vote and become involved in the political processes, banning female circumcision, raising women's awareness of their rights – all are priorities for feminists. Yet nowhere has there been a non-exclusivist attempt to bring these women together as common combatants for *women's* causes. For each is busily believing that 'the Other' is 'the enemy'. In fact, not only is this binarism unproductive as a way of thinking, but 'the enemy' is more likely to be the group(s) which hegemonize(s) and benefit(s) from all the infighting and bickering among feminists – i.e. state and Islamisms.

A politics of difference based on feminist theoretical analysis is an untried agenda in Egypt, and in fact in much of the Arab and Muslim world. Yet, in a situation where hegemony and power can be perceived as indeed circulating, such an agenda may appear to be worth trying at the very least. However, it must be kept in mind that feminist struggles are by no means likely to end with the creation of an alliance enriched by the politics of difference. On the contrary, scepticism of a power-free society is crucial to any feminist and alternative political agendas. Those who struggle must never grow complacent, as victories are often overturned and changes may take on different faces over time, and institutions, once established can always be used for different purposes (Sawicki 1991: 28).

I believe that the group most prepared and capable of advocating a politics of difference successfully are Muslim feminists. Almost by definition Muslim feminism acts as a cultural bridge between more secular ideas adopted by the secularists, and the more stringent ideas espoused by Islamists. In other words, Muslim feminists are the in-between of the two extremes. Any alliance will have to take into account that extremes will not simply meet, but that the role of a go-between is crucial in that regard. It is in the recourse to some form of middle path which seeks to maintain difference whilst looking for the strengths inherent in them, as well as highlighting the commonal-ities, that Muslim feminism paves the way for a politics of difference. Muslim feminists are in the unique position of falling within a hege-monic Islamic paradigm, whilst simultaneously arguing from within it for a diversity of reinterpretations and readings from without. Speak-ing in terms of meta-narratives, Muslim feminism speaks from the platform of a privileged discourse of Islam whilst simultaneously challenging the power of those who speak in the name of the same narrative (Islamists).

It is very significant that 110 men and women from across the political spectrum can successfully set up a Liberties Committee to defend political activists and freedom of speech,[3] whilst feminists are unable to do something similar – despite repeated attempts going back almost a century. Such a Liberties Committee will undoubtedly be countering state ideology and dominance, yet that has not deterred notable individuals from participating in it.[4] Moreover, the Com-mittee successfully brings together Islamists, secularists and Muslim intellectuals. The question that inevitably comes to mind is, what is keeping Egyptian feminists from holding a similar joint platform to fight for basic women's demands like social justice and human rights? Why, in other words, do political affiliations seem most divisive and least productive when it comes to women's issues? I have no answers to this question. Suffice it here to state my conviction that, symbol-ically speaking, feminist activisms are, and will remain, potentially more powerful in altering the status quo than any other social move-ment or force. Hence the attempts to appropriate different agendas in order to quash feminisms and to maintain divisions among its ranks. This reaffirms the fact that *dialogue* between the different feminisms – a dialogue that lingers less on political affiliation and dwells more and constructively on *common* goals developed for and by the different *feminists* – is a social, political and cultural necessity, and one that will have to be made inevitable in the historical development of feminisms in Egypt. The old adage of power in unity need not be dismissed too easily so long as unity and homogeneity are not confused. So far, Egyptian feminists have denied even the identity of a feminist con-sciousness, fearing that it will create divisiveness within the society between men and women. Yet by refuting that aspect of their identity and their politics, they are creating and nurturing the space that divides them from each other.

Notes

1 BACKGROUND AND THEORETICAL CONSIDERATIONS

1. The details of and around these laws will be explained in Chapter 5.
2. AWSA's founding member and chair, the physician and novelist Nawal Al-Sa'dawi, believed that politics and women's issues cannot be separated, and that 'everything is political' (in an interview with the author in November 1991). Al-Sa'dawi was and remains an important Egyptian secular feminist who, through her writings about sex and female circumcision, for example, was the first to attempt to break these various taboos.
3. Cheryl Johnson-Odim makes a distinction, which I use and elaborate upon. Johnson-Odim argues that in the process of making a distinction between different feminisms taking place in differing contexts, gender oppression 'should not be limited to merely achieving equal treatment for women vis-à-vis men. This is where feminism as a philosophy must differ from the shallow notion of "women's rights"' (Johnson-Odim, in Mohanty, Russo and Torres 1991: 20).
4. These activities tend to be developed in urban or urbanized areas, and thus adopt a related bias, though there are numerous small- and large-scale projects for rural women all over Egypt.
5. I am elaborating on Margot Badran's definition in Kandiyoti (1991: 201–36).
6. See Chapter 2.
7. *Jihad* means effort. It is usually linked with *fi sabil Allah* (for the sake of God), i.e. for a religiously commendable aim. This has various meanings. It is often understood as war with society or others, in order to enhance the Islamic character. In other instances, *Jihad* also refers to struggle with one's 'self', in order to overcome one's evil inclinations. Islamists often use the word as synonymous with revolutionary struggle for Islamist ideals.
8. Interview with Heba Ra'uf in May 1993, Cairo.
9. For an interesting and informative comparative situation in Algeria, see Susan Slymoviç's 'Hassiba Ben Bouali, If You Could See Our Algeria: Public Space in Algeria, *MERIP*, No. 192, Vol. 125, No. 1, Jan-Feb 95.
10. Prominent and internationally known writers and theorists who advocate this stance include Fatima Mernissi (Moroccan), Riffat Hassan (Pakistani-American) and Azizah Al-Hibri (Arab-American).
11. *Ijtihad* is independent inquiry into the sources (i.e. the Quran and the exemplary behaviour of the Prophet Muhammad (*pbuh* – peace be upon him) (the Sunna) as transmitted in the *hadith*. The main aim of this inquiry is to come up with interpretations of the religious texts that are appropriate to the conditions and exigencies of modern day life.
12. The role of the Egyptian state in debates about and between feminists and Islamists can best be described as that of sitting on the fence and jumping in whenever politically expedient. On the one hand, much media time and space are given to conservative Muslim preachers who advocate women's

return to the home as a cure for unemployment, congested traffic, and a host of other social ills. On the other hand, the official ruling party line condemns Islamists as a whole as nothing short of terrorists.

13. Information about these *fatwas* can be found in the Egyptian national daily, *Al-Ahram*, of the respective periods.
14. Cf. *Al-Ahram*, 8 December 1981.
15. ICPD is the acronym of the International Conference on Population and Development held in Cairo, September 1994.
16. Specifically the lawyers', journalists', teachers' and doctors' syndicates.
17. Farida Al-Naqqash, head of the Women's Committee in the leftist Tajammu' party, in a personal interview in Cairo, November 1995.
18. Islamization is intended to refer to increasing Islamic consciousness and practice. These processes range from giving classes in mosques, universities and homes, to demanding the application of the shari'a through various groups and institutions.
19. As quoted in William Dalrymple, *The Guardian Weekly*, April (1996: 29).
20. Their emphasis throughout when referring to these terms.
21. This is quoted from the back cover of the *Women against Fundamentalism* journal (No. 5, Vol. 1, 1994).
22. Personal interview with Farida Al-Naqqash in Cairo, May 1993.
23. This was part of her talk in a seminar on 'Women in Egypt', 8 September 1995. The seminar was part of the NGO Forum of the United Nations Fourth World Women's Conference, in Huairou, China. This seminar was organized by the Group of Seven, better known as the Communication Group for the Enhancement of the Status of Women in Egypt. This group is composed of seven women all of whom occupy distinguished and influential social positions in Egyptian society. Dhul-fiqar is one of the members of this group.
24. This will be elaborated in Chapters 5 and 6.
25. This is a summary of conversations held with a great many feminists from diverse orientations – secular, Muslim and Islamist – over a period from September to November 1994. But these statements echoed similar assertions made by others in earlier fieldwork in 1993.
26. The *niqab* is a black shroud that covers the whole body from the head to the feet. Only a small hole (or two) is left for the women to see through, and even the hands are usually concealed by gloves. See Chapter 5 for further elaboration.

2 LIVING FIELDWORK, WRITING ETHNOGRAPHY

1. I have borrowed this title from Marie Gillespie (1995: 48) since I found it to be well formulated in general and apt for my purposes in particular.
2. By situatedness, I mean a 'particular age, sexual orientation, belief, educational background, ethnic identity and class' (Bell 1993: 2).
3. Here she named specifically Yusuf al-Qaradawi, and Sheikh Mohammed Metwalli al-Sharawi, who are two of the Islamist scholars whose books on women I review in Chapter 7: 'Islamism and Gender: Male Perspectives'.

4. The aforementioned Nadia.
5. There were seven Egyptian women, two Sudanese (one man and one woman) and one Malaysian man, all of whom were completing their graduate studies in universities in the West. In the meantime, three of them have completed their MAs, and one has obtained his PhD. The universities they were attached to were mostly in the United States, and the others were also attached to universities in The Netherlands, Belgium, France and Germany.
6. 'Indigenous' is used here in the manner defined by Altorki and El-Solh to mean 'the researcher's membership in a cultural area with which they identify or are identified' (Altorki and El-Solh 1988: 7). The term is also understood and employed as interchangeable with 'insider' and 'native'.
7. I elaborate on this further in Chapter 5.
8. The significance of this latter aspect is highlighted in Chapter 6, where I write of the legal discrimination against children of Egyptian women married to foreign men.
9. Notably those I researched earlier in 1988–90 for my MA thesis, and those whom I had observed during my years as an undergraduate (1985–8).

3 THE STATE AND ISLAMISTS

1. See also Abdel-Malek (1968) and Be'eri (1970).
2. A more detailed discussion of these consequences will be elaborated in the following chapter which deals specifically with how Islamists coped with and reacted to the state regimes, and explains the differences in ideologies and tactics between the different Islamists.
3. The views of some Islamist women activists is elaborated in Chapter 8.
4. At that time Nasser was facing the fiasco of an ill-planned Yemen expedition, the disease of a state bureaucracy that was growing bigger and more inefficient, trouble with the then USSR – Nasser's ally whom the Islamists perceived as the atheistic evil influence – and the dilemmas of the Arab–Israeli wars.
5. For a detailed and highly interesting study of the political role of the Bar Association in the Sadat period, see Baker (1990: 46–78).
6. This was mentioned in one of Sadat's speeches, reported in *al-Ahram* newspaper, 6 September 1981.
7. For an interesting and informative rebuttal of these charges, see *al-Da'wa*, May 1981.
8. The details of the Military Academy Group and the others will be elaborated further in the next chapter.
9. Tilmisani in an interview in *al-Musawwar*, 22 January 1982.
10. It was argued – in many cases rightly – that this alliance cost the Wafd many Coptic supporters and members, and seriously damaged its credibility in the eyes of many intellectuals, who were disillusioned with the whole adoption by a supposedly secular party of religious discourse. Further, the discourse of the political parties *in general* became more 'Islamized' so to speak. With most of them suddenly affirming the need

for Islamic 'guidelines' in policy-making, if not outrightly claiming the necessity of relying on the shari'a (Islamic law) as a basis for politics and society.

11. Despite these claims of openness it is well known among analysts that Egypt has an apathetic electorate (since the one-party initiated by Nasser), which does not demonstrate a dynamic response to the electoral process.

12. There are many reports on the Brotherhood's repeated claim to the government that by granting them political party status, the radical Islamist regimes will become far less influential (and thus less of a problem) because adherents will flock to the 'legitimate Islamic political party' (meaning the Brotherhood).

13. Yet, the Saudi Arabian regime also provides financial donations to the Egyptian state. A possible interpretation of this seemingly contradictory position may be the Saudi interest in maintaining a certain political instability in neighbouring countries, with the aim of enhancing its own role as regional leader. See also Black et al. (1992/1993: 45–6).

14. This was repeatedly pointed out to me by secular and Muslim feminists alike.

4 ISLAMISMS AND THE SEEDS OF DISCIPLINARY POWER

1. After all, as wives and daughters and sisters of male activists, it is not inconceivable that these women would have exerted their influence.

2. Umar al-Tilmisani was leader of a splinter faction in the Muslim Brotherhood, as well as editor of its mouthpiece, *al-Da'wa* magazine.

3. The group's real name was the Society of Muslims. But *al-Takfir wal Hijra* literally means declaring Muslims as unbelievers (*Kufar*) and migration, which is what the group, in many ways, stands for. In fact, it was easier to identify them thus because the literal Arabic translation of 'Society of Muslims' would confuse it with another Islamist group, the *Jama'at Islamiyya*.

4. This ministry manages Islamic religious property and acts as mouthpiece for official Islam.

5. Such as rejecting Friday prayers that were not led by a member of the society and refusing to pray in mosques that were not erected by the society's leaders or followers.

6. These are religious counsels which serve as sanctions for either policies or specific actions. These decrees usually cite precedents or Islamic justifications.

7. His influence is still felt today as his religious interpretations are aired on state television. Al-Sha'rawi's discourse on women is analysed in Chapter 7.

8. *Dar al-Islam* literally means the house of Islam. This term is used to refer to the domain of Muslims or the Muslim lands. It is to be contrasted with *Dar al-harb*, which is the house or domain of war.

9. Umar al-Tilmisani, the previously referred to editor of *al-Da'wa*, was the leader of that group.
10. This party was founded in Palestine in 1950 partly as a reaction to the Arab defeat in the 1948 war with Israel, and partly due to the assassination in 1949 of Hasan al-Banna (founder of the Muslim Brotherhood). Unlike the Muslim Brotherhood who sought to preach to the Muslim masses about the need to Islamize society, the Islamic Liberation Party held that political power first had to be seized in a *coup de force*. Islamism would then be instituted from above. Because of its objectives, the party was outlawed everywhere and its members were hunted down (see Kepel 1985).
11. Mainly by organizing public prayers – particularly in the two most famous Muslim feast-days – during which the *Jama'at* would both preach and recruit followers.
12. This had been more or less the voice and reporter of the *Jama'at* since their inception.
13. *Dhimmi* is a word that has been used since the early days of Islam. Basically, it means those who are not Muslims but who are protected by the state in return for payment of an obligatory tax – the *Jizya*.
14. The same tactics were visible later in June 1981 in the poverty-ridden Cairo neighbourhood of *al-Zawiya al-Hamra*. The incidents that took place in this area between the two communities are noted for the horrific violence that occurred. Several people from both communities were killed in a barbarous and bizarre manner. It is officially reported that the *Jama'at* instigated this conflict – among others – in its attempt to undermine the role of the state.
15. For a more detailed study of this group, see Youssef (1985) and Guenena (1986). I use the terms *al-Jihad* and *Jihad* interchangeably.
16. The concept of Pharaoh used here is intended to refer to both ruler of the country as well as tyrant – these are the traditional images (or stereotypes) of the rulers of ancient Egypt. According to this Islamist discourse, the president of the country is alluded to as autocratic and ruthless, whilst being simultaneously distanced from Islam and Islamic history.
17. Which was conveniently and strategically organized into two main head-quarters:one in Cairo and the other in Middle Egypt.
18. A blind professor at the al-Azhar faculty of Asyut who had links with Karam Zuhdi from 1974. Kepel relates that this professor would forbid female students from directly asking him a question lest he be committing adultery by the ear! The female students, therefore, would write out their question and their male colleagues would then read it out. This is the same man who was sentenced in the United States in October 1995 for 'seditious conspiracy'. He was charged with being the mastermind of a plot (uncovered by the US Federal Bureau of Investigations) to bomb buildings and tunnels in New York.
19. It is often said that another instance in which they were assured of their entry to heaven was when they killed Coptic goldsmiths during robberies committed to finance the organization. Michael Youssef, however, points out that this was denied during the trials of *al-Jihad* members.
20. Khalid Al-Islambuli was to participate in a parade in which the head of state would be present.

21. Since, along with his comrades, he had formed a group with deep roots in the regional Muslim clans, from which he could draw invaluable solidarity and support when needed.
22. The most prominent of these activities were attacks on the tourist industry, successfully aimed to discourage tourists from coming to Egypt. A major source of foreign revenue for the state was indeed badly hit. What the Islamists did not count on, however, or perhaps did not care to take into account, is the repercussion of such a policy on the many millions of Egyptians who earn their livelihoods from the tourist industry, as well as the many who were caught up and hurt in the violence.
23. Particularly the phenomenon of Islamic investment companies which proliferated in the 1980s, some of which were rumoured to be financing Brotherhood activities.
24. The peace treaty with Israel being a case in point, along with the government's stance in the Gulf War.
25. Elaboration on how men and women Islamist activists – and Islamist feminists in particular – perceive women's issues is given in Chapters 7 and 8.

5 FEMINIST VOICES AND WOMEN'S ORGANIZATIONS

1. Many detailed studies have been carried out on the nineteenth-century feminist movement in Egypt. Among the numerous studies see Tucker (1985), Khalifa (1973), Jayawardena (1986: 43–56) and Khater and Nelson (1988: 465–83).
2. For further readings on Huda Sha'rawi's feminist activism, see Badran (1995) and Abdel Kader (1987).
3. Such a massive work has already been undertaken by two women researchers in Cairo: Amany Qandil and Sara Ben Nafissa (1994).
4. The name of the body concerned with women's issues actually differs from one party to another. The NDP have a 'women's secretariat', the Nasserists refer to it as the 'women's committee', and the Tajammu' refer to it as the 'progressive women's union'.
5. This quote and all the following are from an interview taken in October 1994.
6. This and all subsequent quotations are based on a personal interview in November 1994.
7. See Chapter 3.
8. I had met Farida al-Naqqash twice in 1993. On these occasions, she was extremely helpful and generous with her time and her information.
9. As with other political parties in the making, the now Nasserist Party had to go to court and fight a legal battle in order to obtain permission from the court to exist and act as a political party. Many initial petitions or requests to form political parties are thwarted and refused by the government.
10. This and all following quotes, unless otherwise specified, come from a personal interview in September 1994.

11. These reasons were elaborated by Mrs Farida Al-Naqqash, in personal interviews in 1993 and 1994. Al-Naqash is an active and founding member of the central committee of the women's union in the Tajammu' Party. She was herself imprisoned during the 'purge' of political opponents that Sadat carried out in September of 1981.
12. In this case, the group is viewed as a 'non-profit company' and therefore avoids the Ministry of Social Affairs and is listed with the Authority for Land and Real Estate Registration instead.
13. AHED works on women's health issues as part of an overall policy 'to promote the understanding of health and environmental development based on the social, economic and behavioral backgrounds peculiar to the Egyptian environment and the health care delivery system' (AHED pamphlet, n.d.)
14. One such project also concerns legal aid, i.e. helping women both to know about and receive aid to fight for their legal rights. This project is carried out both by the New Woman Research Centre and the Association for the Development and Enhancement of Women (ADEW).
15. The ICPD is the International Conference on Population and Development, held in Cairo in September 1994.
16. The quote is from a personal interview conducted in October 1994. The following quotes are from the same source and time.
17. This situation has changed somewhat in the last few months of 1996, with the government moving towards a more comprehensive ban. This occurred after an outcry by many women and human rights groups, as a result of the death of several young girls due to this operation.
18. See Chapter 1.
19. Hana, personal interview, Cairo, May 1993.
20. For convenience, those from the Muslim Brotherhood will have 'MB' after their quotes, and those from the Jihad group will have 'J'.
21. For an elaboration on this, see Chapter 8.
22. This is a famous Nasserist motto, which was reiterated by some of the Nasserist women's committee members.

6 CURRENT DEBATES ON WOMEN'S LEGAL RIGHTS IN THEORY AND PRACTICE

1. These women, seven in total, worked from a purely personal and voluntary initiative. They come from different governmental and non-governmental affiliations. One was the Egyptian ambassador to Vienna, one a journalist, one a professor of sociology at the American University in Cairo (AUC), one is a head of a cultural NGO 'Friends of the People', another a lawyer and partner in a prestigious law firm and the last a teacher of simultaneous translation at the AUC. This highly commendable initiative and result highlights the fluidity of involvement of some women activists in many initiatives and organizations simultaneously.

2. This is a long and interesting issue in and of itself, which is beyond the scope of this research. For detailed information see Dhu-l-fiqar (1995: 118–48).
3. This domain of the law is governed by the Islamic law according to the Hanafite Madhab, and since the 1920s certain parts have been codified and thereby reformed. Other parts (e.g. the *mahr* – explained later) are still governed by pure Islamic law.
4. Jihan was the wife of the late President Sadat. She played a key role in getting the law drafted and pushing for it. Probably knowing it would be controversial, the late president passed it by presidential decree thus avoiding the normal procedure of having it debated in Parliament. Although this law was more favourable to women than its predecessor, it put women's groups in a quandary owing to their principled disagreement with Sadat's undemocratic rule.
5. In addition, the marriage must be publicly announced, and the contract notarized and signed by two witnesses who are of legal age (i.e. 18 and above).
6. First, no international observers were allowed. Second, the largest opposition source, the Muslim Brotherhood members, were rounded up, imprisoned and subjected to military court trials on trumped up charges. Third, opposition parties claimed widespread vote-rigging. And fourth, the number of people killed during the elections (according to some reports up to 50 people) raises questions as to the validity of the results.
7. *'Idda* is laid down in the Quran as a period of three months, or three menstruation periods. It is meant as a means of ascertaining whether the wife is pregnant or not, but above all as a period wherein tempers cool down and reconciliation between the spouses is facilitated. During the *'idda* period the husband can unilaterally revoke his repudiation and resume marital life, even against his wife's wishes.
8. These are not listed according to any order of importance.
9. Mona al-Nahhas, 'Personal Status Gets a Facelift', *Al-Ahram Weekly*, 20–26 January 1994 (p. 2).
10. All criticisms of the Criminal Code are obtained from Bahiy Al-Din (1994).
11. This was said during the ICPD (International Conference on Population and Development) September 1994, in a seminar entitled 'Egyptian Women's Equality before the Law'.
12. There were reports of arrests made and some lawyers 'disappearing'.
13. An interview with an Islamist, A. Badr, in September 1994.
14. This was said repeatedly by many Islamist women I spoke to, from the *Jihad* group especially.
15. Nermeen El-Nawawi, 'Women Seek Political Space', in *Al-Ahram Weekly*, 7–13 March 1996, p. 2.
16. Amal Mahmud Amal at the time of this seminar (8 March 1991) was representative of the Nasserist party-to-be. Now she is the Secretary General of the women's committee within the newly formed party; see Chapter 5 for details.
17. Paper written by Farida al-Naqqash, founding member of the Union of Progressive Women within the Tajammu' Party (n.d.) pp. 7–8.

18. Ayida Saif Al-dawla, interview (June 1993).
19. *Statistical Yearbook*, June 1991 (Cairo: Central Agency for Mobilization and Statistics).
20. Interview with Farida Al-Naqqash, May 1993.
21. See Anker and Anker (1995: 148–76) and The National Population Council of Egypt *Women and Development Report* (1994).
22. Paper prepared by The Committee on The Position of Arab Women within the Arab Lawyers' Union (1993: 30–1).
23. This is quoted from an Annex on the stipulations of the New Unified Labour Law, which came with a report on the NUL, prepared by the New Woman Research Centre (Cairo, October 1994), and presented to the Centre for Labour and Syndicate Services.
24. This was narrated by a woman activist during the ICPD, September 1994.
25. Rape cases did not become 'public knowledge' until the late 1970s and early 1980s, not because they were previously non-existent, but rather because they were too much of a taboo issue. The legal system became more detailed about punishments for such an offence only in the early 1980s, as a result of several well-publicized rape incidents and a consequent public outcry.
26. Personal interview with Saif al-Dawla (June 1993), reiterated in *The New Woman Journal* (1985: 11–14).
27. All feminists agree that prostitution is not an affordable activity for the average Egyptian man.
28. *New Woman Journal*, p. 12.
29. Interview with Zainab (June 1993).
30. Precious few issues were saved from scathing criticism by the Islamists and conservatives in general. But issues on sexuality and/or sexual orientation especially roused bitter anger and intense condemnation.
31. I was witness to their speeches and arguments both in the ICPD and in the media about this issue.

7 ISLAMISM AND GENDER: MALE PERSPECTIVES

1. Faraj Fuda was a well-known writer and strong critic of the Islamist ideology and those who argue for it. He was threatened and then gunned down (in 1992) by Islamist extremists. Najib Mahfuz is an Egyptian novelist who won the Nobel Prize for Literature in 1994. He was repeatedly threatened for one of his novels, which the extremists alleged was blasphemous and injurious to Islam. In 1994 he was attacked and stabbed in the throat, but miraculously managed to survive.
2. The Personal Status Law, see Chapter 6.
3. *Al-Mar'a al-Muslima* is published as part of a series in *Jaridat al-Umma al-Islamiyya* (The Journal of the Islamic Nation, 1992).
4. In 1970, the ratio of divorce to marriage was 21 per cent, see Rugh (1985). It is expected that with the increase in population, and more than 20 years later, this rate may be higher.

5. The idea being that members of both the man and the woman's families would intervene to try to resolve their dispute, and were that to fail, then the couple are supposed to part with mercy and in peace.

6. These are al-Sha'rawi's words, in Tariq 'Abd al-Hamid, 'Raising the Issue of "Circumcision" aims to destroy the Image of Islam', in *Al-Sha'b* (the weekly newspaper of the Labour Party), 30 September (1994: 2).

7. Al-Gawhari, 'Introduction', in Al-Sha'rawi (1992: 3–11).

8. Or those who pander to Western ideas. This category also includes liberals and leftists.

9. See *Ruz Al-Yusuf*, issues August to September 1992.

10. See Chapter 1.

11. The reference is to long-distance travel, as he specifically mentions the pilgrimage (*hajj*) and student trips outside the normal contours of travel.

12. Such as female infanticide and the practice of taking more than one wife per man.

13. See Chapter 6.

14. Husayn's article is found in the Labour Party monthly journal, *Minbar Al-Sharq* (Pulpit of the East). This particular issue was largely devoted to the topic of 'Islam and Woman', to which many authors contributed.

15. It is commonly interpreted that men inherit twice as much as women (though this is highly qualified and not to be understood as a general rule) and that a woman's testimony counts as half that of a man.

8   GENDER AND ISLAMISM: THREE GENERATIONS OF WOMEN'S PERSPECTIVES

1. See the discussion in Chapter 1 under 'Feminism'.

2. Not a relation of Sheikh Al-Ghazali, mentioned in Chapter 7.

3. See Chapter 5 for notes on Huda Sha'rawi.

4. In this case she advocates the Quranic stipulation of the husband beating the disobedient wife, which she elaborates in her article.

5. This is after being transferred to the women's prison from the military prison where she was tortured.

6. Personal interview, October 1994.

7. See Chapter 3.

8. Personal interview, October 1994.

9. Personal interview, October 1994.

10. Personal interview, October 1994.

11. Dina Ezzat, 'Liberation through God's Word', *Al-Ahram Weekly*, 2–8 March, (1995: 3).

12. Personal interview.

13. Personal interview.

14. Personal interview, November 1995.

15. Interview with Dina Ezzat, *Al-Ahram Weekly*.

16. Interview with Dina Ezzat, *Al-Ahram Weekly*.

17. Personal interview, May 1993.

18. The Arabic word for homosexuality is *shudhudh*, which means deviance.

19. Personal interview, October 1995.
20. Personal interview, October 1995.
21. Personal interview, November 1994.
22. Ra'uf approaches most of these young university women, who flock to her side when they see her, in an older sister/respected mentor manner. She listens to their problems and offers sought-after advice and counsel on emotional and personal matters; she encourages them in their work and advises them as to what subjects to specialize in, and what courses to take which would serve them best in terms of future jobs; and shares in the joys of their academic and personal successes. I witnessed some of these interactions whilst accompanying her on a visit to the American University in Cairo (AUC). I was struck by how warmly and enthusiastically Ra'uf was greeted. Almost all the veiled women we came across at AUC, clustered round her to enjoy her warmth, friendliness and advice. Even the security guard at the door of the university seemed to welcome her, and though security measures oblige the guards to check the bags of all entrants into the building, Ra'uf was respectfully smiled at and silently allowed in.
23. Al-Sha'b is a weekly opposition newspaper published by the Muslim Brotherhood and the Labour Party Alliance.
24. In a personal interview, November 1994.
25. Statement made during ICPD, September 1994.
26. Personal interview, September 1994.
27. Personal interview, November 1994.
28. Ra'uf elaborated on this during a talk given at the International Conference on Population and Development (ICPD), which was held in Cairo in September 1994. Significantly, Ra'uf was sharing a panel with a high-ranking member of the Islamist-dominated Labour Party.
29. See also previous chapter.
30. Statement made by Ra'uf during ICPD, September 1994.
31. This was Ra'uf's main argument during her ICPD talk.
32. ICPD, September 1994.
33. ICPD, September 1994.
34. Statement made during ICPD, September 1994.
35. Personal interview, November 1994.
36. I must admit my own responsibility for the latter expounding and interpreting of some of Ra'uf's ideas. Ra'uf is still busy with her thesis and I am not aware of any written or published material of hers which expounds such elaborations.
37. See Chapter 5.
38. See Chapter 5.

9 CONCLUSION: FEMINISM, ISLAMISMS AND THE STATE

1. Here secularism is understood in the same sense as secular feminists apply it: a non-religious discourse, which perceives religion and politics as two different and separate domains.

2. Having the *'isma* means that the wife shares in the right to divorce. See Chapter 6.
3. Dina Ezzat, 'Intellectuals Set Up Liberties Committee', in *Al-Ahram Weekly*, 4–10 April, (1995: 2).
4. Participants include the secular feminist Farida al-Naqqash mentioned earlier.

Bibliography

Abd Al-Baki Hermassi, Mohammad, 'The Islamicist Movement and November 7', in I.W. Zartman (ed.), *Tunisia: The Political Economy of Reform*, Boulder, CO and London: Westview Press, 1991.

Abdalla, Ahmed, *The Student Movement and National Politics in Egypt 1923–1973*, London: Al-Saqi Books, 1985.

Abdalla, Ahmad (ed.), *Al-Wa'y Al-Qanuni li Al-Mar'a Al- Masriyya* (The Legal Awareness of Egyptian Women), Cairo: Amideast and the Arab Lawers Union, 1995 (in Arabic).

Abdel Fattah, Nabil, *Al-Quran wal Sultan: Al-Niza' Bayna Din wa Dawla fi Masr* (The Qur'an and the Sword: The Conflict Between Religion and State in Egypt), Cairo: Madbouly Publishers, 1984 (in Arabic).

Abdel Khader, Soha, *Egyptian Women in a Changing Society: 1899–1985*, London: Lynne Rienner, 1987.

Abdel-Malek, Anouar, *Egypt: Military Society*, New York: Random House, 1968.

Abdel-Malek, Anouar (ed.), *Contemporary Arab Political Thought*, London: Zed Books, 1983.

Abdel Wahab, Nadia and Amal Abd El-Hadi (eds.), *Al-Haraka Al-Nisa'iyya Al-'Arabiyya: Abhath wa Mudakhalat Min Arb'a Bilad 'Arabiyya: Tunis, Falastine, Misr wa Al-Sudan* (The Arab Feminist Movement: Research and Investigation from Four Arab Countries: Tunisia, Palestine, Egypt and Sudan), Cairo: New Woman Research Centre, 1995 (in Arabic).

Abdel Hamid, Tariq, '*Ulama' Al-Islam wa Asatithat Al-Tib: Itharat Qadiyyat Al-Khitan Tahdaf letashweih Surat Al-Islam*' (Ulama of Islam and Professors of Medicine: The Issue of Circumcision is Meant to Darken the Image of Islam), in *Al-Sha'b*, 20 September 1994 (in Arabic).

Abu El-Teij, Mervat, ''Namoudhaj Wad'e Al-Mar'a fi Qanun Al-Jinsiyya Al-Misri' (An Illustration of the Position of Women in the Egyptian Citizenship Law), in Ahmad Abdallah (ed.), *Egyptian Women's Legal Awareness*, Cairo: Amideast and The Arab Lawyers' Union, 1995 (in Arabic).

Abu-Lughod, Leila, *Veiled Sentiments: Honour and Poetry in a Muslim Society*, Berkeley and Los Angeles and London: University of California Press, 1986.

Abu-Lughod, Leila, 'Fieldwork of a Dutiful Daughter', in Soraya Altorki and Camillia Fawzi El-Solh (eds.), *Arab Women in the Field: Studying Your Own Society*, Syracuse, NY: Syracuse University Press, 1988.

A Group of Women Concerned with Affairs Relating to the Egyptian (Aziza Husain, Inji Rushdi, Saniyya Salih, Awatif Wali, Mervat Ittalawi, Muna Zulficar, Magda Al Mufti) *Al Huquq al qanuniyya lil mar'a al 'arabiyya bain al nadthariyya wa al tatbiq* (The Legal Rights of the Egyptian Woman: Theory and Practice), Cairo: Dar al-Kutub, 1988 (in Arabic).

Ahmed, Leila, *Women and Gender in Islam: Historical Roots of a Modern Debate*, New Haven CT and London: Yale University Press, 1992.

Al-'Arawi, Abdallah, *Mafhum Al-Dawla* (Concept of the State), Casablanca: Al-Markaz Al-Thaqafi Al-Arabi, 1981.

Al-Azmeh, Aziz, *Islams and Modernities*, London and New York: Verso, 1993.

Al-Ghazali, Mohammed, *Qadaya Al-Mar'a: Bayn Al-Taqalid Al- Rakida wa Al-Wafida* (Women's Issues: Between Old and Incoming Traditions), Cairo: Dar Al-Shuruq, 1992 (in Arabic).

Al-Ghazali, Zainab, 'Al Jam'iyyat al nisa'iyya' (Feminist Organisations), in *Al Da'wa*, No. 42, November, 1979 (in Arabic).

Al-Ghazali, Zainab, 'Athar wa Mukhallafat Al-Isti'mar' (Effects and Residue of Colonization), in *Manar Al-Islam*, December 1983 (in Arabic).

Al-Ghazali, Zainab, 'Dawr Al-Mar'a fi Bina' Al-Mujtama'' (The Role of Woman in the Building of Society), unpublished paper presented at the Conference of Muslim Women, Lahore, November 1985 (in Arabic).

Al-Ghazali, Zainab, *Ayyam min hayati* (Days of My Life), Cairo: Dar Al Shuruq (8th printing), 1986 (in Arabic).

Al-Ghazali, Zainab, 'Ibnati Hadhihi Al-Sutur Elayki' (My Daughter These Lines are For You), in *Lewa' Al-Islam*, 11 December 1988a (in Arabic).

Al-Ghazali, Zainab, 'Dawr Al-Mar'a Al-Muslima' (The Role of the Muslim Woman), in *Al-Umma*, October 1988b (in Arabic).

Al-Ghazali, Zainab, 'Ja'ani Ma'n' (They Came to Me Together), in *Liwa' Al-Islam*, Vol. 12, March 1989 (in Arabic).

Al-Ghazali, Zainab, *Return of the Pharaoh: Memoir in Nasir's Prison*, trans. Mokrane Guezzou, London: The Islamic Foundation, 1995.

Al-Hashimi, Ibn, *Humum al-Mar'a Al-Muslima wal da'iyya Zaynab Al-Ghazali* (The Muslim Woman's Woes and the Preacher Zaynab Al-Ghazali), Cairo: Dar Al-'Itisam, 1990.

Al-Jawhari, A., 'Muqaddema' (Introduction), in Muhammad Al- Sha'rawi, *Al-Mar'a al-Muslima* (The Muslim Woman), Cairo: Maktabet Zahran, 1992 (in Arabic).

Al-Masri, Sana', *Khalf al-Hijab: Mawqif Al-Jama'at al-Islamiyya min Qadiyyat al-Mar'a* (Behind the Veil: The Position of Islamist Groups on the Woman's Issue), Cairo: Sina, 1989 (in Arabic).

Al-Nafeesy, Abdallah (ed.), *Al-Haraka Al-Islamiyya wa Ru'ya Mustaqbaliyya* (The Islamic Movement and a Future Outlook): Papers on Self-Criticism, Cairo: Madbouli, 1989 (in Arabic).

Al-Qaradawi, Yusuf, *Fatawi Mu'asira li Al-Mar'a wa Al-Usra Al-Muslima* (Contemporary Fatwa for the Muslim Woman and Family), Cairo and Oman: Dar Al-Ira' and Dar Al-Dia'a, 1991 (in Arabic).

Al-Sa'dawi, Nawal, *The Hidden Face of Eve: Women in The Arab World*, trans. and ed. Sherif Hetata, London: Zed Books, 1988a.

Al-Sha'rawi, Muhammad, *Al-Mar'a Al-Muslima* (The Muslim Woman), Cairo: Maktabet Zahran, 1992 (in Arabic).

Al-Said, Rif'at, *Hassan Al-Banna, Mata, Kaifa wa Limatha?* (Hassan Al-Banna: When, How and Why?), Cairo: Madbuli, 1977.

Altorki, Soraya, 'At Home in the Field', in Soraya Altorki and Camillia Fawzi El-Solh (eds.) *Arab Women in the Field: Studying Your Own Society*, Syracuse, NY: Syracuse University Press, 1988.

Altorki, Soraya and El-Solh, Camillia Fawzi (eds.), *Arab Women in the Field: Studying Your Own Society*, Syracuse, NY: Syracuse University Press, 1988.

Altorki, Soraya and El-Solh, Camillia Fawzi, 'Introduction', in Soraya
    Altorki and Camillia Fawzi El-Solh (eds.), *Arab Women in the Field:
    Studying Your Own Society*, Syracuse, NY: Syracuse University Press,
    1988.
Amin, Qasim, *Tahrir al mar'a* (The Liberation of the Woman), Cairo, 1899 (in
    Arabic).
Amin, Qasim, *The New Woman: A Document in the Early Debate on Egyptian
    Feminism*, trans. Samiha Sidhom Peterson, Cairo: American University in
    Cairo Press, 1995.
Amnesty International, 'Egypt: Security Police Detentions Undermine the
    Rule of Law', *Summary*, January 1992 (AI Index: MDE 12/01/92).
Anker, Richard and Anker, Martha, 'Measuring Female Labour Force with
    Emphasis on Egypt', in V. Moghadam and N. Khoury (eds.), *Gender and
    Development in the Arab World: Women's Economic Participation, Patterns
    and Policies*, Tokyo: United Nations University Press and London: Zed
    Books, 1995.
Anonymous, 'No Easy Exit from Slavery Behind the Veil', in Saad Eddin
    Ibrahim and Nicholas S. Hopkins (eds.), *Arab Society in Transition: A
    Reader*, Cairo: The American University in Cairo Press, 1977(1985).
Ansari, Hamied N., 'The Islamic Militants in Egyptian Politics', in *Interna-
    tional Journal of Middle East Studies*, Vol. 16, No. 1, 1984: 12–144.
Arkoun, Muhammad, *Rethinking Islam*, Washington, DC: Center for Con-
    temporary Arab Studies, Georgetown University Press, 1987.
Asad, Talal, *Genealogies of Religion: Discipline and Reasons of Power in
    Christianity and Islam*, Baltimore, MD and London: The Johns Hopkins
    University Press, 1993.
Ashmawi, Sa'id M., *Al-Islam al-Siyasi* (Political Islam), Cairo: Sina, 1987.
Association for Health and Environmental Development (AHED), *Aims and
    Objectives*, Cairo: AHED, n.d.
Atkinson, Paul, *The Ethnographic Imagination: Textual Constructions of Real-
    ity*, London and New York: Routledge, 1990.
Ayubi, Nazih, *Bureaucracy and Politics in Contemporary Egypt*, London:
    Published for the Middle East Centre St Antony's College Oxford by Ithaca
    Press, 1980.
Ayubi, Nazih, *Political Islam: Religion and Politics in the Arab World*, London
    and New York: Routledge, 1991a.
Ayubi, Nazih, *The State and Public Policies in Egypt Since Sadat*, Reading:
    Ithaca Press, 1991b.
Ayubi, Nazih, *Over-Stating the Arab State: Politics and Society in the Middle
    East*, London and New York: I.B. Tauris, 1995.
Badie, Bertrand, '"State", Legitimacy and Protest in Islamic Culture', in Ali
    Kazancigil (ed.), *The State in Global Perspective* Paris/Aldershot/Vermont:
    Unesco/Gower, 1986.
Badran, Margot, 'Competing Agenda: Feminists, Islam and the State in 19th
    and 20th Century Egypt', in Deniz Kandiyoti (ed.), *Women, Islam and the
    State*, London: Macmillan, 1991.
Badran, Margot, 'Gender Activism: Feminists and Islamists in Egypt', in
    Valentine Moghadam (ed.), *Identity Politics and Women: Cultural Reasser-*

tions and Feminisms in International Perspective, Oxford, San Francisco and Boulder: Westview, 1994.

Badran, Margot, *Feminists, Islam, and Nation: Gender and the Making of Modern Egypt*, Princeton, NJ: Princeton University Press, 1995.

Bahiy Al-Din, Amira, 'Al-Tamyeez Did Al-Mar'a Fi Qanun Al-'Uqubat: Dirasa Awwaliyya' (Discrimination Against Woman in The Criminal Code: A Preliminary Study), unpublished paper, 1994 (in Arabic).

Bahiy Al-Din, Amira, 'Wad'e Al-Mar'a Al-Qanuni fi Qanun Al-Ahwal Al-shakhsiyya' (The Legal Position of Women in the Family Law), in Ahmad Abdallah (ed.), *Egyptian Women's Legal Awareness*, Cairo: Amideast and the Arab Lawyers' Union, 1995 (in Arabic).

Baker, Raymond W., *Egypt's Uncertain Revolution Under Nasser and Sadat*, Cambridge MA: Harvard University Press, 1978.

Baker, Raymond W., *Sadat and After: Struggles for Egypt's Political Soul*, Cambridge, MA: Harvard University Press, 1990.

Basu, Amrita, 'Introduction', in Amrita Basu (ed.), *The Challenge of Local Feminisms: Women's Movements in Global Perspective* Boulder, CO: Westview Press, 1995.

Basu, Amrita (ed.), *The Challenge of Local Feminisms: Women's Movements in Global Perspective*, Boulder, San Francisco, Oxford: Westview Press, 1995.

Battaglia, Debbora (ed.), *Rhetorics of Self-Making*, Berkeley and Los Angeles: University of California Press, 1995.

Battaglia, Debbora, 'Problematizing the Self: A Thematic Introduction', in Debbora Battaglia (ed.), *Rhetorics of Self-Making*, Berkeley and Los Angeles: University of California Press, 1995.

Bax, Mart, 'Religious Regimes and State Formation: Towards a Research Perspective', in Eric Wolf (ed.), *Religious Regimes and State Formation: Perspectives from European Ethnology*, New York: SUNY Press, 1991.

Be'eri, Eliezer, *Army Officers in Arab Politics and Society*, Jerusalem and New York: Praeger and Pall Mall, 1970.

Behar, Ruth and Deborah Gordon (eds.), *Women Writing Culture*, Berkeley, Los Angeles, London: University of California Press, 1995.

Bell, Dianne, Pat Caplan and W.J. Karim (eds.), *Gendered Fields: Women, Men and Ethnography*, London and New York: Routledge, 1993.

Benhabib, Seyla, *Situating the Self: Gender, Community and Postmodernism in Contemporary Ethics*, Oxford: Polity Press, 1992.

Benhabib, Seyla, Judith Butler, Drucilla Cornell and Nancy Fraser, *Feminist Contentions: A Philosophical Exchange* (Introduction by Linda Nicholson), London and New York: Routledge, 1995.

Binder, Leonard, *Islamic Liberalism: A Critique of Development Ideologies*, Chicago and London: The University of Chicago Press, 1988.

Black, I., Pugh, D., Tisdal, S., Evans, K. and Plommer, L., 'Militant Islam's Saudi Paymasters', in *Women against Fundamentalism* (Special Issue) Winter 1992/93: 45–46.

Boulares, Habib, *Islam: The Fear and the Hope*, London and New Jersey: Zed Books, 1990.

Brown, Richard, H., *Postmodern Representations: Truth, Power and Mimesis in the Human Sciences and Public Culture*, Urbana and Chicago: University of Illinois Press, 1995.

Burke, Edmund III and Lapidus, Ira M. (eds.), *Islam, Politics and Social Movements*, London: I.B. Tauris, 1988.

Burgat, François, *L'Islamisme en Face*, Paris: La Découverte, 1995.

Butterworth, Charles E. and Zartman, William (eds.) *Political Islam*, London: Sage, 1992.

Callaway, Helen, 'Ethnography and Experience: Gender Implications in Fieldwork and Texts', in Judith Okely and Helen Callaway (eds.), *Anthropology and Autobiography*, London and New York: Routledge, 1992.

Caplan, Lionel (ed.), *Studies in Religious Fundamentalism*, New York: State University of New York Press, 1987.

Cassell, J., 'The Relationship of Observer to Observed in Peer Group Research', in *Human Organization*, Vol. 36, No. 4, 1977.

Choueiri, Youssef M., *Islamic Fundamentalism*, London: Pinter Publishers, 1990.

Clifford, James, *The Predicament of Culture*, Cambridge, MA: Harvard University Press, 1988.

Clifford, James, and Marcus, George (ed.), *Writing Culture: The Poetics and Politics of Ethnography*, Berkeley: University of California Press, 1986.

Cole, Juan R.I. (ed.), *Comparing Muslim Societies: Knowledge and the State in a World Civilization*, Ann Arbor, MI: The University of Michigan Press, 1992.

Chow, Rey, 'Violence in the Other Country: China as Crisis, Spectacle, and Woman', in C.T. Mohanty et al. (eds.), *Third World Women and The Politics of Feminism*, Bloomington: Indiana University Press, 1991.

Cocks, Joan, *The Oppositional Imagination: Feminism, Critique and Political Theory*, London and New York, Routledge, 1989.

Denzin, Norman K., 'The Poststructuralist Crisis in the Social Sciences: Learning from James Joyce', in Richard H. Brown (ed.) *Postmodern Representations: Truth, Power, and Mimesis in the Human Sciences and Public Culture*, Urbana and Chicago: University of Illinois Press, 1995.

Dessouki, Ali E. (ed.), *Islamic Resurgence in the Arab World*, New York: Praeger Publishers, 1982.

Dhu-l-fiqar, Mona, *'Wad'e Al-Mar'a Al-Misriyya fi Daw'a Al-Ittifaqiyya Al-Dawliyya li-l-Qada' 'ala Kafat Ashkal Al-Tamyeez Did Al-Mar'a'* (The Position of Egyptian Women In Light of The International Convention for the Elimination of All Forms of Discrimination Against Women), in Ahmad Abdalla (ed.) *Legal Awareness of Egyptian Women*, Cairo: Amideast and the Arab Lawyers' Union, 1995 (in Arabic).

Diamond, Irene and Lee Quinby (ed.), *Feminism and Foucault: Reflections on Resistance*, Boston: Northeastern University Press, 1988.

Dreyfus, Hubert and Rabinow, Paul, *Michel Foucault: Beyond Structuralism and Hermeneutics*, Chicago: The University of Chicago Press, 1982.

Eickelman, Dale and Piscatori, James, *Muslim Politics*, Princeton, NJ: Princeton University Press, 1996.

Eisenstein, Zillah, 'The Relative Autonomy of the Capitalist Patriarchal State', in Zillah R. Eisenstein (ed.), *Feminism and Sexual Equality: Crisis in Liberal America*, New York: Monthly Review Press, 1984.

El-Guindy, Fadwa, 'Veiling *Infitah* with Muslim Ethic: Egypt's Contemporary Islamic Movement', in *Social Problems*, Vol. 28, No. 4, 1981: 465–85.

El-Guindy, Fadwa, 'Veiled Activism: Egyptian Women in the Contemporary Islamic Movement', in *Peuples Meditérraneens*, Vol. 22–3, January–June, 1983: 79–89.

El-Sayed, Moustapha, 'The Islamic Movement in Egypt: Social and Political Implications', In Ibrahim Oweiss (ed.), *The Political Economy of Contemporary Egypt*, Washington: Center for Contemporary Arab Studies Georgetown University, 1990.

El-Sayed, Moustapha, 'A Civil Society in Egypt?', in Augustus R. Norton (ed.), *Civil Society in the Middle East*, Volume 1, Leiden: E.J. Brill, 1994.

El-Solh, Camillia Fawzi, 'Gender, Class, and Origin: Aspects of Role During Fieldwork in Arab Society', in Soraya Altorki and Camillia Fawzi El-Solh (eds.), *Arab Women in the Field: Studying Your Own Society*, Syracuse, NY: Syracuse University Press, 1988.

El-Solh, Camillia Fawzi and Mabro, Judy (eds.), *Muslim Women's Choices: Religious Belief and Social Reality*, Oxford: Berg, 1994.

Emerson, Robert Rachel Fretz and Linda Shaw, *Writing Ethnographic Fieldnotes*, Chicago: The University of Chicago Press, 1995.

Esposito, John L., *Women in Muslim Family Law*, Syracuse, NY: Syracuse University Press, 1982.

Esposito, John L. (ed.), *Voices of Resurgent Islam*, Oxford: Oxford University Press, 1983.

Esposito, John L., *Islam: The Straight Path*, Oxford: Oxford University Press, 1988.

Esposito, John L., *The Islamic Threat: Myth or Reality?*, New York and Oxford: Oxford University Press, 1992.

Ezzat, Heba Ra'uf, 'An Islamic Women's Liberation Movement?', in *Middle East Report*, Vol. 24, No. 191, November–December 1994: 26–7.

Fischer, M.J. and Mehdi Abedi (eds.), *Debating Muslims: Cultural Dialogues in Postmodernity and Tradition*, Wisconsin: The University of Wisconsin Press, 1990.

Fontana, Benedetto, *Hegemony and Power: On the Relation Between Gramsci and Machiavelli*, Minneapolis and London: University of Minnesota Press, 1993.

Foucault, Michel, *Power/Knowledge: Selected Interviews and Other Writings 1972–1977*, ed. Colin Gordon, trans. Colin Gordon et al., New York: Pantheon Books, 1980a.

Foucault, Michel, 'The History of Sexuality: An Interview', trans. G. Bennington, in *Oxford Literary Review*, Vol. 4, No. 2, 1980b.

Foucault, Michel, *The History of Sexuality*, Volume 1: 'An Introduction', trans. R. Hurley, New York: Pantheon, 1978.

Foucault, Michel, *Discipline and Punish: The Birth of the Prison*, trans. A. Sheridan, London: Penguin Books, 1977.

Foucault, Michel, *The Archaeology of Knowledge*, trans. A. M. Sheridan Smith, New York: Random House, 1972.

Geertz, Clifford, *The Interpretation of Cultures*, New York: Basic Books, 1973.

Geertz, Clifford, *Works and Lives: The Anthropologist as Author*, Oxford: Polity Press, 1988.

Geuijen, Karin, Raven, Diederick and Wolf, John de (eds.), *Postmodernism and Anthropology: Theory and Practice*, Assen: Van Gorkum, 1995.

Gillespie, Marie, *Television, Ethnicity and Cultural Change*, London and New York: Routledge, 1995.

Gilsenan, Michael, 'State and Popular Islam in Egypt', in Fred Halliday and Hamza Alavi (eds.), *State and Ideology in the Middle East and Pakistan*, London: Macmillan Education, 1988.

Göcek, Muge and Balaghi, Shiva (eds.), *Reconstructing Gender in The Middle East: Tradition, Identity and Power*, New York: Colombia University Press, 1994.

Gramsci, Antonio, *Selections from the Prison Notebooks*, London: Lawrence & Wishart, 1971.

Grant, Judith G., *Fundamental Feminism: Contesting the Core Concepts of Feminist Theory*, London and New York: Routledge, 1993.

Guenena, Nemat, 'The Jihad: An Islamic Alternative in Egypt', *Cairo Papers in Social Science*, Vol. 9, Monograph 2, Summer 1986.

Halliday, Fred and Alavi, Hamza (eds.), *State and Ideology in the Middle East and Pakistan*, London: Macmillan Education, 1988.

Halliday, Fred and Alavi, Hamza, 'Introduction' in Fred Halliday and Hamza Alavi (eds.), *State and Ideology in the Middle East and Pakistan*, London: Macmillan Education, 1988.

Hammersley, Martyn, *Reading Ethnographic Research: A Critical Research*, London and New York: Longman, 1990.

Hammersley, Martyn, *What's Wrong With Ethnography*, London and New York: Routledge, 1992.

Harding, Sandra (ed.), *Feminism and Metholodology: Social Science Issues*, Bloomington and Indianapolis: Indiana University Press, and Milton Keynes: Open University Press, 1987.

Harding, Sandra, 'Introduction: Is There a Feminist Method?', in Sandra G. Harding (ed.), *Feminism and Methodology: Social Science Issues*, Bloomington and Indianapolis: Indiana University Press, and Milton Keynes: Open University Press, 1987.

Harding, Sandra, 'Conclusion: Epistemological Questions', in Sandra G. Harding (ed.), *Feminism and Methodology: Social Science Issues*, Bloomington and Indianapolis: Indiana University Press, and Milton Keynes: Open University Press, 1987.

Hartsock, Nancy C.M., 'Foucault on Power: A Theory For Women?', in L. Nicholson (ed.), *Feminism/Postmodernism*, London and New York: Routledge, 1991.

Hastrup, Kirsten, 'The Ethnographic Present: A Reinvention', in *Cultural Anthropology* Vol. 5, No. 1, 1990: 45–61.

Hastrup, Kirsten and Hervik, Peter (eds.) *Social Experience and Anthropological Knowledge*, London and New York: Routledge, 1994.

Hervik, Peter, 'Shared Reasoning in the Field: Reflexivity Beyond the Author', in Kirsten Hastrup and Peter Hervik (eds.), *Social Experience and Anthropological Knowledge*, London and New York: Routledge, 1994.

Hippler, Jochen and Lueg, Andrea (eds.), *The Next Threat: Western Perceptions of Islam*, trans. Leila Friese, London: Pluto Press, 1995.

Hirsch, Marianne and Keller, Evelyn Fox (eds.), *Conflicts in Feminism*, New York and London: Routledge, 1990.

Hoffman, Valerie J., 'An Islamic Activist: Zaynab al-Ghazali', in Elizabeth Warnock Fernea (ed.), *Women and the Family in the Middle East: New Voices of Change*, Austin, TX: University of Texas Press, 1985.

Hoffman-Ladd, Valerie J., 'Polemics on the Modesty and Segregation of Women in Contemporary Egypt', in *International Journal of Middle East Studies*, Vol. 19, 1978: 23–50.

Holub, Renate, *Antonio Gramsci: Beyond Marxism and Postmodernism*, London and New York: Routledge, 1992.

Hooks, Bell, *Yearning: Race, Gender and Cultural Politics*. Boston: South End Press 1990.

Hull, Gloria and Smith, Barbara, 'The Politics of Black Women's Studies', in *All The Women are White, All the Blacks Are Men, But Some of Us are Brave: Black Women's Studies*, eds. G.T. Hull, P. Bell Scott and B. Smith. New York: Feminist Press, 1982.

Hopwood, Derek, *Egypt: Politics and Society 1945–1984*, London: Allen & Unwin, 1985 (2nd edn 1991).

Humm, Maggie, *The Dictionary of Feminist Theory*, New York: Prentice-Hall, 1989.

Humm, Maggie (ed.), *Modern Feminisms: Political, Literary, Cultural*. New York: Colombia University Press, 1992.

Husayn, Adel, 'The Arab Woman: A Future Perspective', in *Manbar Al-Sharq*, No. 5, January 1993: 5–28.

Hussain, Aziza, 'Recent Amendments to Egypt's Personal Status Law', in Elizabeth Warnock Fernea (ed.), *Women and the Family in the Middle East: New Voices of Change*, Austin, TX: University of Texas Press, 1985.

Hutcheon, Linda, *The Politics of Postmodernism*, London and New York: Routledge, 1990.

Ibrahim, Saad Eddin, 'Anatomy of Egypt's Militant Islamic Groups: Methodological Notes and Preliminary Findings', in *Journal of Middle East Studies* Vol. 12, 1980: 423–53 and 481–99.

Ibrahim, Saad Eddin, 'Islamic Militancy as a Social Movement: The Case of Two Groups in Egypt', in Ali E. Dessouki (ed.), *Islamic Resurgence in the Arab World*, New York: Praeger, 1982.

Ibn Al-Hashemy, *Humum Al-Mar'a Al-Muslima wa Al-Da'iya Zaynab Al-Ghazali* (The Muslim Woman's Woes and the Preacher Zaynab Al-Ghazali), Cairo: Dar Al-'Itisam, 1990 (in Arabic).

Jaganathan, Pradeep and Ismail, Qadri (eds.), *Unmaking the Nation*, Colombo: Social Scientists' Association, 1995.

Jansen, G.H., *Militant Islam*, London and Sydney: Pan Books, 1979 (1981).

Jayawardena, Kumari, *Feminism and Nationalism in the Third World: In the Early 19th and 20th Centuries*, The Hague: Institute of Social Studies, 1982 and London: Zed Books, 1986.

Johnson-Odim, Cheryl, 'Common Themes, Different Contexts: Third World Women and Feminism', in C.T. Mohanty et al. (eds.), *Third World Women and the Politics of Feminism*, Bloomington: Indiana University Press, 1991, pp. 314–27.

Joll, James, *Gramsci*, Glasgow: Fontana/Collins, 1977 (1979).

Kandiyoti, Deniz (ed.), *Women, Islam and the State*, London and New York: Macmillan Academic and Professional Ltd, 1991.

Kandiyoti, Deniz, 'Introduction', in Deniz Kandiyoti (ed.), *Women, Islam and the State*, London: Macmillan Academic and Professional, 1991.

Kandiyoti, Deniz, 'Contemporary Feminist Scholarship and Middle East Studies', in Deniz Kandiyoti (ed.), *Gendering the Middle East: Emerging Perspectives*, London and New York: I.B. Tauris, 1996.

Kandiyoti, Deniz (ed.), *Gendering the Middle East: Emerging Perspectives*, London and New York: I.B. Tauris, 1996.

Karam, Azza M., *'Fundamentalism', 'Modernity' and Women's Groups in Egypt: Activist Women's Realities*, Amsterdam: Middle East Research Associates, Occasional Paper No. 20, December 1993.

Karam, Azza M., 'Gender in Egypt: Between Islamism, Feminism and the State, Perspectives of Some Women Activists', in *VENA Journal*: Gender, the Family and The State, Vol. 6, No. 1, June 1994.

Karam, Azza M., 'Islamismen/Feminismen' (Islamisms/Feminisms), in *Lover: Literatuuroverzicht over feminisme, cultuur en wetenschap* (Lover: Literature Survey of Feminism, Culture and Science), Amsterdam, September 1995 (in Dutch).

Karam, Azza M., 'Feminismo o islamismo en Egipto: en busca de nuevos paradimas' (Feminism and Islamism in Egypt: In Search of New Paradigms), in *Papeles: Cuestiones Internacionales de Paz, Ecologia y Desarrolo*, Madrid: Centro de Investigacion para la Paz, No. 55, 1995 (in Spanish).

Karam, Azza M., 'Muslim Feminists in Western Academia: Questions of Power, Matters of Necessity', *People's Rights*, No.4, 1997 (Cairo: Legal Research Centre on Human Rights) pp. 14–15.

Karam, Azza M. and Arends, Inge, 'Postmodernism and Women's Groups in Egypt', in Inge Boer et al. (eds.), *Orientations: Changing Stories: Postmodernism and the Arab-Islamic World*, Amsterdam and Atlanta: Rodopi, 1995.

Kazancigil, A. (ed.), *The State in Global Perspective*, New York: Unesco, 1986.

Keddie, Nikki R., 'Ideology, Society and the State in Post-Colonial Muslim Societies', in Fred Halliday and Hamza Alavi (eds.), *State and Ideology in the Middle East and Pakistan*, London: Macmillan Education, 1988.

Kepel, Gilles, *The Prophet and Pharaoh: Muslim Extremism In Egypt*, London: Saqi Books, 1985.

Khalifa, Ijlal, *Al-Haraka al-Nisa'iyya al-haditha* (The Modern Women's Movement), Cairo: Dar al Kutub, 1973.

Khater, Akram and Nelson, Cynthia, '*Al-Harakah Al-Nisa'iyya*: The Women's Movement and Political Participation in Egypt', in *Women's Studies International Forum*, Vol. 2, No. 5, 1988: 465–83.

Khuri, Fuad I., *Imams and Emirs: State, Religion and Sects in Islam*, London: Saqi Books, 1990.

Krämer, Gudrun, 'The Integration of the Integrists: A Comparative Study of Egypt, Jordan and Tunisia', in Ghassan Salame (ed.), *Democracy without Democrats: The Renewal of Politics in the Muslim World*, London and New York: I.B. Tauris, 1994.

Kristeva, Julia, 'Women's Time', *Signs*, No. 7, 1981.

Kristeva, Julia, *The Power of Horror*, New York: Colombia University Press, 1982.

Laclau, Ernesto (ed.), *The Making of Political Identities*, London and New York: Verso, 1994.

Laclau, Ernesto and Mouffe, Chantal, *Hegemony and Socialist Strategy: Towards a Radical Democratic Politics*, London: Verso, 1985.

Lather, Patti, 'Fertile Obsession: Validity After Poststructuralism', *Sociological Quarterly*, No. 35, 1993.

Lorde, Audre, *Sister Outsider: Essays and Speeches*, New York: The Crossing Press, 1984.

Lyotard, Jean-François, *The Postmodern Condition: A Report on Knowledge*, Manchester: Manchester University Press, 1986.

Macleod, Arlene Elowe, *Accommodating Protest: Working Women, The New Veiling, and Change in Cairo*, New York: Columbia University Press, 1991.

Mackinnon, Catherine, *Toward a Feminist Theory of the State*, Cambridge, MA and London: Harvard University Press, 1989.

Malinowski, Bronislaw, *Argonauts of the Western Pacific*, New York: E.P. Dutton, 1961.

Malinowski, Bronislaw, *A Diary in the Strict Sense of the Term*, New York: Harcourt, Brace and World, 1967.

Marcus, George E. and Fischer, Michael, *Anthropology as Cultural Critique: An Experimental Moment in the Human Sciences*, Chicago and London: University of Chicago Press, 1986.

Marty, Martin E. and Appleby, R. Scott (eds.), *Fundamentalisms Observed* (Volume I), Chicago: University of Chicago Press, 1991.

Marty, Martin E. and Appleby, R. Scott, *Fundamentalisms and Society: Reclaiming the Sciences, the Family and Education* (Volume II), Chicago: University of Chicago Press, 1993a.

Marty, Martin E. and Appleby, R. Scott, *Fundamentalisms and the State: Remaking Politics, Economics and Militance* (Volume III), Chicago: University of Chicago Press, 1993b.

Marty, Martin E. and Appleby, R. Scott (eds.) *Accounting For Fundamentalisms: The Dynamic Character of Movements* (Volume IV), Chicago: University of Chicago Press, 1994.

Mascia-Lees, Frances, Sharp, Patricia and Cohen, Colleen, 'The Postmodernist Turn in Anthropology: Cautions from a Feminist Perspective', in *Signs*, Vol. 15, No. 1, 1989: 7–33.

McNay, Lois, *Foucault and Feminism*, Cambridge, Polity Press, 1992.

Mernissi, Fatima, *Beyond the Veil: Male–Female Dynamics in Modern Muslim Society* (revised edition), London: Al Saqi Books, 1985 (1987).

Mernissi, Fatima, *Women and Islam: An Historical and Theological Enquiry*, trans. Mary Jo Lakeland, Oxford: Basil Blackwell, 1991.

Migdal, Joel S., *Strong Societies and Weak States: State–Society Relations and State Capabilities in the Third World*, Princeton, NJ: Princeton University Press, 1988.

Mitchell, Richard P., *The Society of the Muslim Brothers*, London: Oxford University Press, 1969 (1993).

Mitchell, Timothy, *Colonising Egypt*, Cambridge and New York: Cambridge University Press, 1988.

Moghadam, Valentine and Khoury, Nabil F. (eds.), *Gender and Development in the Arab World – Women's Economic Participation: Patterns and*

Policies, Tokyo and London: United Nations University and Zed Books, 1995.

Moghadam, Valentine (ed.), *Gender and National Identity: Women and Politics in Muslim Societies*, London and Karachi: Zed Books and Oxford University Press, 1994.

Moghadam, Valentine (ed.), *Identity Politics and Women: Cultural Reassertions and Feminisms in International Perspective*, Boulder, San Francisco and Oxford: Westview Press, 1994.

Moghadam, Valentine, *Modernizing Women: Gender and Social Change in the Middle East*, Boulder and London: Lynne Rienner Publishers, 1993.

Mohanty, Chandra T., 'Cartographies of Struggle: Third World Women and the Politics of Feminism', in Chandra T. Mohanty et al. (eds.), *Third World Women and the Politics of Feminism*, Bloomington: Indiana University Press, 1991.

Mohanty, Chandra T., Russo, Ann and Lourdes, Torres (eds.), *Third World Women and the Politics of Feminism*, Bloomington: Indiana University Press, 1991.

Moore, Henrietta L., *Feminism and Anthropology*, Cambridge: Polity Press, 1988 (1991).

Moore, Henrietta L., *A Passion For Difference*, Bloomington and Indianapolis: Indiana University Press, 1994.

Moore, Henrietta L. (ed.), *The Future of Anthropological Knowledge*, London and New York: Routledge, 1996.

Morsy, Soheir A., 'Fieldwork in My Egyptian Homeland: Toward the Demise of Anthropology's Distinctive-Other Hegemonic Tradition', in Soraya Altorki and Camillia Fawzi El-Solh (eds.), *Arab Women in the Field: Studying Your Own Society*, Syracuse, NY: Syracuse University Press, 1988.

Mortimer, Edward, *Faith and Power: The Politics of Islam*, New York: Random House and London: Faber and Faber, 1982.

Mustafa, Hala, *The State and Movements of Islamic Opposition: Between Consensus and Confrontation, in the Eras of Sadat and Mubarak*, Cairo: Al-Mahrousa, 1995.

Nasser, Gamal Abdel, *Egypt's Liberation: The Philosophy of the Revolution*, Washington, DC: Public Affairs Press, 1995.

Nederveen Pieterse, Jan P., 'Fundamentalism Discourses: Enemy Images', in *Women against Fundamentalism*, No. 5: 1, 1994.

Nicholson, Linda J., *Feminism/Postmodernism*, London and New York: Routledge, 1990.

Nicholson, Linda J., 'Introduction', in Benhabib et al., *Feminist Contentions: A Philosophical Exchange*, London and New York: Routledge, 1995.

Nicholson, Linda J. and Fraser, Nancy, 'Social Criticism without Philosophy: An Encounter Between Feminism and Postmodernism', in Linda Nicholson (ed.), *Feminism/Postmodernism*, London and New York: Routledge, 1990.

Norton, Augustus, R. (ed.), *Civil Society in the Middle East* (Volumes I and II), Leiden: E.J. Brill, 1995 and 1996.

Okely, Judith and Callaway, Helen (eds.) *Anthropology and Autobiography*, London and New York: Routledge, 1992.

Okely, Judith, 'Anthropology and Autobiography: Participatory Experience and Embodied Knowledge', in Judith Okely and Helen Callaway (eds.), *Anthropology and Autobiography*, London and New York: Routledge, 1992.

Okely, Judith, 'Anthropology and Autobiography: Participatory Experience and Embodied Knowledge', in Judith Okely and Helen Callaway (eds.), *Anthropology and Autobiography*, London and New York: Routledge, 1992.

Ong, Aihwa, 'Colonialism and Modernity: Feminist Representations of Women in Non-Western Societies', *Inscriptions*, Vol. 4, No. 3, 1988.

Oweiss, Ibrahim M., *The Political Economy of Contemporary Egypt*, Washington: Center for Contemporary Arab Studies, 1990.

Qandil, Amani, 'Dawr Al-Munadhamat Ghair Al-Hukumiyyah fi Mahw Al-Ummiyya Al-Qanuniyya li Al-Mar'a' (The Role of NGOs in Eliminating Women's Legal Illiteracy), in Ahmad Abdallah (ed.), *Egyptian Women's Legal Awareness*, Cairo: Amideast and The Arab Lawyers' Union, 1995.

Qandil, Amani and Bin Nafissa, Sara, *Al-Jam'iyyat Al-Ahliyya Fi Misr* (Private Voluntary Associations in Egypt), Cairo: Al-Ahram Center for Political and Strategic Studies, 1995 (in Arabic).

Qazim, Safinaz, *'An Al-Sijn wa Al-Hurriyya* (On Prison and Freedom), Cairo: Al-Zahra' li Al-'Elam Al-Arabi, 1986 (in Arabic).

Qazim, Safinaz, *Fi Al-Sufur wa Al-Hijab* (On Non-Veiling and Veiling), Cairo: Maktabet Wahba, 1982 (in Arabic).

Qazim, Safinaz, *'Al Ra'ida Nabawiyya Musa wa In'ash dhakirat al umma'* (The Pioneer Nabawiyya Musa and the Reviving of the Nation's Memory), in *Majallat al hilal*, January, 1984 (in Arabic).

Qazim, Safinaz, *'Al-Mar'a Al-Muslimma wa Al-Tahaddiyyat'* (The Muslim Woman and the Challenges), in *Zahrat Al-Khaleej*, 4 December 1993 (in Arabic).

Qazim, Safinaz, *'Al-Feminism: Harakat Al-Getto Al-Nissa'iyya'* (Feminism: The Ghetto Feminist Movement), in *Al-Mussawar* 24 June 1994a (in Arabic).

Qazim, Safinaz, *'Madha Ya'ni an Takouni Mar'a Muslima?'* (What Does it Mean To You to be a Muslim Woman?), in *Zahrat Al-Khaleej*, 29 January 1994b (in Arabic).

Qazim, Safinaz, *'Badihiyat Tama Nisyaniha'* (Forgotten Basics), in *Zahrat Al-Khaleej*, 12 March 1994c (in Arabic).

Qutb, Mohammad, *Tahrir Al-Mar'a* (The Liberation of Woman), Cairo: Maktabet Al-Sunna, 1981 (1991).

Qutb, Sayyid, *Milestones*, Delhi-6: Markazi Maktaba Islami, 1991, 3rd edition.

Rabinow, Paul, *Reflections on Fieldwork in Morocco*, Berkeley: University of California Press, 1977.

Rabinow, Paul (ed.), *The Foucault Reader: An Introduction to Foucault's Thought*, London: Penguin, 1984.

Ra'ef, Ahmad, *Al-Bawwaba al-Sawda': Safahat Min Tarikh Al-Ikhwan Al-Mulsimin* (The Black Gate: Pages from the History of the Muslim Brotherhood), Cairo: Al-Zahra' Lil 'Ilam Al-Arabi, 1985 (in Arabic).

Radwan, Zainab, *Bahth zahirat al hijab bain al jami'iyyat* (A Study of the Phenomenon of the Veil among University Women), Cairo: National Centre for Sociological and Criminological Research, 1982 (in Arabic).

Rich, Adrienne, 'Toward a Woman-Centered University', in *On Lies, Secrets, Silence: Selected Prose 1966–1978*. London: Virago, 1980.

Rosaldo, R.I., 'Grief and a Headhunter's Rage: On the Cultural Force of Emotions', in E.M. Bruner (ed.), *Text, Play and Story: The Construction and Reconstruction of Self and Society*, Washington: American Anthropological Association, 1984.

Rosenau, Pauline M., *Postmodernism and the Social Sciences: Insights, Inroads, and Intrusions*, Princeton, NJ: Princeton University Press, 1992.

Rubin, Barry, *Islamic Fundamentalism in Egyptian Politics*, London: Macmillan, 1990.

Rugh, Andrea, *Family in Contemporary Egypt*, Cairo: American University Press, 1985.

Sadat, Anwar M., *Those I Have Known*, London: Jonathan Cape, 1984.

Sahgal, Gita and Yuval-Davis, Nira, 'The Uses of Fundamentalism', *Women against Fundamentalism*, Vol. 1, No. 5, 1994.

Salame, Ghassan (ed.), *The Foundation of The Arab State*, London and New York: Croom Helm, 1988.

Salame, Ghassan (ed.), *Democracy without Democrats: The Renewal of Politics in the Muslim World*, London and New York: I.B. Tauris, 1994.

Saleh, Saneya, 'Women in Islam: Their Status in Religious and Traditional Culture', in Saad Eddin Ibrahim and Nicholas S. Hopkins (eds.), *Arab Society in Transition: A Reader*, Cairo: The American University in Cairo Press, 1977 (1985).

Sangren, Steven P., 'Rhetoric and the Authority in Ethnography', *Current Anthropology* Vol. 29, No. 3, June 1988.

Sassoon, Ann S., *Gramsci's Politics*, New York: St. Martin's Press, 1980.

Sassoon, Anne (ed.), *Women and the State*, London: Hutchinson, 1987.

Sawicki, Jana, *Disciplining Foucault: Feminism, Power and The Body*, London and New York: Routledge, 1991.

Sayyid, Bobby, 'Sign O'Times: Kaffirs and Infidels Fighting the Ninth Crusade', in Ernesto Laclau (ed.), *The Making of Political Identities*, London and New York: Verso, 1994.

Schrijvers, Joke, 'Motherhood Experienced and Conceptualized: Changing Images in Sri Lanka and the Netherlands', in Dianne Bell et al. (eds.), *Gendered Fields: Women, Men and Ethnography*, London and New York: Routledge, 1993.

Schuler, Margaret (ed.), *Empowerment and the Law: Strategies of Third World Women*, Washington: OEF International, 1986.

Seidman, Steven and Wagner, David (eds.), *Postmodernism and Social Theory*, Oxford: Basil Blackwell, 1992.

Sha'rawi, Shaikh, *Al Mar'a kama aradaha allah* (The Woman as God Wanted Her to Be), Cairo: Maktabat Al Quran, 1980 (in Arabic).

Silva, Purnaka L. de, 'Studying Political Violence and Its Cultural Constructions', *FOLK: Journal of the Danish Ethnographic Society*, Vol. 36, 1995a.

Silva, Purnaka L. de, 'The Efficacy of 'Combat Mode': Organization, Political Violence, Affect and Cognition in the Case of the Liberation Tigers of Tamil Eelam', in Praddep Jeganathan and Qadri Ismail (eds.), *Unmaking the Nation: The Politics of Identity and History in Modern Sri Lanka*, Colombo: Social Scientists' Association, 1995b.

Sivan, Emmanuel, *Radical Islam: Medieval Theology and Modern Politics*, New Haven and London: Yale University Press, 1985.

Slyomovic, Susan, 'Hassiba Ben Bouali, If You Could See Our Algeria: Women and Public Space in Algeria', in *MERIP Middle East Report*, Vol. 125, No. 1, January–February 1995.

Strathern, Marilyn, 'An Awkward Relationship: The Case of Feminism and Anthropology', in *Signs*, Vol. 12, No. 2, 1987a.

Strathern, Marilyn, 'Out of Context: The Persuasive Fictions of Anthropology', in *Current Anthropology*, Vol. 28, No. 3, 1987b.

Sullivan, Denis J., *Private Voluntary Organizations in Egypt: Islamic Development, Private Initiative and State Control*, Orlando: University Press of Florida, 1994.

Sullivan, Earl L., *Women in Egyptian Public Life*, Syracuse, NY: Syracuse University Press, 1986.

Tadros, Marleen, Abdel Aziz El-Shibiny and Amira Abd Al-Hakim, *Al-Muwatana Al-Manqusa: Tahmish Al-Mar'a fi Masr* (The Incomplete Citizenship: Marginalization of Women In Egypt), Cairo: Centre for Legal Information and Studies on Human Rights, 1995.

Tedlock, D., *The Spoken Word and the Work of Interpretation*, Philadelphia: University of Pennsylvania Press, 1983.

The Arabic Strategic Report: 1989, Cairo: Al-Ahram Centre for Political and Strategic Studies, 1990 (also, 1992, 1993, and 1994).

The Committee on the Position of Arab Women Within the Arab Lawyer's Union 'The Position of Arab Women', paper presented at the 18th Conference of the Arab Lawyers' Union, Casablanca, Morocco, May 1993.

The Communication Group for the Enhancement of the Status of Women in Egypt, *Legal Rights of Egyptian Women in Theory and in Practice*, Cairo: Dar El-Kutub, 1992.

The National Population Council of Egypt, *Women and Development Report* Cairo: 1994.

The New Woman Research Centre, '*A Report on The New Unified Labour Law*', Cairo: 1994.

The New Woman Research Centre, 'Hadith Ma'a 'Ayida Saif Al-Dawla' (interview with Ayida Saif Al-Dawla). In *The New Woman Journal*, Issue No. 1, November 1985.

Tucker, Judith E., *Women in Nineteenth-Century Egypt*, Cambridge: Cambridge University Press, 1978 (1985).

Tucker, Judith E. (ed.), *Arab Women: Old Boundaries, New Frontiers*, Bloomington and Indianapolis: Indiana University Press, 1993.

Turner, Bryan S., *Orientalism, Postmodernism and Globalism*, London and New York: Routledge, 1994.

Tyler, Stephen, A., *The Unspeakable: Discourse, Dialogue and Rhetoric in the Postmodern World*, Wisconsin: The University of Wisconsin Press, 1987.

Tyler, Stephen, A., 'Post-modern Ethnography: From Document of the Occult to Occult Document', in James Clifford and George Marcus (eds.), *Writing Culture: The Poetics and Politics of Ethnography*, Berkeley: University of California Press, 1986.

Van Maanen, John (ed.), *Representation in Ethnography*, London and New Delhi: Sage, 1995.

Vatikiotis, P. J., *Islam and the State*, London and New York: Routledge, 1987a.

Vatikiotis, P. J., *The Egyptian Army in Politics: Pattern For New Nations?*, Bloomington: Indiana University Press, 1987b.

Vatikiotis, P. J., *The History of Modern Egypt: From Muhammad Ali to Mubarak* (4th edition), London: Weidenfeld and Nicolson, 1991.

Visweswaran, Kamala, 'Defining Feminist Ethnography', *Inscriptions*, Vol. 4, No. 3, 1988.

Waterbury, John, *The Egypt of Nasser and Sadat: The Political Economy of Two Regimes*, Princeton, NJ: Princeton University Press, 1983.

Watt, W. Montgomery, *Islamic Fundamentalism and Modernity*, London and New York: Routledge, 1988.

Westkott, Marcia, 'Women's Studies as a Strategy for Change: Between Criticism and Vision', in *Theories of Women's Studies*, eds. G.B. Bowles and R. Duelli-Klein. London: Routledge, 1983.

Wolf, Eric (ed.), *Religious Regimes and State Formation: Perspectives from European Ethnology*, New York: SUNY Press, 1991.

Young, Robert, *White Mythologies*, London and New York: Routledge, 1990.

Youssef, Michael, *Revolt against Modernity: Muslim Zealots and The West*, Leiden: E.J. Brill, 1985.

Yuval-Davis, Nira and Anthias, Floya (eds.), *Women–Nation–State*, London: Macmillan, 1989.

Zaalouk, Malak, *Power, Class and Foreign Capital in Egypt: The Rise of the New Bourgeoisie*, London and New Jersey: Zed Books, 1989.

Zakaria, Fouad, 'The Standpoint of Contemporary Muslim Fundamentalists', in Nahid Toubia (ed.), *Women of the Arab World: The Coming Challenge – Papers of the Arab Women's Solidarity Association Conference*, trans. Nahed El Gamal, London: Zed Books, 1988.

Zakaria, Fouad, *Al-Sahwa Al-Deeniya fi Mizan Al-Aql* (The Religious Revival in the Balance of the Mind), Cairo: Dar al-Fikr, 1989 (in Arabic).

Zakaria, Rafiq, *The Struggle Within Islam: The Conflict Between Religion and Politics*, London: Penguin Books, 1988 (1989).

Zartman, William (ed.), *Tunisia: The Political Economy of Reform*, Boulder, Colorado and London: Westview Press, 1991.

Zubaida, Sami, *Islam, the People and The State: Political Ideas and Movements in the Middle East*, London: I.B. Tauris, 1993.

Zuhur, Sherifa, *Revealing Reveiling: Islamist Gender Ideology in Contemporary Egypt*, New York: SUNY Press.

Index

280   *Index*

coercion, 25
Committee on Islamic Jurisprudence, 123
Communication Group for the Enhancement of Women, 150, 153, 160
consciousness-raising, legal, 129, 142, 143
consent, 30
  manufacture of, 25, 29, 65
contraception, 172
Copts, 91, 93
counter-culture, 98
Criminal Code, 150–1
cultural identity, 91
cultural inauthenticity, 12
cultural politics, 17

Dâr al-harb, 85
Dâr al-Ifta', 14
Dar al-Islam, 85
decentralization, 22
decolonization, 22
democracy, 56
demonization, 17
dhimmi, 91
Dhul-fiqar, Mona, 24, 142
dignity, female, 10, 166
discourse
  feminist, 42
  Islamist, 246
divorce, 102, 143–4, 145, 147
  grounds for, 148
  rights to (*'isma*), 146, 184–5, 190–1, 196
dominance, intellectual, 25
domination, 27
  consent to, 30

economic essentialism, 109
economic participation, 156
Egyptian Constitution (1923), 56
Egyptian Constitution (1956), 59
Egyptian Constitution (1980), 65
Egyptian Feminist Union, 208
Egyptian Women's Union, 101
electoral registration, 152, 154
epistemology, feminist, 9
equal rights, 6

equality of sexes, 6
  critique of, 10, 180–2, 189, 193–5, 199–200
equity, 6
Esposito, John, 17
ethnography, 32, 37–8
  modes of authority, 43

family, primacy of, 177–9; *see also* motherhood
family, extended, 34
Family Law, 1, 3, 14, 102, 144
  debates on, 1, 3, 33
family planning, 172; *see also* abortion; contraception
Faraj, 'Abd al-Salam, 14, 92–3
female circumcision, 35, 127, 173–4, 179
female employment
  criticism of, 182, 193, 201–3
  dependency ratio, 161
  exclusion from, 162
  exclusion from judiciary, 161
  laws governing, 158–60
  participation rate, 161
  productivity 161
  retirement age, 163
  sex discrimination, 161
female literacy, 108
feminism, 119, 231, 234
  Black, 41
  criticism of, 186, 191–2
  as cultural imperialism, 6
  Egyptian, 4–9, 101
  Islamist, 9–11
  Muslim, 9, 11–13, 131
  postmodern conceptualizations, 8–9, 234
  radical, 30
  rejection of, 121
  secular, 9, 13–14, 234
  Western, 7, 10, 38, 231
feminisms, Egyptian, 5
feminist consciousness, 6
Foucault, Michel, 3–4, 26–9, 86
Fourth World Women's Conference (Beijing), 6, 54, 128, 146, 154